The Elected Circle

Laurence Stapleton

Princeton University Press    1973

# The Elected Circle

*Studies in the Art of Prose*

# Preface

It has seemed to me possible, and desirable, to bring together in this study some collaborators in "the democratic art of prose." The phrase is Virginia Woolf's, who used it in an essay, "The Narrow Bridge of Art." There she speculated about the way the novelist of the future might give expression to capacities of life that had earlier been in the province of poetry. Her essay of 1927 was written before modern poets had captured any of the protean shapes of the novel.

As the Introduction to this study proposes, I am concerned with a different yet related question: the art of prose that is *not* fiction, and does not pretend to be like poetry. I do believe that the art of prose is "democratic" in the best sense—speaking to the hearer or reader as an individual. This may seem a strange way to think of John Donne's sermons, for example, or T. S. Eliot's essays. Yet compare the careful Lincoln's Inn sermons delivered to learned men who had known Donne as a law student, with the honest eloquence of his sermons as Dean of St. Paul's. In the congregation at St. Paul's were women and children as well as many kinds of men.

I once heard a truck driver in a small restaurant disown the humdrum conservatism of a political candidate while praising the articulate conviction of his opponent —a judgment of meaning in terms of style. If anyone asks why T. S. Eliot's essays exemplify "the democratic art of prose," it is because he could write as perceptively about a music hall performer (Marie Lloyd) as about Lancelot Andrewes, and because he made clear the difference between the man who suffers and the mind that creates.

I wish to express my thanks to scholars who have shared my interest in the subject of this book and whose advice and encouragement has aided its completion, especially to Professor Arthur Barker, to the late Rosalie Colie, and to Professor A. Walton Litz. And appreciation is a mild word to offer for the courtesy of Professor Wallace E. Williams who, with James H. Justus, is now editing Emerson's Later Lectures for future publication. Professor Williams checked my quotations from the lectures grouped under the title "Natural History of Intellect" and gave me information hitherto unavailable about the dates of some of these lectures. He is of course not responsible for any approximation in my own way of referring to this phase of Emerson's writing.

To Mrs. Valerie Eliot I am grateful for her kind permission to quote passages from some of T. S. Eliot's uncollected articles and reviews, as well as brief excerpts from her Introduction to the facsimile edition of *The Waste Land*. The copyright remains Mrs. Eliot's.

It is a pleasure to thank Pamela Reilly and other members of the staff of Canaday Library at Bryn Mawr College. Marie Burtenshaw deserves my thanks for her careful typing.

Particular thanks are due to Kathrin Platt for her intelligent assistance in the final preparation of the typescript.

*Laurence Stapleton*

# Acknowledgments

Permission to quote excerpts from copyright material in the following works is here gratefully acknowledged as follows:

From *The Sermons of John Donne*, ed. by George R. Potter and Evelyn M. Simpson, originally published by the University of California Press, 1953-62; reprinted by permission of the Regents of the University of California.

From *The Works of Sir Thomas Browne*, ed. by Geoffrey Keynes (Chicago, 1964), first published in 1928 by Faber & Faber Ltd. Published in this new edition in 1964, reprinted by permission of The University of Chicago Press and Faber & Faber, Ltd.

From *Sir Thomas Browne* by Frank L. Huntley (Ann Arbor, 1962), reprinted by permission of The University of Michigan Press.

From *The Complete Works of William Hazlitt*, ed. by P. P. Howe (London and Toronto, 1930), reprinted by permission of J. M. Dent & Sons, London.

From *The Early Lectures of Ralph Waldo Emerson*, ed. by Stephen E. Whicher, Robert E. Spiller, and Wallace E. Williams (Cambridge, 1959-1971), reprinted by permission of The Belknap Press of Harvard University Press.

*All quotations from the work of T. S. Eliot are reprinted by permission of Mrs. Valerie Eliot and Faber & Faber Ltd.*, with permission from other publishers as specified.

From the Introduction to *The Waste Land, a Facsimile and Transcript of the Original Drafts*, ed. by Valerie Eliot (New York, 1971), reprinted by permission of Harcourt Brace Jovanovich, Inc.

From *The Sacred Wood* by T. S. Eliot (2nd ed., London and New York, 1928), reprinted by permission of Methuen & Co., Ltd., and Random House, Inc.

From *Selected Essays* by T. S. Eliot (New York, 1950), reprinted by permission of Harcourt Brace Jovanovich, Inc.

From *The Use of Poetry and the Use of Criticism* by T. S. Eliot (Cambridge, Mass., 1933), reprinted by permission of Harvard University Press.

From *On Poetry and Poets* by T. S. Eliot (New York, 1957) and *To Criticize the Critic* by T. S. Eliot (New York, 1965), reprinted by permission of Farrar, Straus & Giroux, Inc.

# Contents

| | | |
|---|---|---:|
| | *Preface* | v |
| | *Acknowledgments* | ix |
| | *Introduction* | 3 |
| 1 | John Donne: The Moment of the Sermon | 17 |
| 2 | Sir Thomas Browne and Meditative Prose | 42 |
| 3 | The Graces and the Muses: Felltham's *Resolves* | 73 |
| 4 | William Hazlitt: The Essayist and the Moods of the Mind | 93 |
| 5 | The Virtù of De Quincey | 119 |
| 6 | Emerson and the Freedom of the Reader | 166 |
| 7 | Thoreau: The Concrete Vision | 195 |
| 8 | T. S. Eliot: The Dialogue of the Writer | 233 |
| | *Notes* | 269 |
| | *Index* | 287 |

The Elected Circle

# Introduction

Prose is the younger art; in English the "rise of literary prose" chiefly dates from the sixteenth century. But this fact does not account for the lack of attention to its possibilities as an art. A long line of remarkably distinguished poet-critics have made the terms of criticism chiefly relevant to poetry, although in the course of this endeavour they have worked out principles applicable to literature generally. As, more slowly, attention has turned to prose the chief beneficiary has been the novel. In this book I am not concerned with fiction, except where as a limiting case it casts light upon that kind of imaginative prose for which we have only the term non-fiction.

For a point of reference as to what constitutes imaginative prose, I take Coleridge's definition (not the reverberations of his primary and secondary imagination, but the passage where he is thinking more specifically of qualities of writing): "a more than usual state of emotion with more than usual order; judgment ever awake and steady; self-possession with enthusiasm and feeling profound or vehement."[1]

These are qualities that in varying degree appear in the prose of the writers I have chosen to discuss. There is more to be pondered in the grain and texture of life than can be communicated in a story, or crystallized in a poem. And here the writer of imaginative prose has his range. His work permits and encourages self-knowledge in a way that is less indirect than fiction, more open and speculative. His exterior form may be governed by tradition, as in the sermon, or relatively free, as in the periodical essay. But in either case, what counts is the intensity that he achieves in his recreation of experience and the conduct of his discourse. Some writers travel one of these two routes more successfully than the other.

There have been special studies of the evolution of prose style, such as the many articles of Morris Croll and Williamson's *The Senecan Amble*. George Saintsbury's pioneer *History of English Prose Rhythm* is still worth reading; James Sutherland has made discriminating observations.[2] Literary histories have dealt widely with prose, casting the net to include travel books, political pamphlets, biographies—all of which have their fascination. Nevertheless, except in studies of individual authors, few critics have concerned themselves with the interaction of the prose writer's sense of human life and his means of identifying it in language. It is my belief that something more about the art of prose may be discovered by placing side by side explorations of a selected group of masters of related forms, such as the sermon and the essay, or new kinds of narrative, or forms for which we hardly have a name.

It will be clear, then, that the purpose of this book is not to deal with style alone, much less with what is at the moment termed "stylistics." I am concerned with the press of meaning upon structure, the varying ways in which the inner themes of these writers unfold, with their adaptation of existing kinds of discourse. Sometimes such questions lead to a consideration of metaphor or rhythm, or the words that must be obeyed to be reborn. Sometimes more elusive qualities of tone, or the relative interest of smaller and larger units in an imaginative work deserve attention. I do not propose a primarily formal, nor a historical analysis; instead I wish to consider the central nature of prose in eight selected authors, all of whom I think have something in common, individual as they are.

The reason that I have deliberately not tried to follow any uniform pattern of analysis with the different writers here considered is that such a method would do injustice to them, and misrepresent the possibilities of the subject. Whatever the shortcomings of this study —and I could list some of them—nevertheless it is true that there isn't any book like it. Perhaps one may therefore be allowed some leeway in a novel enterprise. With each writer discussed here, I have tried to point out choices that had to be made, the opportunities offered and resources available, the achievement in reconciling or adapting them to each other.

For the most part "genre" in imaginative non-fiction is less identifiable than in poetry—also, I believe, less controllable. But because of the less well-defined path the writer of imaginative prose has to take, if he is not a novelist, we as readers may at times see more clearly what is above and below and beside it, that lets light into meaning. That is part of the fascination of a protean form like the essay—is the writer changing it to meet the reader's expectations or to escape them? Questions of this kind may refresh our sense of the life in literature, where there is no means but nature makes that means.

A word on "the intentional fallacy."[3] I do not think it a fallacy to use any evidence we may have of a writer's intentions to alert ourselves to qualities actually present in his writing. With the argument of Mr. Wimsatt and Mr. Beardsley, that we should not attempt to decide on the *success* of a work by the author's intention, I am in agreement. Once written the work becomes independent, and must be judged for itself. But we may be assisted in appraising it by whatever clues we have to the author's literary insight. We are better readers of Henry James's novels for knowing the notebooks and the prefaces.

By my metaphor, "the elected circle," I seek to unite a perspective and a dimension. In the first instance, there is the hope that this group of studies may point to a center open to other approaches than my own. James said of one of his novels that "the conceived arrangement" opened the door wide to ingenuity.

> In sketching my project . . . I drew upon a sheet of paper . . . the neat figure of a circle consisting of a number of small rounds disposed at equal distance around a central object. The central object was . . . my subject in itself . . . and the small rounds represented so many

distinct lamps . . . the function of each of which would be to light with all due intensity one of its aspects.[4]

The circle created by the group of studies here presented is not as Euclidean as James's, but the possibility of seeing something more about the nature of imaginative prose by these small lamps is, I think, a real one.

In the other instance, the elected circle is that recognized by the principal prose writers themselves. This is not necessarily equivalent to a subjective aim. The elected circle is partly described by the chance offered by the given form at a given time—sermon, essay, or special narrative. But, equally, the purpose or intention disclosed by a piece of imaginative prose is not predetermined, and must be generated by the work as it proceeds. As it evolves in the writer's mind and feelings, it may shift course. It is targeted upon itself.

Some brief explanation of the choice of authors should clarify these points; and perhaps I should comment more briefly on the omission of two or three.

Donne is chosen because he is to me the greatest of the seventeenth-century sermon writers. *Pace* T. S. Eliot, I think those who have read the complete sermons of Donne and of Andrewes would agree; and *pace* Coleridge and De Quincey, I think a similar comparison not between selected passages, but between the complete sermons of Donne and of Taylor, would likewise produce agreement. Part of the reason is that Donne as a young man and even into his middle years had probably never thought he would write a sermon. His early command of language, his intensity of feeling, led him to unique experiments with satire, with the lyric and the long meditative poem. After the trials of his early manhood, the "heave of the will" that led him into the ministry required a new ordering of his experience. It is not extravagant to suppose (and statements of his confirm it) that he had to think about the nature of the sermon as neither Andrewes or Taylor was compelled to do. For him it became a literary as well as a religious calling. We can see this in the great Potter and Simpson edition, which gives twentieth-century readers a chance to know Donne's prose that a struggle with the Alford edition could not provide (and access to the folios was limited to a few). For Donne the sermon liberated imagination, and restricted it. The vaulted structure in which Donne unfolds his cadences, leads to his climactic questions, weights his pauses and his refrains, makes nonsense of the vicious fallacy of "prose poetry." Doubtless he could not have written such prose had he not been a poet, but he knew the difference.

Browne for the first time discovered certain possibilities for imaginative prose that no one before him and few since have opened to us. No exterior prompting or need gave the reason for *Religio Medici*. Its author had clearly read Montaigne, but Montaigne's candor and ease (in his later *essais*) takes the form in Browne of a youthful willingness to pursue mysteries without self-defense. His awareness of what he is doing, when he reveals it, is one of the reasons for thinking of his "elected circle." There is an underlying unity in all his prose, but at different times in his life his immediate interests as a writer varied considerably. Browne also is of immense importance because in his prose writing there are seeds of growth for others, most notably Emerson and Thoreau. There is no English writer before Browne, in all his books except *Pseudodoxia Epidemica*, who found an unprecedented new form; yet *Religio Medici, Urn Burial* and the *Garden of Cyrus*, although cousin to the essay, are books from beginning to end. In a century when the sound brought the sense alive, Browne equals Donne and Taylor, and in the whole shape of his three greatest books he succeeds in what they only partly attempted.

Of seventeenth-century prose writers, Owen Felltham is a good one, unduly neglected. He has a special place here in that his writing was not stimulated by his calling, as Donne's was, or initiated by financial need, as Hazlitt's and De Quincey's. We may hazard the guess that his first precocious book was born of a mixture of conscience and pleasure. Later expansions of this book show delight in the resources of language; equally, they show limitations of the early practice of the moral essay built from *sententiae*, limitations not overcome until Emerson and Thoreau experimented with and remolded this form. The more light-hearted sequences of Addison and Steele have some ancestry in Restoration comedy and look forward to the novel rather than to the further development of imaginative prose. A consideration of Felltham belongs in this study partly because he perfected a form, "the resolve," that did not survive except as inner *resolution* in some nineteenth-century writers. The more significant reason why he belongs here is that his theme of "The Graces and the Muses," the interaction of style with the writer's governing faith and insight, applies to all the other figures in this group.

Why have I not included some eighteenth-century writers? For the eighteenth century is remarkable in its number of great prose works, apart from the novel. There are several reasons; but Swift, for example, the most original prose writer of his time, can be discussed only if one deals with the art of satire, and this is beyond my purpose. While satire may heighten other forms, major works of satire demand separate attention. Thus a comparison between Nashe and Swift would be enlightening; but Swift does not belong in the company of Browne or De Quincey. He is a great luminary in another galaxy. Then, with Burke or Gibbon, one cannot examine their accomplishment as prose writers without being led into extraneous materials of political theory or history. The kind of imaginative prose I am discussing must be sufficient in itself, not dependent upon a body of facts or ideas that ask to be judged in another court of appeal. Finally, Dr. Johnson. In almost everything he wrote, including his *Dictionary*, there is a substratum of imagination. He knew its inner fire (speaking for instance of a mistake of Dryden's as caused by "the tumult of imagination"). But for Johnson as a writer, this faculty was always under control, not suffered to explore beyond the bounds his judgment set, and limited by the conventions of discourse he adhered to. Fortunately, W. K. Wimsatt's book on Johnson's prose style[5] and Walter Bate's prefaces to a number of volumes in the Yale edition do justice to Johnson as one of the great masters of expression in our language and as "the most sympathetic of the great prudential moralists."[6] The rediscovery of *The Lives of the Poets* for future readers has yet to be undertaken, but such an enterprise must claim its own terrain.

It is no wonder that both Hazlitt and De Quincey had to reject Dr. Johnson as a generative force in the art of prose—Hazlitt to derive strength from the example of Burke, De Quincey from Browne and Jeremy Taylor (and both of them of course from the great poets of their own time). With Hazlitt and De Quincey imaginative prose revives. Hazlitt shaped the essay to the contours of individual feeling, making room for new encounters of experience and memory. We may see him, De Quincey, Emerson, and Thoreau as writers each of whom had to decide upon, define or perceive his chances and obligations and eventual freedom in untried ways, thereby enlarging the circle of kinds of expression in imaginative prose.

Parenthetically, I might remark that without Coleridge the imaginative instincts of Hazlitt and De Quincey might not have been evoked so early. But, myriad-minded man that he is, Coleridge's books draw us aside to other issues than the art of prose. He is the magnetic mountain before which all compasses deflect, including his own, and the essence of his power cannot be measured in a study such as this. While he has a strong affinity with Donne and Browne (and knew Andrewes, Taylor, and other seventeenth-century prose writers very well), he did not extend this tradition in his own prose.

Hazlitt and De Quincy have particular significance in the balancing of outward incentives (the sometimes desperate need for money, the character of the periodicals in which they were able to publish) and inward ones that the mind proposes to itself. Hazlitt was a slow starter, irked by the conditions of his profession when he turned to essay-writing, and his venture into lecturing seems to have released him from the limitations of his earlier work. As I hope to show, he in turn, by his range and variety of topics, gave a fresh development to this form of writing, emancipating it from the more polite and expectable versions of the eighteenth century. Each of these nineteenth-century prose writers gave serious thought to the language he needed. Hazlitt's explanation of his preference for a conversational style makes room for the flex and reflexes of point of view towards a subject. In his later essays one may see a treatment of time as different from Browne's as from De Quincey's experiments; yet in this respect as in his progress to a symbolic form he, like De Quincey, shows that imaginative prose is comparable to the novel. I do not argue for any influence of Hazlitt on Emerson or Thoreau, yet he fashioned an instrument that they could convert to their own needs.

De Quincey is a central figure in the writers discussed here, for a number of reasons. He had consciously thought of the possibilities of prose as an art, was in fact the first to see it in terms of the organic theory of style articulated by Coleridge. His essay on rhetoric seems to me of paramount importance in this respect— his struggle to understand the capacities of prose in the seventeenth century, his recognition that there is a relationship between the state of society and the themes available to a writer. Each of his principal works is significant from the point of view of the elected circle because in at least one of his aims, that of writing "impassioned prose," he was in my opinion self-deceived. His work offers a chance to discuss so-called prose poetry, also to indicate the way that the novel is a limiting case of some of his special narratives. My study of him suggests a different view of his accomplishment from the usual one. I am convinced that he deserves to be more widely read and more thoroughly read. He has not exhausted the vitality of the kind of prose in which he excels, and I should not be surprised if he were someday to have some great inheritors.

In contemplating Emerson's place as a major writer of imaginative prose, I have again, as with De Quincey, seen somewhat differently the comparative vitality of his several works. Emerson was not summoned by financial need—although as a young man he was poor—or by the opportunities of the periodical press; instead, the writing of essays appeared to him as a calling. It soon coalesced with his early activities as lecturer, yet he maintained the two channels that he had foreseen: to formulate the spirit of the age, and to disclose moral incentive. Certain major seventeenth-century themes were transmitted to Emerson, notably that of a cosmos held together by correspondences. By this yeast he baked a new and nutritive bread. In his prose he recut and freed the lines of meditation from the trammels of argument or dogma. The best of his writings achieve novel patterns of arrangement in ideas. He and Thoreau give a forward impetus to the kind of literature I am concerned with, an impetus that is hard to transfer into other terms than their own.

All the writers given place in this study appeal to the reader's consciousness as part of their subject. But Emerson and Thoreau (like Whitman) find in their experience of the new world a new possible kind of reader. Therefore they can write without the same portmanteau of assumptions. In Emerson's later essays he can give an immediate record of the mind's sensations, which we can find otherwise only in briefer passages in his *Journals*. I have respectfully disagreed with Henry James's belief that Emerson did not find his form. Emerson too approaches a vein of meaning otherwise recoverable only in the novel.

"What can the man do that comes after the king?" Thoreau, owing much to Emerson, and like him belonging to the lineage of seventeenth-century writers yet aware of his contemporaries, needed no kingdom, "too intrinsic for renown."[7] Once underway with his early writing, he begins a kind of narrative highly adaptable and flexible as a way of linking observation with the universal. In this respect he has no peer. Compare for example the personality—the literary personality—of the narrator in *The Confessions of an English Opium Eater* with that of the young voyager in *A Week on the Concord and Merrimack Rivers*. Or the scale of nature in *The Garden of Cyrus* with new graphs of it in Thoreau's *Journals*. He, like Emerson, reconnects batteries of imagination charged by Browne and advances confidently, if also warily, by their current. He did not in his later narratives altogether find the form that he needed; but it is yet to be found by anyone else. I have tried to show how Thoreau notches his own place farthest ahead in a main tradition.

In our own time the dominant phase of prose other than the novel has been literary criticism. And the chief representative of this movement was, and is likely to remain, T. S. Eliot. Without the device of formal speakers, his criticism is the dialogue of a writer with other writers, and with readers.

Many of Eliot's essays have not yet been included in published volumes. One that needs to be known for an understanding of his leap from a gifted writer of reviews or occasional prefaces, to a major critic, a critic for whom imagination was always a calling upon the soul, is his tribute to Bruce Lyttelton Richmond. Eliot relates his meeting with Richmond (then the editor of the *Times Literary Supplement*): "At that time I was still a clerk at Lloyd's bank: but whether my presentation at *The Times* took place at my lunch time, or after bank hours, . . . I cannot now remember. Nor do I remember what was said at this (for me) memorable meeting."[8] He describes the figure of Bruce Richmond, his alertness and courtesy, then continues, "But to be summoned to the presence of the Editor of the *Times Literary Supplement* and to be invited to write for it was to have reached the top rung of the ladder of literary journalism. . . ."

The account given here of the province assigned to Eliot for reviewing (Elizabethan and Jacobean poetry and drama) comes as no surprise to readers of Eliot's first two books of essays. But his modest yet responsible view of the opportunity the *TLS* gave him, and of what he learned ("to moderate my dislikes and crotchets, to write in a temperate and impartial way") is quite relevant to the concept of an elected circle—different elected circles—for the writer at difference stages in his life.

Like Eliot, I find repugnant Arnold's idea that poetry should be a substitute for religion.[9] It is a diminution of both these modes of thought and feeling. Nevertheless it is true that in discourse about literature today many ideas are conveyed that once would have been considered in traditional religious terms. In literary criticism now, we are concerned from the beginning to the end with the human condition. That is the chief reason why criticism has become the dominant phase of modern prose, apart from the novel.

Eliot has done more than anyone to stake out the field of this enterprise. To his cost, his criticism early became identified with certain popular preoccupations —with the metaphysical poets, or with formulations like the "objective correlative." Actually, as I am concerned to show, he proceeds from a more general position about criticism and about literature to an incorporation in each of integrity of experience.

As Eliot's criticism develops, he becomes more simply, less oracularly confident and more confiding. He constantly assumes the courage to disclose questions of great import in relatively clear and simple terms. More and more his prose becomes an honest dialogue with the willing reader and the future writer. Parallel to his poetry, the prose uncovers a vein of moral insight, and in the essay "Goethe as the Sage" approaches the realm of contemplation.

In dealing with each of the writers selected for discussion here, I have tried to convey a sense of his special identity or character. In most cases the titles of the chapters are a clue to this conception. Also, where possible, I have tried to consider the extent to which the prose writings of any one of these individuals constitutes, even if only potentially, an *œuvre*, a sense of filaments connecting one essay with another, or a progress from mastery of one form to experimentation with another.

In the novel, we have characters by whose adventures and encounters we discover our own. But it is a part of life to ponder more openly, and without the aid of fiction, on what we feel, believe, hope, propose.

> Life being all inclusion and confusion, and art being all discrimination and selection, the latter, in search of the hard latent *value* with which alone it is concerned, sniffs round the mass as instinctively and unerringly as a dog suspicious of some buried bone. The difference here, however, is that where the dog desires his bone but to destroy it, the artist finds in his tiny nugget, washed free of awkward accretions and hammered into a sacred hardness, the very stuff for a clear affirmation, the happiest chance for the indestructible.[10]

These chances for the indestructible occur in imaginative prose unforgettably and undiluted, as each of the writers here discussed uniquely demonstrates.

# John Donne: 1

## The Moment of the Sermon

The sermon in our time is no longer an active literary form. The question is, rather, why it achieved such excellence not only for its religious value but as a major channel of literary expression in the seventeenth century. Andrewes, Donne, and Taylor became great prose writers in this medium. Of the three, the sermons of Donne, though not necessarily the finest in every sense, offer the best challenge in appraising this kind of writing, for more of them are independently interesting than those of Andrewes or of Taylor.

Donne's conception of a sermon affirms its literary, as well as its religious, import. For the sermon is to give further scope and meaning to texts chosen from the Bible, and to Donne the Bible gave example of art.

. . . The *Holy Ghost* in his Instruments, (in those whose tongues or pens he makes use of) doth not forbid, nor decline elegant and cheerfull, and delightfull expression; but as God gave his Children a bread of *Manna*, that tasted to every man like that that he liked best, so hath God given us *Scriptures*, in which the plain and simple man may heare God speaking to him in his own plain and familiar language, and men of larger capacity . . . may heare God in that Musique that they love best, in a curious, in an harmonious style, unparalleled by any. For, that also *Calvin* adds . . . that there is no secular Authour . . . which doth more abound with perswasive *figures* of Rhetorique, nor with musicall *cadences* and *allusions* . . . and correspondency of words to one another, then some of the *Secretaries of the Holy Ghost*, some of the authours of some books of the Bible doe (x, 103).[1]

In the Bible, then (and in many sermons Donne reaffirmed this conviction) truth found itself in harmony of language and variety of metaphor. For, if Donne did not adhere to the older allegorical method of interpretation, he made room for something resembling it by his belief that frequently the "secretaries of the Holy Ghost" made use of figurative language.[2] Although in the reading of some books—especially Genesis—"there is danger in departing from the letter," in the reading of others—especially Revelation—there is equal danger in adhering to the letter closely.

The literall sense is always to be preserved; but the literall sense is not always to be discerned: for the literall sense is not always that, which the very Letter and Grammar of the place presents, as where it is literally said, *That Christ is a Vine*, and literally, *That his flesh is bread*, and literally *That* the new Jerusalem is thus *situated*, thus built, thus furnished: But the literall sense of every place, is the principall intention of the Holy Ghost, in that place: And his principal intention in many places, is to expresse things by allegories, by figures; so that in many places of Scripture, a figurative sense is the literall sense . . . (vi, 62).

From this it follows that one of the main functions of the sermon is literary. The sermon as a means to exhort and edify has a practical purpose, which does not in itself favour or require the endeavour of art. Donne often calls attention to this practical purpose, and asks his hearers to listen to "the Sermon of the sermon" rather than its logic or its rhetoric. But more characteristically the sermon is a mode of art that exalts art: "God shall neither take from us, The Candle and the Candlestick, The truth of the Gospel, which is the light, And the cheerfull, and authorized, and countenanced, and rewarded Preaching of the Gospel, which is the Candlestick that exalts the light . . ." (v, 289). It is true that in this passage taken as a whole Donne is, as often, concerned to urge zeal in the outward services of the church, but his conception of preaching as that which exalts the light of the Gospel gives the sermon meaning as an art. Even more revealing is the metaphor of the sermon as the honeycomb to the honey.

For, *verba composita*, saith *Solomon*, chosen words, *studied*, premeditated words, *pleasing* words . . . are as a *Hony-combe*. Now, in the Hony-combe, the Hony is collected and gathered, and dispensed, and distributed from the Hony-combe, And of this the Hony-combe is wax, wax apt for *sealing*, derived too. The distribution of this Hony to the Congregation, The sealing of this

Hony to the Conscience, is in the *outward Ordinance of God*, and in the labour of the Minister. . . . But the *Hony-combe* is not the *Hony*, The gifts of the man, is not the Holy Ghost (viii, 271).

As, in the earlier passage, the Bible itself, work of the Holy Ghost, is the light carried and exalted by the sermon, or candlestick, here the Bible is the honey gathered and dispensed by sermon as the honeycomb. In both cases the sermon, while ancillary to the truth it conveys, serves its purpose more faithfully if it too possesses the skill in expression inherent in the Bible.

Donne was the heir of a long tradition, dating from the Fathers of the Church, in which the sermon writer converted to his own use the conventions of rhetoric developed in classical oratory. In the earlier Renaissance as well as in the seventeenth century the rhetoric of the sermon received the explicit attention of compilers of handbooks. The practice of note-taking by members of the congregation, including young students and even children, encouraged the development of a form that could be easily grasped. Donne does not differ from his principal Anglican contemporaries in following the recognized conventions of a *praecognitio texti*, or proem presenting the text in terms of its setting or occasion, followed by *divisio*, a cutting into parts, (often calling for ingenuity, but allowing simplicity also) of the text to be considered, followed by amplification by means of other Biblical passages, the comments of the Fathers and others, and—rather implicit throughout than separately emphasized—the application to the hearer's spiritual needs. The play on significant words, the paradoxes and conceits of the witty preachers had by Donne's time been exercised in the further development of this basic form of the sermon.

Donne followed the convention and availed himself of the resources of the "metaphysical" sermon writers. The manner in which he did so has been thoroughly discussed by William Fraser Mitchell, by Mrs. Simpson, by William Mueller, and most recently by Joan Webber in her fine book *Contrary Music*.[3] To all these any student of Donne's prose must be indebted. In deciding to include Donne in this study, I wish to place the question of his accomplishment a little differently, to ask what is to be enjoyed and admired in his sermons as they test and prove the capacity of prose? To proceed with reflections on this question will require us in the end to show how the sermon form may have aided or impeded Donne's effort to give independent existence to his chosen themes.

One of the most notable traits of prose writers is the instinctive choice of words and phrases. In some writers the instinct impels an accuracy of reference by means of sensitivity to the root meaning of words. In other writers, there is a tendency to resort to words enhancing emotion. All are likely to have a predilection for some favourite terms that are not so readily housed in the writing of others. Donne's untiring regard for words, rather than any idiosyncratic choice or combination of them, is a mark of his practice. One could choose at random from his sermons passages that might have been written by others in his century. But wherever we open there is a scrupulosity at work. The very procedure of the sermons, the exposition of texts regarded as sacred, impelled Donne to this care. For as he strikingly argues, "In the midst of Paradise grew the *Tree of knowledge*, and the *tree of life*: In this Paradise, the Scripture, every word is both those Trees; there is Life and Knowledge in every word of the Word of God" (VIII, 131). The very start of the sermon was, as he termed it, to "propose words" to the congregation (VII, 94).

But let us take a relatively neutral passage, not an unusually eloquent one, and observe Donne's search for accuracy in the words he emphasizes. For the sake of clarity I have italicized words reflecting a marked choice of meaning. (I have omitted Donne's own italicization of the Latin words, to avoid confusion.)

> . . . would all this satisfie that Inquisition which we have brought, how this assurance of the Resurrection *accrues* to us? Would any of these reasons . . . convince a man, who were not at all *prepossessed*, and *preoccu-pated* with a beliefe of the resurrection, with an assurance thereof? The resurrection was always a *mystery* in it selfe; Sacrum secretum, a holy *secret*, and above the search of reason. For there are secrets and mysteries of two kindes, as the Schoole presents them; some things are so Quia quaedem interposita, Because, though the thing be *near enough* unto me, yet something is *inter-posed* between me, and it, and so I cannot see it: And some things are so, Quia longè seposita, because they are at so remote a distance, as that, though nothing be in-terposed, yet my sight cannot extend to them. In the first sense, the Sacraments are mysteries, because though the grace therein bee neare mee, yet there is Velamen interpositum, there is a *visible figure*, a *sensible signe*, and *seale*, between me, and that *grace*, which is exhibited to me in the Sacrament: In the second sense, the resur-rection is a *mystery*, because it is so *farre removed*, as

that it *concernes* our state and condition in the next world . . . (VII, 98).

One sees that the distinctions made arise out of an effort toward clarity, and a careful logic dominates the contrast Donne is drawing here. At the same time, he moves to terms like *secret, mystery*, and *grace*, which convey not only distinctions but certain reverberations of feeling. As in the poems, logic is the substratum of emotion for Donne.

The exactitude of distinction apparent in all the sermons, the more eloquent as well as the more prosaic, is one propellant toward antithesis, a figure of phrase and sentence noticeable everywhere in Donne's writing, but never or rarely used merely for rhetorical effect.

Frequently a long passage will build to a climax of intensity focused on one such unexpectedly precise word—for example, on the seemingly unsuggestive word *disparagement* in a great sequence from his sermon at the marriage of Margaret Washington. In the middle of this sermon, Donne turns from the duties of human marriage to discuss the spiritual marriage of Christ and the believer.

> And can these persons meet? in such a distance, and
> in such a disparagement can these persons meet? the Son
> of God and the son of man? . . . When I consider Christ
> to have been from before all beginnings, and to be still
> the Image of the Father, the same stamp upon the same
> metall, and my self a peece of rusty copper, in which
> those lines of the Image of God which were imprinted in
> me in my Creation are defaced and worn, and washed
> and burnt, and ground away, by my many, and many,
> and many sins: When I consider Christ in his Circle, in
> glory with his Father . . . and then consider myself in

my circle . . . can these persons, this Image of God, this God himself, this glorious God, and this vessell of earth, this earth itself, this inglorious worm of the earth, meet without disparagement? (III, 250).

Many of Donne's skills are harmonized in this passage; Mrs. Simpson has commented on the subtle alliteration, which is even more evident in some portions that I have omitted, and has pointed out also the antitheses and the repetition of certain fundamental words. What I am emphasizing here is that from the opening simply stated question, where the word *disparagement* is introduced, Donne conducts his hearer to what seems finally undeniable impossibility conveyed by the final ring of *disparagement*. Sometimes the impeccable word gives the central rather than the concluding accent, as does the word *illustrate* in the great passage on mercy soon to be discussed.

In the passage just quoted from the marriage sermon (although it has necessarily been abbreviated here), one observes that the contrasting parallel clauses that are the vaulting of this arch do not conform to any normal grammatical construction. "When I consider. . . when I consider" is led to a conclusion not by "then I . . ." but by the surprising shift to "can these. . . ." This is elliptical and more forceful. Such a freedom of progress—although by symmetrical rises—is characteristic of the variation in ordered units of meaning that is the heart of Donne's rhythm.

His sentences have no typical pattern. As those who have specialized in "baroque" prose style have pointed out, the brief statement or rapid question has as frequent a place as the rounded or loose period. Miss Joan Webber, in her discerning study, has identified a clue to his structure: "the sentence does not always appear to have a central point of focus, but . . . its balance shifts as the reader progresses or speaker continues."[4]

In this style designed for both listeners and readers, the secret is movement, and variety of movement, with, throughout, a courtesy of tone. The key may be disarmingly quiet, a simple telling:

> At the first meeting of *Isaac* and *Rebecca*, he was gone out to meditate in the fields, and she came riding that way, with his fathers man, who was imployed in making that marriage; and when upon asking she knew that it was he who was to be her husband, *she tooke a vaile and covered her face*, sayes that story. What freedome, and nearnesse soever they were to come to after, yet there was a modesty, and a bashfulnesse, and a reservednesse required before; and her first kindnesse should be but to be seen (V, 340).

But when some relation of ideas is to be presented, then Donne more often calls upon a deliberate, accentuated symmetry:

> That soule, that is accustomed to direct her selfe to God, upon every occasion, that, as a flowre at Sun-rising, conceives a sense of God, in every beame of his, and spreads and dilates it selfe towards him, in a thankfulnesse, in every small blessing that he sheds upon her; that soule, that as a flowre at the Suns declining, contracts and gathers in, and shuts up her self . . . whensoever she heares her Saviour wounded by an oath, or blasphemy, or execration; that soule, who whatsoever string be strucken in her, base or treble, her high or her low estate, is ever tun'd toward God, that soule prayes sometimes when it does not know that it prayes (IV, 310).

This passage exemplifies one of Donne's most evident skills: that of a suspension and then a resolution, simultaneous, of the sentence and its meaning. In all the best sermons there are similar way-stations marking the progress.

His rhythm is Donne's most fundamental resource, in his prose as in his poetry. Imagery and metaphor would be soluble colours without the sustaining structure they are let into, or open out of, or upon occasion help to define.

The vitality of Donne's images and metaphors, not their abundance, is what one discovers in a reading of many of the sermons. There may be pages without a trope other than the possible ones turned on the Biblical text. We may be drawn through knotholes of the ruminations of the Fathers, by mere comparison and exegesis, without any new root in experience except the preacher's own modesty and rigour. It may seem surprising to maintain, but I am tempted to propose that the infrequency of imagery and metaphor in the sermons gives them all the more lustre. Certain ones are so frequent—and re-echo also from the poems—that we tend to think the total number great.

While most metaphors contain or suggest some image (some evocation or recreation of our sense experience, visual or auditory, tactile or kinaesthetic), not every image reaches to a metaphor, or finding of similarity in dissimilarity. Pure imagery in Donne is rare. He seems to like not merely the pun on the meaning of Adam, but the redness of red earth, because he so often associates the name with the colour. In his poems there are many image-metaphors drawn from the translation of one mode of appearance into another—world into map, tear into globe, face into image on a coin, light into shadow. Of landscape seen or human features, we find few examples—usually in a negative, like the "five grey hairs" or the sweat upon his mistress's breast. The primrose of Primrose Hill is unaccompanied by other flowers. In the sermons, an awareness of the physical world is more often called upon, but that is perhaps because the Biblical landscape is always in the background. "A fountaine breaks out in the wildernesse, but that fountaine cares not, whether any Man come to fetch water, or no; A fresh and fit gale blowes upon the Sea, but it cares not whether the Mariners hoise saile or no; A rose blowes in your garden, but it calls you not to smell to it" (v, 125). Here are windows let in upon the abstract argument about Christ's calling believers to come to the Church. Donne resorts to no metaphor here, he offers direct impression. Yet within an instant it becomes a means, by contrast, of analogy.

And it is the purpose of analogy, rather than that of opening a sudden new insight into experience, that Donne's metaphors in the sermons chiefly serve—that, and the pleasure of concreteness in an otherwise abstract discourse. Often and often, as in the poems, the figures are of voyaging, ships, seas, maps, harbours, discoveries. "[God] hath not discovered, but made that Northerne passage, to pass by the frozen Sea of calamity, and tribulation, to Paradise, to the heavenly Jerusalem" (vi, 212). This is as vivid and quick as Herbert's "The land of spices, something understood"—yet Herbert's equivalence for prayer is more truly a metaphor than Donne's analogy of the frozen Northwest Passage for death, and Cathay for Paradise. Not that one is better than the other, certainly; they perform different functions. The rareness of truly denotative metaphors in Donne's prose—metaphors which instantly evoke an identity not otherwise perceptible—makes them all the more effective when they do occur ("this Song of Deborah were enough . . . to slumber any storme," or the remarkable "herb of grace," which speaks pages of meaning in three words). Or, in an unusual metaphor evolved from an image of shapes and colours, Donne expresses his imagination of rapture in the contemplation of God: ". . . and like a Lily in Paradise, out of red earth, I shall see my soule rise out of his blade, in a candor, and in an innocence, contracted there . . ." (ii, 210-211). The metaphorical force of candor, especially, has been liberated by the images that precede it. But such a complex of sensation and feeling compacted in an image-metaphor is less frequent than the effort to present logically, as well as concretely, a hypothetical relationship rather than a similarity.

An important service that metaphors perform in the sermons is to articulate the structure of the whole, to serve as knowable architecture. On of the clearest examples of Donne's success in giving, as it were, a visual design to what would otherwise be sheer exposition of dogma is the pair of sermons that open volume ix in the Potter and Simpson edition. These two were preached before King James on the text from Genesis, "And God said, let us make man, in our image, after our likeness." Donne opens the combined discourses with a proem that powerfully creates a sense of the vastness of the earth, its undiscovered lands, uninhabited spaces, the fact that the globe had never been "compassed, till our age," the possibility that heaven contains "many earths, many worlds, as big as this, which we inhabit" (ix, 47-48). Then, in announcing his division of the text in the two sermons, he proposes the idea of a voyage through all the points of the compass, East, West, North, and South, as a guide to the topics he will conduct his hearers through. In turn, *Faciamus*, "Let us make," is East, and stands for the Trinity, since God spoke here in the plural; *Hominem*, Man, is their West, Adam; *Imaginem*, in our image, will be represented as North; and likeness to God suggests knowledge of another world, the last part of the voyage, to be taken as the South.

Thus the congregation is encouraged to enter upon this effort of understanding by an enhancement, the fascination of voyaging, and an encouragement, a reminder at each stage of the distances already spanned. At the end of the first sermon Donne humorously combines the idea of a ship's grounding on sand with a pun on the hour glass that announced this sermon's end: "we are strooke upon the sand; and must stay another Tyde, and another gale for our North, and South" (IX, 67). One wonders if Donne knew the lines from *The Merchant of Venice*:

> I should not see the sandy hour glass run
> But I should think of shallows and of flats
> Vailing her high-top lower than her ribs
> To kiss her burial (I. i. 26-29).

In this pair of sermons the fundamental metaphor has the value, not of insight into an uncommon likeness in things observed, but of giving concrete outward form to what would otherwise seem a mainly abstract discourse. The metaphor here is not "unity in multeity" or "discordia concors," it is a means of ordonnance.

Except for subsidiary ones, metaphor is not as often as we might expect an entrance into the theme itself of the sermon. This does happen in the second of a complex pair Donne wrote out in 1630 from his notes of what was apparently one sermon delivered at The

Hague in 1619. Here, in expanding Christ's call to Andrew and Peter to follow him, and become fishers of men, Donne moves to a climactic last part in which the world is the sea and the Gospel is the fisherman's net. What is interesting about these metaphors is that Donne does not move through them in a logical progress—as for example in the stiff twin compasses conceit of the poem, "A Valediction: Forbidding Mourning," where he is discovering additional resemblances and developing an argument from them. Here, on the other hand, he opens out more varied and to some extent contrasting aspects of likeness between the world and the sea.

> The world is a Sea in many respects and assimilations. It is a Sea, as it is subject to stormes, and tempests; Every man (and every man is a world) feels that. And then, it is never the shallower for the calmnesse, The Sea is as deepe, there is as much water in the Sea, in a calme, as in a storme; we may be drowned in a calme and flattering fortune . . . as irrevocably, as in a wrought Sea, in Adversity; So the world is a Sea. It is a Sea, as it is bottomlesse to any line, which we can sound it with, and endless to any discovery that we can make of it. . . . But yet we are sure the Sea hath a bottome, and sure that it hath limits, that it cannot overpasse; The power of the greatest in the world . . . cannot exceed those bounds, which God hath placed for them . . . (II, 306).

And so on; this refrain-metaphor opens out many other aspects of human life, capped by the last, that the world is like a sea, "in this respect, that the Sea is no place of habitation, but a passage to our habitations" (II, 307). This is followed by development of the metaphor of the Gospel as a net, and the work of the ministry as fishing.

The metaphor of the minister as fisherman with a net tempts Donne to remind his auditory that he is preaching, and that they are hearing a sermon. And this habit of his, which is in itself a token of honesty as well as determination, raises the essential question of the sermon as a form of literature. Where shall we locate the meaning and energy of its themes? For, although rhythm, imagery, and metaphor cause the writing in these sermons to be studied and enjoyed, the realization of these structural values is incomplete unless the themes open into independence.

In a major sense they are handicapped by being predetermined. Christian theology has had a long development by this time; the doctrines of original sin, redemption, resurrection, immortality have taken shapes not to be essentially renewed. Areas of controversy existed between the Anglicans and the Roman Catholics on the one hand or Puritans on the other; here Donne took his part in marking out the path of the *via media*. But the appeal to the reader's experience, the renovation of that experience that we expect from literature, cannot be grounded in some other authority such as that of theology or science—although it may be stimulated by them. Donne's treatment of the traditional terms of Christian doctrine is attentively summarized, for example, in William R. Mueller's *John Donne: Preacher*.[5] Mr. Mueller is concerned to indicate Donne's position from the theologian's point of view—and on this there is even more to say in detail than he attempts. But he does not ask what we must ask: does Donne, can he, *make* of these questions anything that approaches the new coherence of a work of art?

Often the note of individuality is felt directly in Donne's handling of minor themes, which are nevertheless absorbing to him. One of these, for example, is that of the calling. No matter how transcendent the doctrine being elicited from the text—and all lead to an unremitting futurity—Donne makes a place for man's conduct of activity here and now. For a man to walk sincerely in his calling, keep his calling, is itself a primary value. And he sees that value in work of diverse kinds, with a humorous demand for tolerance:

> God in Christ may be had in an active, and sociable life, denoted in the Pigeon, and in the solitary and contemplative life, denoted in the Turtle; Let not Westminster despise the Church, nor the Church the Exchange, nor the Exchange and trade despise Armes; God in Christ may be had in every lawfull calling (vii, 282).

This emphasis on the calling—more often associated with Puritanism—recurs in the sermons and is one evidence of Donne's awareness of the present. A more surprising example of it, almost, is his consistent allowance for man's enjoyment of his lot if it be a fortunate one:

> For, beloved, Salvation it selfe being so often presented to us in the names of Glory, and of Joy, we cannot thinke that the way to that glory is a sordid life affected here, an obscure, a beggarly, a negligent abandoning of all wayes of preferment, or riches, or estimation in this World, for the glory of Heaven shines downe in these beames hither; neither can men thinke, that the way to the joyes of Heaven is a joylesse severeness, a rigid austerity; for as God loves a cheerefull giver, so he loves a cheerefull taker, that takes hold of his mercies and his comforts with a cheerefull heart (iii, 270).

And in a well-constructed sermon on the text "rejoice evermore" Donne counsels men to rejoice "in Temporalibus" that they may anticipate the enjoyment of spiritual goods.

But such attention to the present conduct of life, though observable in the sermons, and genuine, is comparatively infrequent. This fact accounts for the relative lack of first-hand observation of people. There is more in Taylor—his young men with the necks of doves, his children, his portrait of Lady Carberry, much more solidly painted than Donne's of Magdalen Herbert, Lady Danvers. There are moments when we feel Donne alert to human beings and their ways:

> We should wonder to see a Mother in the midst of many sweet Children passing her time in making babies and puppets for her own delight. We should wonder to see a man, whose Chambers and Galleries were full of curious master-peeces, thrust in a Village Fair to looke upon sixpenny pictures, and three farthing prints (IX, 80).

But compared with the Satires or the Elegies we note the lack of realistic observation of others in the sermons. One notable passage is reminiscent of the satires:

> Are there not yet misrepresentations of men in Courts? Is there not yet Oppression in the Country? A starving of men, and pampering of dogs? *A swallowing of the needy? A buying of the poor for a pair of shooes, and a selling to the hungry refuse corn?* Is there not yet Oppression in the Country? Is there not yet Extortion in *Westminster?* . . . Is there not yet Collusion and Circumvention in the City? (IX, 182-183).

This was pressing it home. Donne rarely addressed himself so straightforwardly to the social abuses of his time; his laconic questions and refrain-like repetition here underline his earnestness. A passage like this does something to offset his conventional bows to the monarchy or the seeming complacency that leads him elsewhere to assert that "the incorrigible vagabond is farther from all wayes of goodnesse, then the corruptest rich man is" (VI, 304). (Yet this occurs in a sermon wherein Donne with considerable insight develops his view of the temptations that beset the poor and their need for a calling.)

Another theme appealing in itself is Donne's praise of the sociableness of God—occurring, appropriately enough, in a sermon that emphasizes the infinity of souls to be saved, and in several faiths.

> Our first step . . . is the *sociablenesse*, the *communicablenesse* of God; He loves holy meetings, he loves the *communion of Saints, the household of the faithful . . . his delight is to be with the Sons of men,* and that the Sons of men should be with him: Religion is not a *melancholy*; the spirit of God is not a *dampe* . . . they say we cannot name God, but *plurally*: so sociable, so communicable, so extensive, so derivative of himself, is God . . . (VI, 152).

The generosity and fervour of Donne's conception of deity goes far to offset this otherwise morbid preoccupation with sin and death. Yet he could hardly have foregone emphasis on either, given the closed equation of that Christian theology: original sin, redemption by Christ, grace offered to man, Salvation leading to resurrection after death. The infinitude of life was abbreviated in the framework of these conceptions as they were then entertained. His capacity for metaphor did not save Donne from an incredible literalness of understanding—as, for example, when he imagines the start of existence: ". . . though sin doe not get the start of God, God does not get the start of sin neither. Powers, that dwell so far asunder, as *Heaven,* and *Hell, God* and the *Devill,* meet in an instant in my soul, in the minute of my quickening, and the Image of *God*, and the Image of *Adam*, Originall sin, enter into me at once, in one, and the same act" (II, 59). With a similar breathtaking simplitude he asks, "May I not say, that I had rather be redeemed by Christ Jesus than be innocent? rather be beholden to Christs death, for my salvation, then to Adams standing in his innocencie?" (VI, 183).

This question is a pivot in one of Donne's greatest sermons, and on his greatest theme, that of mercy. It will, finally, be instructive to consider this "exercise" as a whole, for it offers a fair test of the advantages and disadvantages of the sermon as a form of prose.

The text Donne chose—taken from a lesson read in the Anglican Church on Christmas evening—offers no immediate clue to the heart of his discourse: "Therefore the Lord shall give you a signe; Behold, A Virgin shall conceive and beare a son, and shall call his name Immanuel." This Old Testament text constitutes a promise to the obdurate King Achaz. To transform it into a message of mercy, Donne seizes on the first word "therefore," as evidence that God may take *any* occasion to show mercy, and that on this occasion he puts mercy above anger. The *divisio* of the text advises the congregation, then, that mercy will be the first theme; the second part will deal with the particular way of mercy, a sign; the third with the sign's meaning ("Behold, A Virgin," etc.) and in particular with her giving the child the name Immanuel.

Donne never wrote with more generosity, understanding, and music of feeling than in the first part here. Opening the idea that the mercy of God has no limitation in time, and the names of first or last derogate from it, "for first and last are but ragges of time," he proceeds to a moving climax of this section—and all admirers of Donne's prose would agree that here he is at his best:

> God made Sun and Moon to distinguish seasons, and day, and night, and we cannot have the fruits of the earth but in their seasons: But God hath made no decree to distinguish the seasons of his mercies; In paradise, the fruits were ripe, the first minute, and in heaven it is alwaies Autumne, his mercies are ever in their maturity. . . . If some King of the earth have so large an extent of Dominion, in North, and South, as that he hath Winter and Summer together in his Dominions, so large an extent East and West, as that he hath day and night together in his Dominions, much more hath God mercy and judgment together: He brought light out of darkness, not out of a lesser light, he can bring the Summer out of Winter, though thou have no Spring; though in the wayes of fortune, or understanding, or conscience, thou have been benighted till now, wintered and frozen, clouded and eclypsed, damped and benummed, smothered and stupefied till now, now God comes to thee, not as in the dawning of the day, not as in the bud of the spring, but as the Sun at noon to illustrate all shadowes, as the sheaves in harvest, to fill all penuries, all occasions invite his mercies, and all times are his seasons (vi, 172).

Against the swinging of the pendulum of day and night, light and darkness, summer and winter, amid the seasonal fruits and harvests, appears this unquenchable mercy glowing in the metaphor "as the Sun at noon to *illustrate* all shadowes." Here is the symmetry of rhythm varied by the reversed parallels of Donne's sentence structure; here is simultaneous resolution of cadence and meaning at the end.

But the purpose of the sermon is exposition of the text in a manner to "edify and exhort" the congregation. Donne strives to continue on a high level by allusions to God as a circle, the church as his chariot, and mercy as his language, but as he proceeds to consider the giving of signs, he is led into a tortuous path. When he comes to his third section, "Behold, A Virgin shall conceive," he goes off from the theme of mercy to consider the perplexities of a virgin birth, and various opinions of the fathers are invoked. The fundamental unity of the sermon is seriously jeopardized. The necessities of the text, the preacher's reminder to the congregation of the Church's claims, detract from the wholeness of his consideration of mercy. At the end, by his treatment of the name Immanuel, "God with us," Donne finally achieves a level of discourse worthy of his beginning.

The early essayist, like the sermon writer, may take off from one or more quotations, but he cannot so easily avail himself of the treasury of experience and incident in the Bible nor draw a sustained meditation from something like the paradox of God's mercy to King Achaz. In Donne's sermons at their best there is an amplitude, a sustained working through of significant major themes. Thus in the development of imaginative prose the sermon overlaps with the essay and the free organic prose meditation developed in the seventeenth century by Browne and, much later, carried to its height by Emerson and Thoreau. Occasionally in Donne's sermons there is a stretch that, taken separately, could constitute an independent essay.

One remarkable example occurs in his sermon on the theme, "For, where your treasure is, there will your heart be also." In this sermon he expands into a profound exploration of the need for, and threats to, wholeness of heart.

> And yet truly . . . to recollect our selves, . . . to assemble and muster our selves, and to bend our hearts intirely and intensely . . . upon something, is, by reason of the various fluctuations of our corrupt nature, and the infinite multiplicity of Objects, such a Work as man needs to be called upon . . . to do it. Therefore is there no word in Scripture so often added to the heart, as that of intireness; *Toto Corde, Omni Corde, Pleno Corde*: Do this with *all thine heart*, with a *whole heart*, with a *full heart* . . . (IX, 174-175).

He then unfolds various degrees and kinds of incompleteness of heart: "*Cor nullam*, Incogitancy" is the first. It may be bad: "the soul that does not think . . . cannot be said to actuate, but to evaporate." But there may also be a good "nullification" through a rapture— and here Donne reminds us of some passages in Browne: "I come to such a melting and pouring out of my heart, that there be no spirit, that is, none of mine own spirit left in me . . . this is a blessed nullification of the heart" (IX, 177). This gives God a vacuity, a new place to create a new heart in.

A further threat to entirety of the heart that he unfolds is *cor duplex*, the divided or distracted heart. Of this he writes with obvious self-knowledge—for Donne had experienced *cor duplex*. Then he proceeds to show that man may overcome *cor nullam* and *cor duplex* only to succumb to inconstancy, *cor vagam*, "a various, a wandering heart, all smoaks into Inconstancie" (IX,

181). And inconstancy was, in Donne's early poems, a preoccupation.

But after these explorations and without conclusions from them, Donne is led away by the necessities of his text to expatiate on *treasure*, treasures of wickedness and sin, overseen by an Old Testament deity incompatible with the thinking in the early part of the sermon. Only in the last paragraph—and this frequently happens—is Donne able to rise again to a high level of thought and feeling in his portrayal of spiritual treasures.

Donne's approach to a free meditation on entirety of the heart is thus sacrificed to the overriding form of the sermon. Independent commitment to the theme gives way to a predetermined commitment to doctrine and dogma. But even in searching the interstices of meaning in the text, Donne is often engaged in work like that of a modern literary critic. We may follow with a similar enjoyment in the analysis of the question for its own sake.

The shape of the sermon became more nearly enlightening in itself—apart from the import it contained—in Donne's best sermons. We can never afford merely to excerpt from them. I cannot say, as Joan Webber and Mrs. Simpson have said, that the art of his sermons equals that of his poetry. In all the major and many of the lesser poems, not a word can be dispensed with from beginning to end, not a line fails to live with every other line; there is nothing ever extraneous. You cannot maintain this of even a dozen of his sermons. But in them he did achieve a more profound communication than even in the *Devotions*, where, as Miss Webber has said, Donne was "both subject and object of his meditations."[6] In the sermons the "eloquent I" is not Donne himself, but the source of good that he venerates. The lapses into practicality or ephemeral exhortations occur only because his calling obliged him to summon others to belief. If the sermons do not "equal" the poetry as art, it is partly that although both are incomparable, one cannot compare them. And although only the poet could have written these sermons, it was a different kind of work, and the writer knew it to be.

The rhythm of Donne's prose is as unmistakable as Browne's, and essentially different. No other seventeenth-century prose writer had so many channels of meaning at his command: not only rhythm, but words that are like transistors, shining imagery, metaphors that unify thought and liberate feeling, the orchestration of paragraphs and pages.

The essay in its original form—whether Montaigne's more ruminative or Bacon's more aphoristic—does not demand an accompaniment of belief by the reader. Nor does the prose meditation by Browne—although it assumes our willingness to entertain belief. Donne's sermons, many of Emerson's essays, D. H. Lawrence's, appeal powerfully for assent. Of course commitment, or the refusal of it, can be a powerful component in the reader's interest. Or he may be stimulated by his awareness of the stages that led the writer to it.

It is hard to say why the sermon in English reached its height in the time of Andrewes, Donne, and Taylor. The conduct and tenor of the discourse is often sheer delight. One reason is that the harmonics of English prose after fifty years of eager experimentation and discipline had developed such extraordinary resources. The other is the concern of these men with themes that penetrate the contours of experience, whatever the form of the reader's belief. At that time, too, there was the possibility in the sermon of a dialogue of feeling that later had to find different terms. To ponder analogues of these themes more freely for their own sake was the work of Browne, later of Emerson and Thoreau.

# Sir Thomas Browne 2

## and Meditative Prose

Sir Thomas Browne is in one way the most original prose writer of the seventeenth century; not simply for the uniqueness of tone, the individual voice imparted to every sentence, but because he evolved a form of writing that contained the seed of growth. The sermon had no future, the Baconian essay was perfected by Bacon, never to be equalled. Browne's prose, in contrast, created an encounter of thought with observation available for new development long afterwards by writers as different as Dr. Johnson and De Quincey, Emerson and Melville.

In his lifetime Browne published four books (*Religio Medici* 1642, *Pseudodoxia Epidemica* 1646, the related pieces *Urn Burial* and *Garden of Cyrus* 1658). After his death another discourse appeared, *Christian Morals* (1716). Although he may not have finished working on it, its composition is deliberate and represents a further stage in Browne's development.

In the making of *Religio Medici*, Browne was fortunate in being at a remote place where he had little access to books. We need not doubt his statement that it was composed "at leisurable hours" for his own private exercise. As T. S. Eliot has suggested, what is usually called lyric and might preferably be called meditative poetry is written in the first voice, that of the poet speaking to himself or no one. And a consonant voice is the secret of Browne's *Religio*; unlike the sermon or the pamphlet or oration, it is not addressed to an audience, does not seek to convince, persuade, or change commitment. From the outset, there is a turning of thought in the light, an awareness of the dark from which it comes. The progress is not by heaping of proofs or logic, but by an undercurrent of association.

Like a bird circling before landing, Browne begins by reading the bearings he knows, his unbellicose acceptance of Christian faith as channelled through the Reformation and the Church of England. His refusal to judge "heretics" like Jews and Turks, his sympathy with Catholic ceremonies, set a mood for the discussion first of heresies that have appealed to him and then of the experience of belief. All this first part is to prepare for a wider peregrination. He calmly states: "Since I was of understanding to know we know nothing my reason hath beene more pliable to the will of faith; I am now content to understand a mystery without a rigid definition in an easie and Platonick description"[1] (I, 19). And thus he is ready to start his way into the great central themes of *Religio*. His manner of opening them is

significant: "In my solitary and retired imaginations . . .
I remember I am not alone, and therefore forget not
to contemplate him and his attributes who is ever with
mee, especially those two mighty ones, his wisedome and
eternitie . . ." (I, 19-20). The whole first section of
*Religio*, the fundament of Faith, exemplifies Whitehead's finding that religion is what man does with his
solitariness. The result, for Browne, is the contemplation of Wisdom and Eternity in God.

After unravelling initially these two great skeins,
Browne expands upon the theme of wisdom. Throughout his treatment of both themes, however, there is the
recurrent testing of man's capacity for knowledge; if no
man can attain wisdom in the final sense, yet the
thought of it alone makes Browne content that he was
"bred in the way of study" (I, 21). Man is unready for
"Contemplations Metaphysicall" upon the nature of
God's wisdom, he is called to study "those impressions
hee hath left on his creatures, and the obvious effects
of nature" (I, 22). By a great loop of meaning Browne
expands his theme to encompass his reading of the Book
of Nature. He reveals his delight in the study of minute
things, his feeling that nothing is ugly except chaos,
and he rises finally to his declaration that Nature is the
Art of God. Throughout, he is sustained by his conviction of the unity between perceiver and perceived; as
he says, in a sentence Emerson or Thoreau would find
prophetic of their own beliefs, "Wee carry with us the
wonders, wee seeke without us: There is all *Africa*, and
her prodigies in us; we are that bold and adventurous
piece of nature, which he that studies wisely learnes in a
*compendium* what others labour at in a divided piece
and endlesse volume" (I, 24).

In this entrance to the wisdom men may truly seek,

Browne deals inimitably with themes which were, of course, known to, accessible to his potential readers. This is, I think, a reason why the great prose writers of the seventeenth century possess an advantage not shared by their successors of the nineteenth. Because the earlier ones could in a measure take for granted a greater share of assent, they avoid eccentricity, whim, or overemphasis.

The difference between the kind of self-portrait created by, say, Lamb or De Quincey, and Browne's, is the difference between self-consciousness and self-awareness. Browne comes before us as a believer discovering to us only as he does to himself the perspectives of his mind and feelings, which he refuses to regard as fixed forever, yet relies upon. The features of his self-portrait are given at the outset of *Religio*. He tells us how his reverence is awakened, and how he refuses to divide himself from others on the grounds of opinion, and most of all of the nature of his will to believe;

> Some beleeve the better for seeing Christ his Sepulchre, and when they have seene the Red Sea, doubt not of the miracle. Now contrarily I blesse my selfe, and am thankefull that I lived not in the dayes of miracles, that I never saw Christ nor his Disciples; I would not have beene one of the Israelites that passed the Red Sea, nor one of Christs Patients, on whom he wrought his wonders; then had my faith beene thrust upon me, nor should I enjoy that greater blessing pronounced to all that believe & saw not (I, 18).

In Part I the incidental detail of behaviour ("At a solemne Procession I have wept abundantly," I, 13) is rare. What we have is a pattern of positions from which the

commitments of mind and feelings may be observed, in
the "Cosmography of my selfe" (I, 24). What in a self-
portrait by Rembrandt would be conveyed by the expression of the eyes and mouth, the disposition of the
countenance, Browne gives to us by the lineaments of
his convictions. The portrait deepens towards the end
of Part I, as he contemplates death, resurrection, immortality. With a musical deftness, by transitions like
breathing or walking, Browne leads his reader on a
winding but not aimless path. He has, as a human being,
taken his place on the Great Chain of Being to examine
his relationship to angels or devils, spirit or matter.
And as so often, the relationship of man to other forms
of being is to Browne a kind of metaphor in existence
itself; thus in his famous image man is an "amphibium"
living in the two worlds of matter and spirit. In acknowledging death as inevitable to man, Browne's portrait becomes more distinctly that of an individual person. "I am naturally bashfull, nor hath conversation,
age, or travell, beene able to effront, or enharden me;
yet I have one part of modesty, which I have seldome
discovered in another, . . . I am not so much afraid of
death, as ashamed thereof . . ." (I, 51). Accepting death
as part of his condition, he nevertheless takes a deep
reckoning of his lineage in the world. As he was to do
with more vaulting architecture in *Urn Burial*, he
thinks of time's end and its beginning, and his participa-
tion in the whole of it:

> *Before Abraham was, I am*, is the saying of Christ; yet it
> is true in some sense if I say it of my selfe, for I was not
> only before my selfe, but *Adam*, that is, in the Idea of
> God. . . . And in this sense, I say, the world was before
> the Creation, and at an end before it had a beginning;

and thus was I dead before I was alive; though my grave be *England*, my dying place was Paradise, and *Eve* miscarried of mee before she conceiv'd of Cain (I, 68).

In the first part of *Religio*, Browne has achieved a self-understanding that the sermon writer can only touch upon inferentially, and character writer tangentially. In his contemplation of the Wisdom and Eternity of God, Browne has placed himself upon the Chain of Being, and found his place in and throughout time. Throughout his discourse by his responsiveness to the mutual impact of belief and idea Browne has shown that the discovery of Faith and Hope is like an antiphon of the unity and diversity in nature itself.

In Part II, devoted to the theme of Charity, Browne portrays the freedom of attention that comes from tolerance. His liking for variety in people, his being "framed and constellated to all climates," his hatred of useless controversy, and of the hostility of nations to each other, disclose a willingness to measure life that is shadowed only by a dislike of the "Multitude." Although Browne does not tell us as much about himself as Montaigne does, he writes in a similar spirit, with a humour *divers et ondoyant*. We learn of his interest in languages, astronomy, botany, and above all of his susceptibility to music. The dominant theme is that of man as the microcosm, but here, as he brings himself to our notice, he demonstrates that it is indeed the microcosm of his own frame that he casts his eye upon. In spite of the preparation for death and the expectation of an unknowable life thereafter, *Religio Medici*, with its love of mystery, and willingness to permit differences, is a young man's book, a harmony of convictions that are in youth if at all to be harmoniously combined—the portrait of the believer as a young man. Perhaps nowhere until we reach the less closely woven pattern of the early volumes of Thoreau's *Journal* is there a comparable book.

In *Religio*, Browne has made a true advance in the art of prose, developing a form in which an individual sensibility is active in the exploration of ideas, without didacticism. When this book was published, approximately seven years after its composition, Browne must have been preparing his next, much longer one, *Pseudodoxia Epidemica*. For the reader interested in the thought of the seventeenth century, this is an absorbing document. Written in the Baconian spirit, testing popular fallacies by "sense" (experiment) and reason, as well as by a comparison of authorities, *Pseudodoxia* shows some noticeable changes in Browne's thinking. He has developed a new and firm allegiance to "reason" that is quite different from the attitude expressed in *Religio* where he had maintained "this I think is no vulgar part of faith to believe a thing not only above, but contrary to reason, and against the arguments of our proper senses" (I, 19). In *Pseudodoxia*, reason is "the very root of our natures, and the principles thereof common unto all" (II, 49). And Christ himself is praised because his teaching appealed to the mind, and his life "as it was conformable unto His Doctrine, so was that unto the highest rules of Reason" (II, 28).

Both *Religio* and *Pseudodoxia* show the workings of a mind sceptical in T. S. Eliot's sense of the word: "Scepticism—by which of course I do not mean infidelity or destructiveness (still less the unbelief which is due to mental sloth) but the habit of examining evidence and the capacity for delayed decision."[2] In *Religio* the scepticism is directed not against the willingness to believe, but against the arrogance of some believers toward others. In *Pseudodoxia*, scepticism is an exercise in discrimination—for observers, readers, and relayers of uncritically received opinions. But in casting his net so widely to catch popular and obstinate fallacies, Browne is overwhelmed by endless and unrelated particulars. Externally, *Pseudodoxia* has a planned structure. Browne begins with errors respecting the mineral, vegetable, and animal kingdoms, proceeds to deal with fallacies of opinion about man, and reserves to the last those attaching to wide branches of human activity, culture, and learning. But, if there is a formal pattern giving the order of books a seemingly ascending purpose in accord with the Chain of Being, there is no organic relationship of the separate inquiries or larger categories. The book is a collection of fragments, of details oddly assorted, having no unity in themselves, cast up together like the strange cargoes of wrecked ships. The freight is assembled by the driving force of a man's curiosity, which, lacking a central purpose, leaves it in curious heaps. Although in one of his memorable phrases Browne compares this book to a voyage into "the America and untravelled parts of Truth" (II, 5), there is no headway. He provided what is perhaps the best comment on the whole: "although in this long journey we miss the intended end, yet are there many things of truth disclosed by the way; and the collateral verity may . . . requite the capital indiscovery" (II, 481).

From *Pseudodoxia* we can expect no new accomplishment in the art of prose as it builds structure out of theme. The book has, however, a unique value, which may be savoured at random: its individual idiom. Opening the volumes almost anywhere the reader can hear the voice of Browne. I shall take only two examples, the first from a deliberately casual turning of the pages.

Wondrous things are promised from the Glow-worm; from thence perpetual lights are pretended, and waters said to be distilled which afford a lustre in the night; and this is asserted by Cardan, Albertus, Gaudentinus, Mizaldus, and many more. But hereto we cannot with reason assent: for the light made by this animal depends much upon its life. For when they are dead they shine not, nor alwaies while they live; but are obscure or light, according to the protrusion of their luminous parts, as observation will instruct us. For this flammeous light is not over all the body, but only visible on the inward side; in a small white part near the tail. Where this is full and seemeth protruded, there ariseth a flame of a circular figure and Emerald green colour; which is discernable in any dark place in the day; but when it falleth and seemeth contracted, the light disappeareth, and the colour of the part only remaineth. Now this light, as it appeareth and disappeareth in their life, so doth it go quite out at their death. As we have observed in some, which preserved in fresh grass have lived and thrived eighteen days; but as they declined, and the luminous humour dried, their light grew languid, and at last went out with their lives (II, 262).

Not every part of *Pseudodoxia* has the animation and progress of this passage, but many have. Browne's eye and mind are upon the object, some of the finest strokes of phrasing result from the effort towards accuracy and compression—"obscure," "flammeous," "a small white part near the tail." There is no effort to enhance the importance of what he is saying, but his grave and equable concentration on the whole phenomenon is reflected in the alliteration of "perpetual lights are pretended" or of the whole last clause. Even a writer as praiseworthy as Evelyn cannot, for example in his *Sylva*, rival Browne's ability to recapture the reader's attention after he has lost it.

Again, in a section marked by inherent humour, Browne begins his argument as follows:

> Another mistake there may be in the Picture of our first Parents, who after the manner of their posterity are both delineated with a Navel. And this is observable not only in ordinary and stained pieces, but in the Authentic draughts of Urbin, Angelo and others. Which not withstanding cannot be allowed, except we impute that unto the first cause, which we impose not on the second; or what we deny unto nature, we impute into Naturity itself; that is, that in the first and most accomplished piece, the Creator affected superfluities, or ordained parts without use or office (II, 345).

This is elegantly succinct; care of statement governs the central antithesis, the building for emphasis of a sentence on a dependent clause, the coined word "Naturity," and triumphant expression "first and most accomplished *piece*." No one but Browne could have written it.

The little essay on glowworms is based on observation, that on the lack of a navel in Adam and Eve rests upon reasoning from principles as well. In *Pseudodoxia* the one kind of writing rarely derives strength from the other. The errors Browne confutes no longer prevail, but it is the lack of pattern in what he is concerned with that has brought upon his book the decay of obsolescence. When Bacon is engaged in attacking a whole way of thought, to establish another, there is substantial meaning in the contest. But in *Pseudodoxia* Browne often, although not always, wars with trivia, and there is no progress in the campaign as a whole. What rewards the admirer of Browne who stays the course with this book, is the constant presence of a sensibility. Perhaps the shortcoming of *Pseudodoxia Epidemica* is that Browne failed to make his own *persona* a part of the structure itself. Whereas in *Religio* the light and shadows of the writer's moral portrait give the whole both design and intensity, in *Pseudodoxia* types of information govern the pattern. We read, when we do, because the texture of the language conveys an individual idiom, but it is accompaniment, not theme.

Differently planned and executed, *Urn Burial* and *The Garden of Cyrus* open new possibilities of structure, new difficulties, new solutions. Furthermore, there is a bridge of meaning between these two works that discloses a further chance for the writer of "linked analogies."

If Browne had never written the fifth chapter of *Urn Burial*, only specialists would now read the first four. Why did he need to catalogue and survey burial customs to ascend to his meditations on memory, time, immortality? George Herbert once said, "Particulars ever touch, and waken more than generals." But for certain prose writers and some poets the truth is that particulars are specially needed before the writer can approach "generals"—do not take the place, but initiate the larger sense of wonder.

Of all Browne's works, *Urn Burial* and *The Garden of Cyrus* have the clearest structure, and in these two also he finally develops a sustained rhythm of language that corroborates and confirms the central emotion. In *Pseudodoxia Epidemica*, the different stages of life from minerals through plants and animals to human beings provide a merely external framework, a means of classifying the many otherwise unrelated details. But in the prefatory epistles to both *Urn Burial* and *The Garden of Cyrus* Browne discloses themes that will unify the work as a whole, even though they may not achieve an equal presence or resonance in each chapter.

When, in the letter prefatory to *Urn Burial*, Browne tells his friend that "We were hinted by the occasion, not catched the opportunity to write of old things, or intrude upon the Antiquary" (i, 132), he shows that the discovery of the urns at Walsingham did not furnish the subject of his essay, but called upon his previous meditations. He indicates in the epistle the direction in which these meditations will lead. In the first paragraph he establishes the mood of wonder about the relativity of awareness of time, in pointing out that the first generations of men had no expectation of long futurity, and "having no old experience of the duration of their Reliques, held no opinion of such after-considerations" (i, 131). The fact that, nevertheless, later men would dig up and study early relics prompts Browne's initial irony: the uncertainty not only of human expectations, but of most kinds of mortal knowledge, the questions "who knows," "who hath" that will echo through his discourse.

In a way that is more true of Browne than of any other prose writer of the seventeenth century; he incorporates his own point of view toward the subject as at the heart of all he will say, his awareness of the discrepancies between time and human memory. What a difference it made to man's way of thinking, he suggests, when the number of living exceeded the dead!

The dedicatory epistle then informs the reader that death itself is not the subject of *Urn Burial*, but the customs relating to death as a clue to man's sense of his place in time, and of what lies beyond time, and is to be to him infinitely more valuable than fame.

In the chapters that intervene between the suggestive introduction and the sustained andante of chapter five, Browne seldom rises from his intricate patterns of fact to any larger reflection or principle. At the beginning of the first chapter, however, he embarks on a conception that speaks for the central experience of the Renaissance: discovery, the kinds, dimensions and newness of it. Some, he begins disarmingly, would neglect discoveries of the subterranean world, but in so doing they would abridge knowledge itself, for "Nature hath furnished one part of the Earth, and man another" (I, 135). He then links this idea with his underlying theme by announcing time as the mother of discoveries, which reveals old things in heaven, and new parts of the globe itself. This was indeed the startling conjunction for men of his period, the simultaneous acquisition of knowledge about eras of time previously unknown or little known, with that of new areas of the earth, and comparable societies of living creatures of all kinds. The newness of space and the deeper dimensions of the past come together, and more is yet to be learned of both, since "that great Antiquity *America* lay buried for thousands of years; and a large part of the earth is still in the Urne unto us" (I, 135).

From this challenging beginning Browne passes rapidly to the tissue of facts about burial or its alternatives that fill up the first four chapters of his book. He deftly indicates reasons for the different customs in the possible attitudes of the ancients toward the elements themselves: earth, water, air, and fire. After exploring the curiosities as he sees them of kinds of cremation, interment, or exposure, he turns to a consideration of these particular Walsingham urns which have "hinted the occasion" of his whole discourse. His interest here, in explaining why he thinks them Roman, seems to lie in the past of his own land and particularly of Norwich. These puzzling urns contained no coins or medals, and a relic like the blue opal that brings a flicker of colour to Browne's somber pages, was no adequate clue to the time of their depositing.

Throughout this part there are many signs of the closeness of Browne's writing to his notebooks. Incomplete sentences or clauses show hardly any art in the transposition of a detail to the page: "Than the time of these Urnes deposited, or precise Antiquity of these Reliques, nothing of more uncertainty. . . . The Province of *Brittain* in so divided a distance from *Rome*, beholding the faces of many Imperiall persons. . . . A great obscurity herein, because, no medall or Emperours Coyne enclosed, which might denote the date of their enterrments; observable in many Urnes, and found in those of *Spittle* Fields by *London*, which contained the Coynes of *Claudius, Vespasian, Commodus, Antonimus,* attended with Lacrymatories, Lamps, Bottles of Liquor, and other appurtenances of affectionate superstition, which in these rurall enterrments were wanting" (1, 144). Many other examples of rapid jottings and hypothetical queries occur. Sentences end with admissions of uncertainty: "we hold no authentick account"; "we have no historical assertion or denial"; "there is no assured conclusion." These convey not only the honest scepticism that runs through *Pseudodoxia Epidemica,* but also Browne's sense that it would be *desirable* to know more; he contrasts known with unknown customs throughout.

In his description of the Walsingham urns and his

attempt to relate them to other British antiquities, there is a kind of observation similar to an archaeologist's. Browne's commonplace books must have been arranged by topics, or have been extraordinarily well-indexed. He seems fascinated by the particulars of the articles buried with the dead—whether bay leaves, cypress, or other kinds of wood are to be found with some remains—and in this context the blue opal is mentioned again.

Only once in chapter three (at the end) does Browne progress to his larger theme, that the hope of resurrection surpasses a survival of relics:

> Severe contemplators observing these lasting reliques, may think them good monuments of persons past, little advantage to future beings. . . . And if according to learned conjecture, the bodies of men shall rise where their greatest Reliques remain, many are not like to erre in the Topography of their Resurrection, though their bones or bodies be after translated by Angels into the field of *Ezechiel's* vision, or as some will order it, into the Valley of Judgment, or *Jehosaphat* (I, 157).

Here, for almost the first time since the dedicatory epistle, Browne permits his thinking to rise from the mosaic of curiosities to a more inclusive idea. And in chapter four the ascent is continued. *Urn Burial* begins to be knit together as a whole, and chapter four is the keystone of the arch. For while allowing himself still to dwell curiously on varying customs of Christians, the ancient Gentiles (Greeks and Romans), the nub of Browne's questioning is what kind of expectation of futurity human beings have experienced. He strikes great sparks from his flint. The whole inquiry radiates from his comparison of two infants in the womb, debating the state of the world they are to be born into, with the uncertainties of both Christians and others concerning the state after death. "The particulars of future beings must need be dark unto ancient Theories, which Christian Philosophy yet determines in a Cloud of opinions" (I, 162). And he ponders the place of ancient philosophers, Plato, Socrates, and Epicurus, in Dante's fabulous hell. He leads to his conclusion that "Happy are they, which live not in that disadvantage of time, when men could say little for futurity, but from reason" (I, 163). The reader is thus prepared for the longer flight of the final chapter, with its search through layers of the past, offset by the "pious rapture of futurity." From the curious and speculative mood of the opening chapters Browne has emerged into a tone primarily of wonder.

Browne never wrote anything so continuous, so thoroughly composed as the last chapter of *Urn Burial*. No one who has read it needs to be told that there is nothing like it in English prose, except a few sections of its companion piece, *The Garden of Cyrus*. Here are seventeen paragraphs in a sustained, continuous rhythm that rises to a crescendo in the farthest reaches of meaning, and ebbs to a contemplative close. Browne is now emancipated from his notes, perhaps because he has already set down the gist of his readings and explained the objects of his attention. Thought has *preceded* this writing: it brings us the outcome of thought in a unique sensibility. The grave spondees of the opening sentence announce the theme, anticipate the form of the whole chapter by means of an ironic question:

> Now since these dead bones have already out-lasted the living ones of Methusaleh, and in a yard under ground, and thin walls of clay, out-worn all the strong and

specious buildings above it; and quietly rested under the drums and trampling of three conquests; What Prince can promise such diuturnity unto his Reliques, or might not gladly say

> Sic ego componi versus in ossa velim (1, 164).

Here, two stretches of past time are contrasted—the life of the longest-lived man, as briefer than the survival of the dead bones in these urns, and the hope of some contemporary prince for future fame—an expectation to be refuted as mortally deceptive in all that follows. Different levels of history—known lives as against those that have disappeared from memory—lead to the puzzle of contemporary man's place in the whole time-scheme. For Browne, as for many in the seventeenth century, present time is late in history; even those solicitous of fame cannot expect as much of it, because they cannot expect as many generations to succeed them, as could men of Biblical days or the Greeks or Romans. Browne's is a weighty farewell to the value the Renaissance attached to fame, yet the appetite for fame and the accidental loss of it engage his curiosity. His words are moving because he ponders the ties binding generations of men to each other, and shows their frailty compared with the eventual contemporaneity of all in the resurrection that is the end point of his discourse. But he does not propose much about the state, or the content of immortality—very different his concerns, say, from those of Baxter in *The Saints' Everlasting Rest*. Nor does he exhort to belief; unlike Taylor in *Holy Dying* he refrains from adjuration or warning. He simply poses a mighty premise, in the light of which oblivion equals fame, and obscurity, recognition.

The relativity of human computations is minor, when

even the heavens manifest change—a cosmic scale re-
futes the pretensions of the world scale. Thus we are
confronted by the purity of a sheer concept; Browne
does not create an image of individual survival, but reveals that "there is nothing strictly immortall but immortality" (I, 169). At the height of his discourse, affirming that the sufficiency of immortality frustrates earthly
glory, Browne makes a climax with a surprising sentence
—like a new instrument entering. "Life is a pure flame,
and we live by an invisible Sun within us" (I, 169). Affirmation of life, except tangentially and implicitly, is
rare in Browne, rarer in the seventeenth-century sermon
writers. Here his contrast is between the pure flame of
life and "prodigall blazes" of extravagant obsequies. But
the surprise, the climax, is real and essential—what is all
this thirst for immortality but an admiration of life?

The essay as a whole does not deal with, but prepares
for as its solution, "the Metaphysicks of true belief" (I,
171). Browne's vast range of examples, from history,
literature, and travel as well as archaeological evidence,
has to do with human activities. What he has written is
not primarily religious, though it concludes with a revelation of religious feeling. "And if any have been so
happy as truly to understand Christian annihilation, ex-
tasis, exolution, liquefaction, transformation, the kisse
of the Spouse, gustation of God, and ingression into the
divine shadow, they have already had an handsome an-
ticipation of heaven . . ." (I, 170). No argument is here,
only the mystery of steps of suggestion.

Because Browne is not trying to create belief or to
reprove unbelievers, and because at the same time he
could *assume* the presence of belief in his readers, he
was able in the last section of *Urn Burial* to meditate
fully on ideas that are difficult of access. He was able to

speak of human quandaries that elude conversation in our time because we have no terms in which to discuss them. For him the route to this ascent was by observation of many particular habits and ways of men. In *The Garden of Cyrus* his procedure is similar, and in parts of the last two sections at least he reaches the same ease of meditation.

In some respects *The Garden of Cyrus* is the most carefully planned of Browne's works and is striking because he makes his procedure in thinking on the chosen theme an explicit part of the plan. In his autobiography *Safe Conduct,* Pasternak refers to "botany as his first passion in response to the five-petalled persistence of the plant."[3] This was a discovery Browne had made for himself, but it is not clear whether the genesis of *The Garden of Cyrus* lay in his experimental notes on actual observation or whether the fascination arose from his reading two old treatises, by Benoit Court and J. B. Della Porta, describing the "quincunx" or pattern of planting trees and gardens with one tree or plant in the center, the others in the corners of a parallelogram. Whether the printed sources, or his own discerning of patterns in growth and form of every kind, took precedence, is relatively unimportant. What matters is the effort that Browne made in *The Garden of Cyrus* to connect reading and seeing and to elicit from them truth of a contemplative order.

Professor Frank Huntley, whose work on *Urn Burial* and *The Garden of Cyrus* contributes more to our understanding of them than any other study, sees in the five chapters of the latter work an outward conformation of the quincuncial theme. However that may be, in designating the first two chapters as an "artificial" consideration of his theme, the next as "natural" and the last two as "mystical," Browne shows the progress of thinking he likes to follow. The chapters in which the theme is "artificially" seen are to deal, he means us to understand, with the phenomena of art or artfulness— gardens, orchards, plantations, buildings, phalanxes of soldiers, crowns, jewels, textiles, and whatever else of man's contriving shows his indebtedness to this pattern. In a sense it might seem illogical that Browne's treatment of these examples of human craftsmanship should precede his demonstration of patterns of five occurring "naturally." Yet the plan has the advantage of giving an ancient and even exotic history to the topic; it also shows that Browne's love of gardens (emphasized by the title) is symbolically at the heart of his discourse. And even at the outset the sequence is clearly announced to us, as Browne characteristically posits that, Paradise having been planted on the third day, "Gardens were before Gardiners" (I, 179).

If the Biblical overtones of the hanging or pensile gardens of Babylon and the evocation of ancient times enrich the first two chapters, there is on the other hand a more direct, excited kind of description when Browne draws upon his own seeing of "the elegant ordination of vegetables" (I, 192). In Pasternak's expression again of his interest in botany, he remembers "how names, sought out according to the classified text, brought peace to eyes of flowers." It is much the same delight that leads Browne to draw the reader's attention to the "squamous heads" of various plants, the leaves of the artichoke or of "sea wracks" "overwrought with Net-work elegantly containing this order," the head of the teazle, or of kinds of thistles (I, 193). Then the movement to connect and generalize that is carried to its height in the later chapters appears—plants are accompanied by characteristic insects; curious comparisons of relative size may be made, as between an oak and a whale; animal figurations such as the wings of flies, belly of the water beetle, eggs of some butterflies, "neatly declare how nature Geometrizeth, and observeth order in all things" (i, 203). Browne thus sets the mark for those whom he calls "signal discerners."

Taking the bulk of Browne's writings, there can be no doubt that he often worked straightforwardly from the point of view of the natural historian: thus his collections of many kinds, his experiments and dissections. Even in *The Garden of Cyrus* his effort for accuracy impels him to concede the *absence* of the quincuncial pattern where he had expected it, for instance in "the woof of the neat Retiarie Spider" (i, 188). But his purpose is not ultimately the scientific one of classification or systematization, his purpose is the search for its own sake for what he rightly calls *analogies*, in the book of nature, and in the contemplation of these analogies as an incentive to moral or spiritual experience. From the point of view of the scientist, the assemblage of the families of facts that Browne ranges under the quincunx is often misleading, or trivial, or unimportant. But Browne resembles Thoreau—even more than Emerson —in needing to start from the ground of some fact, because as Emerson said of Thoreau, "Every fact lay in glory in his mind."[4]

Yet, as I shall hope to show later, Thoreau had other means than Browne's to let the fact "ascend into a truth." In *The Garden of Cyrus* there is the handicap that Browne leaves standing too much of the scaffolding. In the plan of the whole an attempted architecture is displayed by Browne's proceeding from the theme's being "artificially" and "naturally" to its being "mystically considered." Our reading of these last two sections will determine our interpretation of the whole book and our opinion of its unity.

Before offering my own, I must summarize and pay tribute to Mr. Huntley's elucidation of *The Garden of Cyrus* and his masterly linking of it to *Urn Burial*. After having expounded Browne's central emblem, derived from Plato's *Timaeus*, in the circles bisecting each other in such a way as to symbolize life and death, Mr. Huntley continues:

> As in a Platonic dichotomy, these twin essays are parts of a single whole . . . and there is a "rising" from the lower, or elemental, part, which is *Urn Burial*, to the "higher," or celestial part, which is *The Garden of Cyrus*, the "numerical character" of reality. More particularly, the two discourses are related in at least three ways: (1) in their subject matter, as two parts of a whole, yet eternally opposed; (2) in their epistemologies, as they pass from ignorance to knowledge; and (3) in their images, which take us in circles from darkness to light to darkness again, from womb to urn to new birth, from the "sleep" of death to drowsiness when the "quincunx of heaven runs low" and "the huntsmen are up in America."[5]

And in an even more inclusive statement Huntley concludes:

> That Browne intended us to read the two essays in this manner and in the order he gave them is seen most obviously in the deliberateness of their opposition in subject matter. One concerns death, the other life; one the body, the other the soul; one passion, the other reason; one accident, the other design; one substance, the other form, . . . The first essay treats of time; the second, space.

And together these two concepts delineate the character
of God, in that time is an image of His Eternity, whereas
number and geometrical figures in space are a key to His
Wisdom.[6]

Mr. Huntley as well as Browne has meditated on the
given theme. There can be no question of the brilliance
of his analysis, or of its value. Only, he has done for Sir
Thomas Browne what Browne could not, would not do
for himself. Browne is no philosopher. T. S. Eliot's at
first surprising statement on Henry James, that he had
a mind so fine that no idea could violate it, has a wider
bearing. It is true of some essayists as well as novelists
that the brook is crossed by stepping stones, not a bridge,
and they are sometimes uneven, slippery, and not in a
straight line.

"Mystically" in the seventeenth century could refer to
a mode of spiritual allegory, or it could have the more
tenuous and supple meaning of making out things of
dark conceit. In his last two chapters, in which his theme
is "mystically" considered, Browne is not really more
systematic than in the preceding ones, but he is moving
from further examples of his omnipresent quincunx, to
mysteries discoverable in experience without it, although, for Browne, by means of its aid. Thus in chapter four after flying over the "delights" and "commodi-
ties" of this order, large figures such as how plants are
affected by the effects of wind and water and whether
they are "solisequious," he progresses to the inherent
pleasure of seeing afforded by plantations, and begins to
rise to more general contemplations. His approach to the
theme of light and darkness begins gradually. "Nor are
only dark and green colours, but shades and shadows
generally contrived throughout the great Volume of na-

ture, and trees ordained not only to protect and shadow others, but by their shades and shadowing parts, to preserve and cherish themselves" (1, 217). Thus darkness is a source of life. Then, from the reflection that seeds lie in perpetual shades, Browne prepares for the climax of *The Garden of Cyrus*, in the great passage beginning "Darknesse and light hold interchangeable dominions, and alternately rule the seminal state of things" (1, 218). The sequence, rather than the circles and right lines of the quincunx, reveals the true meaning of Browne's treatise: interdependence of life and death, reciprocity of light and darkness.

The climax itself may now be given out in the paragraph that follows, which, familiar though it is, I must quote in full:

> Light that makes things seen, makes some things invisible: were it not for darknesse and the shadow of the earth, the noblest part of the Creation had remained unseen, and the Stars in heaven as invisible as on the fourth day, when they were created above the Horizon, with the Sun, or there was not an eye to behold them. The greatest mystery of Religion is expressed by adumbration, and in the noblest parts of Jewish Types, we finde the Cherubims shadowing the Mercy-seat: Life it self is but the shadow of death, and souls departed but the shadows of the living: All things fall under this name. The Sun it self is but the dark *simulachrum*, and light but the shadow of God (1, 218).

The central conceptual metaphor is that sounding in the word *adumbration*. Of sixteenth-century origin in English, it could mean, from shading in painting, "a sketch, outline, or shadowy figure." But more suggestively it meant also in Browne's time "a symbolic representation typifying or prefiguring the reality."[7] Thus to Browne the shade, shadow, or darkness both came from light and revealed the otherwise invisible. As he moves from patterns of planting to the source of being and growth, Browne's largest and most suggestive term is *adumbration*. Now, this is both what he has progressed to, and the means of his progression. One thinks immediately of Donne's preoccupation in *Songs and Sonnets* with the shadow. That Browne concerns himself as much with the way of seeing as with the seen, is confirmed by the end of chapter four where the quincunx is described as the pattern of rays from object to retina, and as, in Plato, the motion of man's and the world's soul.

The theme of light and darkness is resumed at the end of chapter five and ends the whole discourse, as it is newly placed in relation to the revolution of day and night. Before Browne can develop this central motif, he ranges side by side phenomena having nothing in common but an association with *five*. Declining "unexcusable Pythagorisme," he nevertheless has little else to justify an assortment of items including the number of fingers and the fifth letter of the Hebrew alphabet as a symbol of generation, the number of acts in a play and the points of "sea-stars." It is a marvel that the writer who could thus link so many discrepant facts retains at the last a hope worthy of the scientist, "to search out the . . . figured draughts of this nature, and . . . to erect generalities . . . not only in the vegetable shop, but the whole volume of nature; affording delightful Truths, confirmable by sense and ocular Observation . . ." (I, 226). The key to his procedure is in his combining the *delight* of truth with observation. His famous last paragraphs marking the time "when the quincunx of heaven runs low" at once affirm that night, and dreaming, are not dependable sources of knowledge because, however appealing their experience, they but anticipate the dawn and the reawakening of the senses. "The huntsmen are up in America" evokes the newness and discovery allied with regeneration and resurrection.

Opinions of *The Garden of Cyrus* have varied greatly. Dr. Johnson called it a "sport of fancy"; to such an enlightened and sensitive admirer of Browne as Mrs. Joan Bennett it is "the least important of the works published in Browne's lifetime."[8] In my discussion of it I have intended to stress that, while there is much in it that is dispensable by the way, the singular items serve to aid Browne's approach to his most original meditative strain. As early as *Religio Medici* he had made articulate the fascination for him of the minute, and the larger reading of God's wisdom in the wonders of the book of nature. These interests are given a new vitality and depth in *The Garden of Cyrus*. And, if Mr. Frank Huntley is perhaps almost too purposeful in his reading of the buried design uniting *Urn Burial* and *The Garden of Cyrus*, I have no doubt that the design is there. My slight difference in emphasis is to suggest that Browne saw this conjunction, as Thoreau would put it, "with the side of his eye." Browne in his preface made an important note on his method of composition. "In this multiplicity of writing," he said, "bye and barren Themes are best fitted for invention. . . . Beside, such Discourses allow excursions, and venially admit of collaterall truths . . ." (I, 175-176). This is the born essayist speaking, who knows it is not from the center of the target that most other circles move. *Urn Burial* and *The Garden of Cyrus* do support each other in a unity of belief, each enhances the other. If the profounder rhythm is heard in *Urn Burial*, the novelty of knowing is released in *The Garden of Cyrus*.

Even without the later *Christian Morals*, Browne's writings showed range, variety, and development. In *Christian Morals* he produced something different from his other works. "These essays," as Dr. Johnson accurately referred to the collection, have been, in comparison with Browne's other major writings, usually undervalued. To the generally admiring Mr. Huntley, for example, "*Christian Morals* is a sententious anticlimax,"[9] although he does advocate further study of it. Probably the lack of attention (comparatively speaking) bestowed upon *Christian Morals* results from the assumption that it was the product of Browne's old age, an intended continuation of *Religio Medici*, culled from commonplace books, and unfinished. From the point of view of its place among Browne's other writings, however, two considerations alter this opinion of *Christian Morals* as late, essentially unfinished work. As has been widely recognized, the first part incorporates many paragraphs that appeared in Browne's *Letter to a Friend*. Now, Professor Huntley's convincing dating of the *Letter* as probably composed about 1656,[10] makes it likely that these paragraphs at least of *Christian Morals* represent Browne's thinking in his middle life. Further, the fact that they were so expertly revised before their incorporation in *Christian Morals* shows the care Browne had bestowed upon the latter work.[11] In comparison with *Religio, Urn Burial,* or *The Garden of Cyrus* it may to some extent be unfinished, as not having the author's final touches and decisions before publication. But it is not fragmentary, not a tangential piece such as we find among Browne's *Miscellanies*, and it is by no means a rough draft.[12]

In fact, it possesses more structure, internal coherence, and unity than has ordinarily been acknowledged. In Part I, all the separate paragraphs of observation revolve about a single axis: the *mood* that is favourable to virtue. Now from this side, now from that, Browne shows the need for a positive generosity, flourish, freedom in the expression of what is good, rather than a narrow, inhibited, cautionary practise. The theme is gathered firmly in Section 9: "Persons lightly dipt, not grain'd in generous Honesty, are but pale in Goodness, and faint hued in Integrity. But be thou what thou vertuously art, and let not the Ocean wash away thy Tincture" (1, 246). This is developed through Browne's advice to every man to study his own economy, his acknowledgment that imperfect men may have valuable qualities, and that " 'tis well, if a perfect Man can be made out of many Men" (1, 254). The final section sums up the whole. Here, fortitude is seen as the foundation of all loyalty, there is a condemnation of small and creeping things, and praise of "bright Thoughts, clear Deeds, Constancy, Fidelity, Bounty" as the gems of noble minds, wherein, says Browne, "the true Heroick English Gentleman hath no Peer" (1, 258).

In this first part of *Christian Morals* there is a deeper knowledge of what is human than in any previous writing of Browne's. True, of *Religio Medici*, that he is, as Emerson noted, "inward"—but he is creating a portrait of himself. In *Christian Morals* he is aware of many more qualities, kinds of human capacity and behaviour.

The second part of *Christian Morals* is a natural outgrowth of the first. Browne illuminates the value of plain willingness to learn, of modesty in learning, and of freedom from meanness of spirit in acknowledging the worth of others. "Bring candid Eyes unto the perusal of men's works, and let not Zoilism or Detraction blast well-intended labours" (I, 260). The need to be tentative in discourse, and at the same time not to be over-impressed by pretensions to learning on the part of others, is compatible with the ability to admit worth in younger spirits. There are many variations in the paragraphs that touch upon these related themes, but all circle about a willing response to merit, a refusal of closed-mindedness. Only in the last paragraph does Brown shift to a topic at first sight unrelated, the ways men have found to death. In his advice that "to learn to dye is better than to study the ways of dying" he prepares for the last part of *Christian Morals* (I, 269).

Part III has a closer affinity with *Religio* than any other. Browne now deals directly with man's relation to himself and to God, and as in *Urn Burial*, with his place in time. He starts from the characteristic thought that the longevity of men in the first ages of the world must have enhanced either their virtues or their vices. This caused him to think it difficult to find any whole age to imitate. He regrets our ignorance of the early ages obliterated by the flood that "so shut up the first Windows of Time, leaving no Histories of those longevous generations, when Men might have been properly Historians, when Adam might have read long Lectures unto Methuselah, and Methuselah unto Noah" (I, 271). Thus many possibilities of instruction from history are lacking, and we must elect the better course of self-knowledge. It is impossible to recreate the richness and essential unity of the related ways Browne celebrates the life of contemplation. The nucleus of the active whole is in Sections 14 and 15: "Let Intellectual Tubes give thee a glance of things, which visive Organs reach not. Have a glimpse of incomprehensibles, and Thoughts of things

which Thoughts but tenderly touch. . . . Behold thy self
by inward Opticks, and the Crystalline of the Soul" (1,
280-281). All in the tenor of living thought and devotion
prepares for the "vivid eschatology,"[13] as Mr.
Huntley terms it, that provides the conclusion of *Christian Morals*, wherein "The created World is but a small Parenthesis in Eternity" (1, 289). But this does not derogate
from man's earthly existence, for "to palliate the shortness of our Lives, and somewhat to compensate our brief
term in this World, it's good to know as much as we can
of it, and also so far as possibly in us lieth to hold such
a Theory of times past, as though we had seen the same"
(1, 290). And, as if to forge one further link of his meditations, Browne ends *Christian Morals* deliberately with
a sentence from the end of *Urn Burial*.

In this piece of writing, which may well have been
the fruit of his meditations over many years, even if
composed, as we now have it, late, Browne achieved a
compression and directness beyond any previous effort
of his. Perhaps some readers find *Christian Morals* too
compressed. But it is a mistake, I think, to regard the
work as merely a collection of *sententiae*. To the extent
that it may partly be characterized so, *Christian Morals*
could be compared with Felltham's *Resolves*. But the
sentences of Browne are freer, more articulate, as his
exploration of potential human freedom in the thought
of virtue is at once gentler, more profound, more generative. Almost every paragraph of *Christian Morals*
is sufficiently well-knit to be an essay, but the company
of these paragraphs with each other is intelligible, as I
have tried to show, in larger shapes of purpose and idea.
Perhaps there is nothing really to resemble *Christian
Morals* until Emerson's *Journals* and his *Natural History of Intellect*. There are some readers who would

prefer these nuggets melted to a seemingly more ductile quality, but the ductility is in the direct release of energy from one to the other, not in the expansiveness of ordinary logical persuasion.

Various forms of energy are captured and released, then, in the writings of Sir Thomas Browne, the most central one his rapt absorption in his own and man's capacities for life and knowledge. The forms in which these capacities appear and appeal to him have the characteristic religious cast of his time, in most of his writing; but as he deals with his themes, he sets free profound enjoyment in the art of contemplation. Throughout this discussion I have been concerned to point out that Browne's love of the way of seeing matches his fascination with the things seen. In an otherwise sensitive essay Mr. Peter Green states that Browne was "honestly indifferent to literary art as an end in itself."[14] His subjective point of view we cannot recover, but the delight of a deliberate art is incorporate in phrase, sentence, paragraph, and in the later works, architecture of design. He tried different subjects, discovered new rhythms, and, by his skill, imaginative prose first fully revealed its power.

The Graces and the Muses:    3

Felltham's *Resolves*

Little is known of Owen Felltham; but in an age
when most writers supported themselves by some other
profession, many as clergymen, his lot was to become
steward of an estate.[1] As a boy of perhaps twenty he had
published a small book, *Resolves,* destined to be reprinted, with additions and changes, eleven times within
a century and several times after 1800.[2] The book, listed
in the Stationer's Register of 1623, probably came out
that year. It contained a hundred short essays on questions of faith or conduct, moving to or incorporating a
determination upon some course of action or behaviour
—hence its title. In the second edition Felltham added
another "century" of resolves; and evidently preferring

them to the original set, in later editions he placed them first in order.

Perhaps a decade after the first appearance of his book, Felltham took up service with the family of the Earl of Thomond, and lived at their country seat, Great Billing, in Northamptonshire. He had some connection with literary men—he wrote an elegy for Ben Jonson as well as an answer to "Come leave the loathed stage," and was himself saluted by the poet Thomas Randolph. Whether he knew these men in his youth, in London, or stole away from Northamptonshire for rare city recreations, we cannot say. As a steward he was persevering, honest, even self-sacrificing in his duties as rent collector and custodian of accounts. The dowager countess, to whom he dedicated the eighth enlarged edition of *Resolves*, testified in a law suit that he was "just and ffaithful . . . in all . . . the affaires this defend$^t$ intrusted him w$^{th}$ and shall still soe Continue her beleife till shee finds very good reason to the Contrary w$^{ch}$ shee hopes shee never shall."[3] Nevertheless, he was not like other stewards. His *Resolves* place him as a conscious moralist, who cared for the written word.

These two commitments of his, as moralist and stylist, cannot be separated in intention, although they sometimes are in execution. Virtue, he thought, "is better by being communicated" (II. 27, p. 310)—but cannot be so without a good style. "The muse" to him stands for virtue; style is attended by "the graces." By serving both, he invented a variation of that mutable form, the essay.[4] The *Resolves* differ from most other essays of his time or of later periods by being usually led to, rounded off with, a declaration of will or faith. Thus he saw his purpose: "I may refine my speech without harm: but I will endeavour more to reform my life. It is a good grace both of oratory, or of the pen, to speak or write proper: but that is the best work, where the graces and the muses meet" (p. 311). When they did not meet for him, it was because his moral insight flagged. Then it was the muse who failed him, although he had preferred her.

Felltham is often described as a Stoic, or a Christian Stoic, but in his treatment of virtue he is more Aristotelian than Stoic and more Christian than either.[5] True, he often brings Cicero or Seneca or Lipsius to his aid, even when writing "Of the Soul." Like the Stoics, he makes his bow to the sway of Fate or Fortune, and advocates control of the passions. But the attitude does not represent the marrow of his belief. The proud self-sufficiency of Stoicism is not his. Where Seneca would counsel indifference to poverty, Felltham is acutely aware of its inhuman grip. "Poor men are perpetual sentinels, watching in the depth of night, against the incessant assaults of want. . . . If the land be russetted with a bloodless famine; are not the poor the first that sacrifice their lives to hunger?" (I. 18, p. 53). And he sympathizes not only with the physical suffering but with the mental afflictions that go with them. "Continual care checks the spirit; continual labour checks the body; and continual insultation, both." Here is no Stoic sense of superiority to circumstance, rather a compassionate attention to the handicaps it may impose. Along with sympathy, a certain worldliness appears in his meditation on poverty: the miseries of hunger, the checks of care are harsh, but lack of esteem is "another transcendent misery" and "Poor men, though wise, are but like satins without a gloss . . ." (p. 54).

The end of this little discourse shows clearly two characteristic turns of Felltham's thought. Aristotle's presentation of virtue as a mean between two extremes appealed to him: poverty is worse than abundance, but he sees the defects of riches also. "He that hath too little, wants feathers to fly withal: he that hath too much, is but cumbered with too large a tail" (pp. 55-56). The Aristotelian mean accommodates itself to the *via media* of Anglicanism; the Christian and man of experience speak last: "Questionless, I will rather with charity help him that is miserable, as I may be; than despise him that is poor, as I would not be" (p. 57).

This statement discloses the practicality and prudence that exist alongside Felltham's moral sincerity. He is aware of a world of rivalry, and it has made him cautious. "It is an inconvenience for a man to be accounted wiser than ordinary" (I. 28, p. 83). He would not adventure too far in search of knowledge. Sir Thomas Browne enjoyed pursuing his reason to an *O altitudo*, but Felltham exclaims that they live most happily who know only what is necessary (I. 27, p. 81). In choosing his friends, he resolves to avoid angry men and drunkards—as if both were equal and equally frequent menaces. He observes that some associates are too extravagant in the courtesies they proffer, others niggardly, and decides, "I will so serve others, as I injure not myself; so myself, as I may help others" (II. 42, p. 326). His praise of silence follows similar guidelines. Everywhere it "is a safe safeguard: if by it I offend, I am sure I offend without a witness" (II. 8, p. 292). Therefore to save both himself and his auditors, he will so speak as to be "free from babbling garrulity," and so be silent, as his hearers may not account him "blockishly dull" (*ibid.*). In company, one would be grateful for his discretion. As a reader, one cannot help thinking of the deeper value attached to silence by Carlyle or by

Thoreau. At once we see Felltham's chosen circle. He is not prophet or see-er. He is always apprehensive of a potential judge of his actions, whether God or man.

Yet he is independent—and this is one of the clear impressions of him as a person that emerge from the *Resolves*. He disliked being indebted to anyone. Writing on the topic "Of Courtesies" he records, "I know not that I am ever sadder, than when I am forced to accept courtesies that I cannot requite" (I. 75, p. 177). This gives a sense of the man. He goes even further: "If ever I should affect injustice, it should be in this, that I might do courtesies, and receive none." His thoughts revolve on the same theme in "Of Bounties" and "Of Reward and Service." In the latter there is perhaps some reflection of his position as steward in a noble household, his relation to his masters and to those under him leading to the observation that service is "a condition, which is not found in any creatures of one kind, but man" (II. 7, p. 14).

Although cautious, prudent, and independent, Felltham does not give much attention to the questions of policy that Bacon anatomizes. Without doubt he owes something to Bacon, as a literary model. But the range of his observation, as well as his constitutional temper, is different. He does not live in the environment of the courtier or the man of state. He is aware of it, has seen something of it. Those few of his resolves that may be called "political" reflect it. They are seldom concerned with issues of government but rather with what was then deemed policy: human conduct in a public world. He has read his Machiavelli and occasionally quotes him without too great disapproval, as he does in his essay "Of Dissimulation." This may be compared with Bacon's of a similar title. Bacon is forthright in seeing deception as a sign of weakness, "for it asketh a strong wit and a strong heart to know when to tell truth and to do it." But he is hard-headed in his classifying of different types of dissimulation and their use by particular kinds of men in specific situations. His sense of the disadvantages is clear and sharp, the noblest of them coming last, "that it depriveth a man of one of the most principal instruments for action, which is trust and belief." He closes with a curt decision on strategy. "The best composition and temperature is to have openness in fame and opinion, secrecy in habit, dissimulation in seasonable use, and a power to feign if there be no remedy."

Felltham places the problem solely in the world of policy, "[which] is but circumstantial dissembling," and finds that "as the world is, it [dissimulation] is not all condemnable" (II. 42, p. 119). But even granting its use to princes, he deplores the extent of it, which makes state policy "an irreligious riddle" (p. 120). Unlike Bacon, he never wholly sets aside the requirements of a Christian ethic. He comes to an honourable if somewhat melancholy conclusion: "If I must use it, it shall be only so, as I will neither by it, dishonour Religion, nor be a cause of hurt to my neighbour" (p. 121). Bacon's handling of this topic is more incisive and is based on a wider experience of affairs of state and of intrigue for power. Although undeceived by the ruses of ambition, he is willing to reckon with them. Felltham has encountered this world and remembers historical examples of its demands. His treatment of the question is both more literary and more meditative. He feels a deeper personal concern for the moral issue presented.

Felltham at his desk pondering his Greek or Roman history, or his Horace or Lucretius—in the earlier *Re-*

*solves,* he quotes Roman authors more frequently than the Bible—reveals too little of his own disposition or tastes. But it is clear that he was capable of enthusiasm. Although in essay after essay he indicates the solution of a problem as the finding of a *via media,* he dislikes coldness, indifference. "Moderation may become fault," he warns. "To be but warm, when God commands us to be hot, is sinful. We belie virtue into the constant dulness of a mediocrity" (I. 45, p. 126). Again, he shows a height of feeling when he declares, "I care not for his humour, that loves to clip the wings of a lofty fame" (I. 50, p. 141). He admired distinction of lineage if reinforced by character; nobility joined with virtue was to him "How glorious" (II. 43, p. 380). And while clear in his admiration of modesty, he would not have faint-heartedness. "In any good action, that must needs be bad, that hinders it: of which strain . . . is . . . a blushing shamefacedness" (I. 77, p. 210). He was not faint-hearted himself in appreciation of beauty. In an essay intended to warn against seeming attractiveness in a wicked person, he thinks in contrast of true beauty and suddenly exclaims "Beauty is the wit of nature put into the frontispiece. If there be any human thing may teach Faith reason, this is it: in other things we imagine more than we see; in this we see more than we can imagine" (II. 78, p. 364).

One other sympathetic trait that appears in the *Resolves* is Felltham's attitude toward women, and fairness to them. His essay on this topic is spirited and amusing. A strict examination of the sex, he says, "makes more for their honor, than most men have acknowledged" (I. 30, p. 90). He holds man to be superior, but thinks he was not so before the fall. "If place can be any privilege; we shall find [woman] built in Paradise, when man was made without it" (p. 91). He sees a value in the mind of woman and thinks she is more temperate, modest, and merciful than man. He returns to this topic in his essay "Of Marriage and Single Life" (again, how different from Bacon's), and expresses his conviction that "It is the crown of blessings, when in one woman a man findeth both a wife and a friend" (I. 85, p. 234).

The sphere of interest described by the *Resolves* is enlarged in the eighth edition, which was printed in 1661, and furnished the text for subsequent ones. In the preface Felltham indicates his dissatisfaction with that part of his book which was originally printed as the first century, then placed second, and was now to be drastically altered. Speaking in the third person, he notes that "being written when he was but Eighteen," these early pieces now seem to him "to have too many young weaknesses, to be still continued to the World: though not for the Honesty; yet, in the Composure of them" (10th ed., A 3). Accordingly he rewrote and expanded more than half of the original resolves, omitted the remainder, and added twenty-seven new pieces.[6] The resulting Second Century, as it stands in the eighth, ninth, tenth, and eleventh editions, contains a total of eighty-five rather than one hundred resolves. The new material is valuable both for the widened scope of ideas and as evidence of Felltham's deliberate practice as a writer.

Many of the added essays are on secular topics. "Of History," "Of Memory," "Of Civility," and even "Of Dancing" appear for the first time. The revised essay "Of Apparel" is a good example of the less somber cast of Felltham's mind in these latter essays, of a developing vein of humour, and an equally spirited expression, often more adequately sustained. The usually orthodox author is now more willing to indulge in speculation, for example when he tells us, "As it is my belief, that Man was created mortal before he sinned; so I could incline to believe, he might have come to Garments, although he had not faln" (10th ed. II. 52, p. 263). While Felltham adheres to his old pursuit of the mean between extremes, even in the choice of clothing, there is perhaps an increased worldliness in his observation that "as the world is, a man loses not by being rather above his rank, than under it . . . Socrates himself, when he went to a Feast, was content to be smug'd up and essenc'd in his Pantophles . . ." (*ibid.*, pp. 264-265). Years of responsibility for the management of the Thomond estates influence his welcoming "Of Business." He pities the man that is not brought up to it. "If a man with a Syth should mow the empty Air, he sooner would be weary than he that sweats with toyl to cut the standing Corn. Business is the Salt of Life, that only gives a grateful smack to it . . ." (10th ed. II. 67, p. 300). We are not surprised to learn from students of the meager facts of Felltham's career that he had become moderately wealthy. A whole point of view is implicit in such a phrase as "the Plausibilities and Benignities of life" (10th ed., p. 330), which he sought to defend against untrustworthy, self-seeking men. The more constricted world of the young author of eighteen, preoccupied with his own moral resolution, also aware somewhat abstractly of practical concerns, has expanded to a more active scene.

In addition to reflecting the point of view of an older and more expansive man, both the new and the enlarged essays show some changes in manner of writing. Mr. McCrea Hazlett, who has systematically studied the revisions, emphasizes Felltham's stronger concern for

public improvement and his increased desire to persuade. He thinks that this change in attitude accounts
for the increased use of formal argument, citation, anecdote, and metaphor. This is a valid point; but there is
also the fact that Felltham had become a more practiced
and perhaps at the same time a more indulgent writer.
He now exploited more obviously his recognized skill in
metaphor and pointed sentences. Wider reading had increased his knowledge of and pleasure in relevant anecdote. We must balance the richer experience and greater
freedom of expression in the later essays against their
occasional long-windedness and their sacrifice of the
tone of simplicity, the voice of an individual witness, the
effective brevity of the early resolves. A direction of the
meditation inward is lost by the removal or displace-
ment of the personal resolution that had been the culmination of the early essays. But in cases where the first
version offered only a string of curt sentences, inadequate to stimulate the reader's interest or win his consent, the later, more energetic treatment is often to be
preferred. And much more of the writer's attitude toward his own time emerges as we read of his abhorrence
of the Civil War, his adulation of Charles I, distrust of
Quakers, scorn of Protestant nonconformists but belief
that "heathens" might be saved.

These expansions and revisions almost amount to a
third century. In it we have added variety and a fuller
portrait of the writer's mind. But the whole body of
work, early and late, does not record a marked shift of
interests such as we find in the 1612 and 1625 collections
of Bacon's *Essays*, compared with those of 1597. As Mr.
Jacob Zeitlin has shown, many essays in the 1612 edition evince "a different moral atmosphere . . . a general
loftiness of tone . . . a generous disdain of all that is

ignoble," whereas those introduced in 1625 often deal with "topics which are either aesthetic or scientific and involve no ethical values."[7] In comparison, Felltham's sphere of interests expands more predictably. And certainly we find nothing similar to the developing perspectives of Montaigne's second and even more of his third book of essays, when contrasted with his first.[8] No, even in these later "resolves" Felltham moves without purpose or progress from topic to topic, turning without discomposure from "Of Play and Gaming" to "Prayer most needful in the Morning." Only the last four in his revised edition suggest a sequence: "Of Law," "Of Conscience," "Of Peace," "Of Divine Providence," but the possibility inheres more in the titles than in the discourse.

This seesawing of attention is the occupational fault of the writer expert in *sententiae*, especially when his philosophical (or in Felltham's case religious) beliefs have no organic connection with his methods of observation. Later essayists like Emerson and Thoreau, also specialists of the sentence, could evolve a moulded paragraph out of the sentences and, at their best, perfect the larger structure of chapter or book because their convictions about what can be seen into were organically related to concrete ways of seeing. But Felltham's occasionally Stoic attitudes or pervasive Christian conviction rarely act upon his faculties of perception. What lends life to his writing is accuracy of language. He observes with words given by words rather than with words given by eyes or ears.

Seventeenth-century admiration and imitation of the style of Seneca is well-known, and Felltham is usually taken as an exponent of this school. Thomas Randolph —like Felltham, a friend of Ben Jonson and a writer to

whom Henry Vaughan was indebted—praised the Senecan qualities of prose in the *Resolves*.

> I mean the stile, being pure and strong and round,
> Not long but Pythy: being short breath'd, but sound.
> Such as the grave, acute, wise *Seneca* sings,
> That best of Tutours to the worst of kings.
> . . . . . . . . . . . . . . . . . . . . . .
> Well setled full of nerves, in breife 'tis such
> That in a little hath comprized much. . . .[9]

And the modern scholar who has made the most thorough study of this tendency, George Williamson in his
*Senecan Amble*, concludes that in addition to violence
of metaphor, Felltham's "ornament derives from Senecan antithesis, with some parallelism and a touch of
alliteration to set it off; again he is like the character-
writers."[10]

But to classify Felltham's prose in this way is too
limiting. What matters is that he was a deliberate and
knowing writer: a devoté of the "Graces" as well as a
seeker of his muse. If he preferred the *style coupé*, the
short coupled sentence, to the Ciceronian period, he
merely shared a widely prevailing taste. It is more important that he had thought about style as the discipline
that shapes meaning. In his elegy on Ben Jonson he expressed his knowledge that language to be commanded
must be obeyed.

> The Boy may make a Squib: But every *line*
> Must be *considered*, where men spring a *mine*.
> And to write things that Time can never staine,
> Will require *sweat*, and rubbing of the *braine*.[11]

His essay "Of Preaching" reveals Felltham's admiration for the dramatic poetry of his age, superior in its

"weighty lines" to the bad oratory and vain tautologies of many sermons. He is concerned with the preacher's opportunity to recapture the auditory which deserts him for the stage, or slumbers in the church. But apart from the various means he thinks available to this end, he has much to say that applies to writing generally, the best parts of which must be quoted:

> A man can never speak too well, where he speaks not too obscure. Long and distended clauses, are both tedious to the ear, and difficult for their retaining. A sentence well couched, takes both the sense and the understanding. I love not those *cart-rope* speeches, that are longer than the memory of man can fathom. . . . And this is *Seneca's* opinion: Fit words are better than fine ones. I like not those that are injudiciously made, but such as be expressively significant; that lead the mind to something, beside the naked term. And he that speaks thus, must not look to speak thus every day. A combed oration will cost both sweat, and the rubbing of the brain: and combed I wish it, not frizzled, or curled. . . . And even the Scriptures, (though I know not the Hebrew) yet I believe they are penned in a tongue of deep expression: wherein, almost every word, hath a metaphorical sense, which does illustrate by some allusion (i. 20, pp. 62-64).

Here we see the essentials of Felltham's thinking on style. First comes insistence on concision, especially by means of shorter sentences (not the only, not in every case the best means, one must add). Then, he is sensitive both to the aptness of words and their expressive significance. Words alone may lead us into metaphor.

Let us look at the vitality of these elements in Felltham's own writing, leaving to the last his sentence rhythm, and beginning with words. His idiom gains force from its exactitude. "They are bad works," he wrote "that need rewards to *crane* them up withal" (I. 19, p. 61). He transmits his feeling for the action in verbs; he drafts nouns as verbs with good effect, observing for instance that base people "worship and *knee* them to the spending of a fair inheritance" (I. 53, p. 149) or that while poor men are sentinels against want, "the rich lie *stoved* in secure reposes" (I. 18, p. 53). The vigilant mariner who launches his boat with the first wind may meet a gale, but may "find the blast to *womb* out his sails more fully" (II. 61, p. 347). Felltham, like his mariner with the wind, is quick to take advantage of a strong word, but on the whole his vocabulary like his ethic represents a *via media*. He avoids ink-horn terms. An occasional specialism lends interest, as when we read that "A covetous man's kindness is like the fowler's *shrape* [snare]" (II. 70, p. 356) or that Satan's wiles are like the spots of the panther, "concealing the *torvity* [grimness] of her countenance" (II. 89, p. 376).[12] On the whole, there is little in Felltham's language that has become obsolete.

I do not share Mr. Williamson's view that we find in him a violence of metaphor. On the contrary, many of his metaphors serve a chiefly functional purpose: to clarify, make plainer or more memorable. The reader of idle books is like one who angles where he is sure "to strike the Torpedo, that instead of being his food, confounds him" (II. 1, p. 284). A virtuous man is compared to a lighthouse whereby mariners sail aright (II. 24, p. 307). Self-commendation "is an arrow with too many feathers: which we levelling at the mark, is taken with the wind, and carried quite from it" (II. 3, p. 287). Metaphors in which an image comes alive are less frequent: "What a skein of ruffled silk is the uncomposed man"

(I. 2, p. 3). Sometimes a single word generates the life of the comparison: "Gold that lay buried in the buttock of the world: is now made the head and ruler of the people" (I. 34, p. 103).

The best metaphor discovers what otherwise could not be named. Of these we find few in Felltham. We start with interest, on reading that grief, like mist, "spoils the burnish of the silver mind" (I. 36, p. 105). Two of the most memorable metaphors in the *Resolves* are reincarnated in the poems of Vaughan: the soul as "a shoot of everlastingness" (I. 64, p. 174) and the ring of eternity. But by Vaughan's setting them in a slightly altered phrase they are infinitely enhanced.

Of the "Senecan" brevity of Felltham's sentences enough has perhaps been said by others, except that it should be added that he does not write in the abrupt manner known in his time as "Lipsius his hopping style."[13] His statements fall into the tone of suggestion, and the turning over of an idea, and usually avoid curtness. The fact that his essays in most cases lead to his own resolve allows him to take a smoother road than the humped imperative. Although he does not often shape his sentence to a rhythmic line, he can at times produce a rhythmic progress: "With what a cheerly face the golden sun chariots through the rounding sky? How perpetual is the maiden moon, in her just and horned mutations? . . . In the air, what transitions? and how fluctuous are the salted waves?" (I. 48, p. 134).

But this contemplative sequence is perhaps less characteristic than the brief aphorism ("An arrow aimed right, is not the worse for being drawn home") (I. 45, p. 127) or the neat array of parallels or contrasts by alliteration: "I will in all losses, look both to what I have lost, and to what I have left" (II. 14, p. 298).

From these qualities of Felltham's style, from his success in achieving a conscious standard, we see that he had sought and been attended by the Graces. I proposed earlier that when he lags or is too obvious, it is the Muse that fails him. Often a title alone will prompt us to say "Of course—how can you bother to debate it?" as when, for instance, he sets forth to prove "That Policy and Friendship are scarcely compatible." We do not expect much from resolves with titles like "That man ought to be extensively good" or "That Religion is the best Guide." We feel impatient when Felltham is unobservant enough to believe that we may sometimes obtain good counsel from bad men (I. 33) or "that Man is neither happy nor miserable, but by Comparison" (I. 72, p. 196). We see that while the humane wisdom as well as the profounder insight of religious literature now suffer some neglect, in earlier periods the widespread and conventional acceptance of Christianity imperiled freshness of thought. Felltham is limited when he speaks most obviously to the condition of his generation. The Muse and the *Zeitgeist* are sometimes at odds.

But of the more than two hundred resolves that Felltham composed, the majority will give some reinforcement of knowledge, mood, or conviction to the thoughtful reader. In some, the current runs deeper, the whole discourse becomes memorable. In "Of Logic" he delights the reader by his ardent confrontation of all schemes of reasoning with the nakedness of truth. Unlike Montaigne, Felltham seldom makes room in his essays for the recreations of his mind—except as he allows us to see the use he makes of reading. But in "Of Poets and Poetry" his affectionate comments on the ways and disposition of poets show that he had been deservedly in their company.

The theme that truly united Felltham's powers is to be found in "Of Charity" (I. 86). "Charity is communicated goodness," he begins, and we know at once that he will emancipate rather than confuse the inherent possibilities of meaning. He is himself emancipated here by faith and feeling. We notice this again in his treatment of related themes: his scorn "Of Arrogancy," and repelling "Of Detraction." And he is fit to praise humility as "of all moral virtues . . . the most beautiful" (II. 2, p. 285). He sees that magnanimity and humility are not opposed, they are "cohabitants" (II. 71, p. 357). He detests pride and cruelty as "curs of the same litter" (II. 97, p. 384). This ardent zest for decency rises to perception of the prime goodness in "Of Charity." In this essay he transcends the *via media* for once:

> The world, which is chained together by intermingled love, would all shatter and fall to pieces, if charity should chance to die. There are some secrets in it, which seem to give it the chair from all the rest of virtues. With knowledge, with valour, with modesty, and so with other particular virtues, a man may be ill with some contrary vice: but with Charity we cannot be ill at all (I. 86, pp. 235-236).

Here, the Graces and the Muses meet; this time Felltham might truthfully say "Both them I serve, and of their train am I." In comparison with the more prudential tone of many of the other *Resolves*, in those radiating out of the theme of charity "Thought that was frozen up under stern experience gushes forth in feeling and expression. There is a freshet which carries away dams of accumulated ice."[14] His thought on this subject is always inspired by a generous sympathy for suffering. "Of Libelling against them that are fallen" (II. 56), or

"Of Arrogancy" (I. 6) as well as the new essay "Of Alms"
(10th ed. II. 79) reflect the instinctive desire to cham-
pion the modest, impoverished, or unfortunate against
the overbearing and powerful. This current of Christian
feeling is not only stronger than the traces of Stoicism
that appear in the *Resolves*; it also has a liberating influence on Felltham's writing.

He chose a form of expression, the meditation on
conduct leading to a resolution of the will, that suited
the seventeenth-century meditative man but did not
survive that century. The writer of miscellaneous prose
is like an archer who, aiming at an outer circle of the
target, may sometimes lodge his arrow in the center.
Felltham's modesty led him to think that his prose, like
his ethics, represented a mean between extremes. In the
address to the reader provided for the later editions
(surely his own, though couched in impersonal terms),
it is said that his resolves "were written to the middle
sort of people. For the wisest, they are not high enough;
nor yet so flat and low, as to be only fit for fools. . . ."
But this does not give a true sense of his endowments
or of his delight in workmanship. Again he returned to
deliberate on a writer's aim, and expanded his early essay "A Rule in Reading Authors." Again he sought to
relate the Graces and the Muses. He found them in the
same path. "A good style, with good matter, consecrates
a work to Memory; and sometimes while a man seeks
but one, he is caught to be a servant to the other" (10th
ed., p. 216). He finds that it may become a man both
"to precept himself into the practice of Virtue, and to
fashion both his Tongue and Pen, into the exercise of
handsom and significant words" (p. 215). It is as if he
knew himself that the Graces would lead him in the direction of the Muses when he maintains that "Wit is

very near a kin to Wisdom" (p. 214). The later reader may stimulate his interest in human and humane convictions by turning over the leaves of Feltham. Or he may take more interest in the conscious stylist, expert in pointed sentences and brisk antitheses. But what is most likely to continue Feltham's hold on some favouring readers is his ability, in a sufficient number of his compositions, to link his charitable will, his steady grasp of experience, and his control of statement.

Feltham and Sir Thomas Browne were near-contemporaries, although the first edition of *Resolves* appeared almost twenty years before *Religio Medici* was published. The range, the diversity, the unfathomable imagination of Browne's prose make it irrelevant to compare them; yet humane qualities of mind and unique traits of expression make it allowable to set them side by side. The 1661 edition of *Resolves* is closer to the temper of Restoration prose; perhaps these later pieces by Feltham have some ancestral affinity with adept eighteenth-century essay writers who owe nothing to Browne.

But the incentives and temptations of writing for the periodical press differentiate Addison, Steele, and even Goldsmith from Feltham, who is never whimsical or arch, never constructs a personality for himself, and does not assume a social gathering as the milieu of the reader. The inwardness of the resolve, and the incorruptibleness of Feltham's primary muse, make it possible to see in him a partial predecessor of Thoreau.

After the victory of the plain style in the latter part of the seventeenth century, and Dryden's shaping of it into a more conversable and secular instrument, the fuller orchestration of Donne and Browne could not be used again. Its latent powers had to be regenerated in the nineteenth century, for new minds and new convictions.

Underlying the explorations of Emerson and Thoreau particularly, the openness to wonder was prepared for by individual resolve.

These writers, and Hazlitt and De Quincey as well, were quite aware of the need to bring the graces and the muses into the same, or concentric circles. Dr. Johnson looked to neither of these visitors. He had learned from Browne, but nothing that he could really develop. His muse was his own indomitable will; he stands alone like the rock of Cashel.

William Hazlitt:  4

The Essayist and the Moods

of the Mind[1]

Hazlitt speaks in his own person. His is not the grave impersonal voice of "counsels, civil and moral," nor the brisk sociable presence of a Bickerstaff or Spectator, or the smiling mask of Elia. He comes forward and utters an incisive sentence reflecting a straight personal conviction.

This freedom from the assumed persona might be thought to owe something to a decision of Leigh Hunt, when he founded his Round Table in the *Examiner*. Here Hazlitt published his first essays. Hunt wrote, in presenting this series, "we have avoided the trouble of adding assumed characters to our real ones; and shall talk, just as we think, walk and take dinner, in our

proper persons."[2] But in fact, although in his own con-
tributions Hazlitt avoids an assumed character, he
speaks often in the tone of an editorial plural, is less
actively the marked individual speaker he was to become
as he went on writing.

Before he found his central path writing for the *Examiner* the essays to be published in his book, appropriately called *The Round Table*, Hazlitt as a man of
thirty-seven had travelled two byways unsuccessfully.
The first was, to use his own proud term, as "metaphysician." Before he took the enchanted road to Nether
Stowey and Alfoxden, on his visit to Coleridge and to
meet Wordsworth, Hazlitt had confided to Coleridge
his plan for an *Essay on the Principles of Human Action*. Although he had formulated the argument in his
mind, several years passed before he could get it on
paper. And after it was published, it drew no attention.
Hazlitt made some further efforts in this direction with
his lectures on philosophy. But generally speaking philosophy was not a channel for the powers that he possessed.

Nor was painting to be his true profession, although
he practiced it too hopefully and for too long. In these
two premature choices of profession, Hazlitt nevertheless experienced a sense of unity in important branches
of perception and of feeling. This unity brings into relationship the various "moods of the mind"[3] that Hazlitt
later presented and explored in his essays.

In the *Essay upon the Principles of Human Action*
Hazlitt made imagination, a term he was to invest with
central significance, the clue to belief in the reality of
concern for the betterment of the human condition.
Determined to refute systems asserting the primacy of
self-interest, Hazlitt argued that "The imagination, by

means of which alone I can anticipate future objects, or be interested in them, must carry me out of myself into the feelings of others by one and the same process by which I am thrown forward as it were into my future being, and interested in it" (1.1-2). If his dry and crabbed analysis failed of influence on other minds, it provided a theoretical foundation for his commitment to the aims of the French Revolution and sustained his own beliefs when the heroes of his youth, Wordsworth and Coleridge, became conservative.

Imagination found another stimulus in the unsuccessful effort to become a painter, for "The humblest painter is a true scholar; and the best of scholars—the scholar of nature,"[4] and "From the moment that you take up the pencil . . . you are at peace with your own heart."[5] From his copying of masterpieces in the Louvre, as well as from attempts to paint an old woman or his father's portrait, Hazlitt developed a certain kind of faith that underlies many of his best essays. Before he embarked on the career of journalist, before he created, considered, battled with, remembered, and set off the various moods of his prose, he had attained a possible unity of mind and emotion. He attained a faith with which he never became disillusioned. He was stunned, and often bitter, because those who had shared his political hopes not only abandoned them, but openly allied themselves with the forces of repression. But insofar as these men also remained "scholars of nature" he respected them, and even his antagonism starts from an affirmative source.

Many of Hazlitt's essays, early and late, are not rooted in these fundamental beliefs of his, but belong to the realm of discourse or opinion. They remind us of the derivation of essay from *exagium*, a weighing, but they lack the sinuosity of Bacon or the undulance of Montaigne. Instead of threading his way through *sententiae* of diverse kinds, Hazlitt brusquely contrasts attitudes, often taking it on himself to rebuke the favoured ones. But here again, he is asserting a mood of the mind.

At the head of his *Round Table* he placed an early essay on an inviting topic, "On the Love of Life." But soon the spirit of contrariety takes over, and we read, "The proof that our attachment to life is not absolutely owing to the immediate satisfaction that we find in it, is, that those persons are commonly found most loth to part with it who have the least enjoyment of it, and who have the greatest difficulties to struggle with, as losing gamesters are the most desperate," and "We would willingly . . . sacrifice not only the present moment, but all the interval (no matter how long) that separates us from any favourite object" (4.1-2). Is this the author who could write of gusto as "power or passion defining any object"? Yes, but that is gusto in art, and from art Hazlitt could recover the tone of feeling which sometimes forsook him in his contemplation of a commoner range of experience. Hence many of his essays worry opinions back and forth, and the structure is governed by the vein of antithesis, or by marked sequences of emphatic disavowal (as in "On the Ignorance of the Learned").

Two different kinds of opportunity seem to have liberated Hazlitt from the more limited scope of the papers in *The Round Table*. One was perhaps the experience of lecturing, the other the greater amount of space available in the hospitable columns of *The London Magazine*. And more space meant room to diversify the patterns of mood and feeling entering into these essays.

With Hazlitt's lectures as such we are not chiefly concerned, since his interest as a writer ultimately derives more from the variety of his essays than from his intermittent activity as a literary critic. But the variety itself, and the direction of the writer's talent, was, I believe, liberated by the reading and thinking that he did to prepare the lectures.

Compared with most of the essays in *The Round Table*, the *Lectures on the English Poets* (1818) have a more sustained current of feeling and a further reach of thought. In these lectures Hazlitt developed more fully concepts of imagination that link together many of his later pieces. In distinguishing the qualities of related poets, such as Chaucer and Spenser, he is admirable in showing the different possibilities open to the poet, or closed to him, the different ways he may choose to, or be impelled to, use his gifts. Perhaps most important of all, his way of understanding Shakespeare, the approach to Shakespeare's elusive creativity, unanalyzable in terms of any one moral scale—the approach to Shakespeare that underlies Keats's attribution to the poet of "negative capability"[6]—tended, I believe, to emancipate Hazlitt from the restrictive prejudices that mar some of his discourses. The decisive passage is this:

The striking peculiarity of Shakespeare's mind was its generic quality, its power of communication with all other minds—so that it contained a universe of thought and feeling within itself, and had no one peculiar bias, or exclusive excellence more than another. He was just like any other man, but that he was like all other men. He was the least of an egoist that it was possible to be. . . . His genius shone equally on the evil and on the good, on the wise and the foolish, the monarch and the beggar. . . . He was like the genius of humanity, changing places with all of us at pleasure, and playing with our purposes as with his own (5.47).

Toward the end of this part of his lecture Hazlitt adds "Nothing is made out by formal inference and analogy, by climax and antithesis: all comes, or seems to come, immediately from nature" (5.50). I venture to suggest that without having developed this generous insight, Hazlitt would not have grown the power that sets apart such essays as "The Indian Jugglers" and "The Fight."

His *Lectures on the English Comic Writers* (delivered 1818, published 1819) are also in a sense preparatory to his own finest essays, in the grasp shown of certain kinds of prose writing by his predecessors. The lecture on the periodical essayists is significant. One notices the nature of his preliminary tribute to Montaigne as the first essayist "who had the courage to say as an author what he felt as a man," and "who wrote not to make converts of others . . . but to satisfy his own mind of the truth of things" (6.92-93). In his discussion of Addison and Steele Hazlitt notes the "fictitious and humorous disguise" assumed, and the direction to "the more immediate and passing scenes of life, to temporary and local matters," from which the philosopher and wit "brings home little curious specimens of the humours, opinions and manner of his contemporaries, as the botanist brings home different plants and weeds" (6.95). Hazlitt's preference for Steele's essays over those of Addison is instructive: they have "more of the original spirit, more of the freshness and stamp of nature. The indications of character and strokes of humour are more true and frequent; the reflections that suggest themselves arise more from the occasion, and are less spun out into regular dissertations" (6.97).

Hazlitt was now ready, and the beginning of *The London Magazine* gave him the opportunity, for the freer, more substantial essays published in his *Table Talk* (volume I, 1821, volume II, 1822). In fact, the collection in book form includes a number of essays written independently rather than for *The London Magazine* or the *New Monthly*, to which Hazlitt had transferred the series. This is evidence that he had reached an independent goal, even though he had been aided by the hospitality of these magazines, and perhaps stimulated by the quality of their other contributors, including Lamb and De Quincey. As Addison said, "Great contemporaries whet and cultivate each other."

Some of Hazlitt's most memorable essays are contained in the two volumes of *Table Talk*. In "On the Pleasures of Painting" he drew directly from personal experience in a way that he was to do later even more adeptly. Who can doubt his veracity when he tells us that "to look at Nature is to be . . . free from the temptation to combat, to strain a point, or crush an adversary"?[7] One regrets for his sake but does not question the statement that in comparison with painting he takes little pleasure in his essays. Doubtless he never could understand why he had the one kind of skill and not the other. As a painter he could not, and as a writer he could, recreate the brown face of the old lady to whom he hoped to do the justice of a Rembrandt. On the page, the face speaks movingly to the reader, as does that of Hazlitt's father, at the end of this essay.

The love of painting—the effort to do it, the unenvied glory of admiring the true masters of it—is a particular mood of the mind that Hazlitt explores in *Table Talk*. I cannot avoid singling out the brilliant piece "On a Landscape of Nicolas Poussin," where in the writing as well as the summoned image of the painting "we are thrown back on the first integrity of things" and taught a major difference when we read that "He could give to the scenery of his heroic fables that unimpaired look of original nature, . . . or deck it with all the pomp of art, with temples and towers and mythologic groves."[8] Thus Poussin could both "give us nature, such as we see it," a power "well and deserving of praise" and could "give us nature, such as we have never seen, but have often wished to see it," a better power, "and deserving of higher praise."[9] From rediscovering for us particular paintings, Hazlitt is led at the same time or other times to ponder terms like imagination, nature, genius, originality. Marianne Moore once said, in a conversation about Wallace Stevens, "One might think that it would kill afflatus to extol imagination as a theme." But for Stevens it did not, nor for Hazlitt. For the latter, here was opportunity to try to identify regions of feeling that he well knew, even if only abstract terms could name them. And he saved himself as a mature writer from the aridity of abstraction that had accompanied his early efforts as "metaphysician." In "On Genius and Common Sense," for example, he unites the disparate terms by acknowledging the importance of feeling as underlying common sense. He likewise brings genius closer to comprehension by his deserved use of symbolic examples, from Shakespeare, Rembrandt, and Wordsworth.

The Paris edition of *Table Talk* (1825) carried an "Advertisement" by Hazlitt which sets forth an indispensable comment by him on the tone, the structure and the contrasting types of essays this book contains.

The title may perhaps serve to explain what there is of peculiarity in the style or mode of treating the subjects. I had remarked that when I had written or thought upon a particular topic, and afterwards had occasion to speak of it with a friend, the conversation generally took a much wider range, and branched off into a number of indirect and collateral questions, which were not strictly connected with the original view of the subject, but which often threw a curious and striking light upon it, *or upon human life in general* [italics added], it therefore occurred to me as possible to combine the advantages of these two styles, the *literary* and *conversational*; or, after stating and enforcing some leading idea, to follow it by such observations and reflections as would probably suggest themselves in discussing the same question in company with others. The same consideration had an influence on the familiarity and conversational idiom of the style which I have used (8.333).

He goes on to speak of a contrasting kind of essay, in which he has perhaps "too frequently attempted to give a popular air and effect to subtle distinctions and trains of thought." There can be no question in which of the two kinds Hazlitt excelled. And it is essential to recognize that his idea of conversation, while it included idiom, extended also to the flex and reflexes of point of view towards a subject. Of conversation in this sense there is hardly an example before him. Bacon never conceived it so, Addison and Steele were chatty, impromptu, casual, but did not structurally follow the moods of the mind. Lamb assumes an appealing role in which he may apostrophize or cajole the reader (often addressed as "thou") but he seldom opens the chance of an exchange of ideas or a contrasting pattern in experience. He more often writes from a single point of view.

The pondering of a specific time of discovery is what distinguishes some of the most celebrated essays in *Table Talk*, such as "On Going a Journey." Hazlitt sets out to tell the reader why on a considerable walk he would have no companion, and he makes him one. The unwished-for accompanist heartily agrees that a "continual comparing of notes interferes with the involuntary impression of things upon the mind."[10] He sees the ferry over the Severn, and the girl controlling the boat, he remembers an hour when he too read a book as beguiling as the *Nouvelle Heloise*, over something like the cold chicken and glass of sherry—and he rejoices that this day was Hazlitt's birthday. The name of Coleridge as the man Hazlitt is walking to see evokes a new sensation, and the expression of an unfathomable regret at his changed faith, from youth to older years, brings the reader close to Hazlitt. He, now, has fashioned a kind of essay in which past and present interanimate each other. The finding of this on the road to Langollen far excels the interest of such abstract discourse as we find in a general essay like "On the Past and Future."

In "The Indian Jugglers," Hazlitt has fashioned another kind of composition that is uniquely his own and anticipates the great uncollected ones of his last years. The ascent and the descent from the central massif, the evocation of the Indian juggler's art, and the mastery of Cavanagh, the fives player, are flashing with light and

motion. The Indian juggler is before us, in the perfection of his skill.

> To catch four balls in succession in less than a second of
> time, and deliver them back so as to return with seem-
> ing consciousness to the hand again, to make them re-
> volve round him at certain intervals, like the planets in
> their spheres, to make them chase one another like
> sparkles of fire, or shoot up like flowers or meteors, to
> throw them behind his back and twine them round his
> neck like ribbons or like serpents . . . to laugh at, to play
> with the glittering mockeries, to follow them with his
> eye as if he could fascinate them with its lambent fire . . .
> there is something in all this which he who does not
> admire may be quite sure he never really admired any-
> thing in the whole course of his life.[11]

Hazlitt is led to compare this perfection or that of the
rope-dancer, master of his art, with the seemingly less
controlled skill available to him in writing his essays.
"The tact of style is more ambiguous than that of
double-edged instruments,"[12] he observes. And thinking of a painter such as Reynolds, in comparison with
the rope-dancer, or the juggler, he concludes that although the painter's effort to do what nature has done
can never wholly succeed, nevertheless admiration for
the painter must be greater. He is then stimulated once
more to approach topics central to his writing, and to
deliver himself of some of his most enlightening statements about them.

> Nature is also a language. Objects, like words, have a
> meaning; and the true artist is the interpreter of this
> language, which he can only do by knowing its applica-

tion to a thousand other objects in a thousand other situations. . . . The more ethereal, evanescent, more refined and sublime part of art is the seeing nature through the medium of sentiment and passion, as each object is a symbol of the affections and a link in the chain of our endless being.[13]

And as if he, the author, knows that we, the readers, sometimes have difficulty in sorting out the terms of his conversation with us, he tells us that *genius, imagination, feeling,* are the same power.[14] Progressing further to contrast cleverness with inherent greatness, he shows that the latter imparts knowledge and being to others.

It was an inspired decision to conclude this essay by adding at the end of it the notice Hazlitt had written for the *Examiner* in 1819 of the death of John Cavanagh, the fives player. The incredible speed and versatility with which Hazlitt describes his strokes and his strategy match the player's art. This portrait at the end recalls the differing style and skill illustrated by the juggler at the beginning, and gives to the essay as a whole a balance and natural symmetry rare with Hazlitt.

His underlying unity of conviction connects some of Hazlitt's essays with others, but many are on wholly unrelated topics. He was now to produce a book with a potential unity of purpose, his *Spirit of the Age* (1825). Reformers like Bentham and Godwin, apostles of reaction like Malthus, writers like Wordsworth, Coleridge, and Scott, parliamentarians like Sir James Mackintosh, the Tory cabinet members Canning and Lord Eldon, an activist like Cobbett—such figures were represented in Hazlitt's gallery.

The seventeenth-century "character," whether Theophrastan or historical, presenting the type or the individual, is a collateral form with the essay, and Hazlitt's sketches in *The Spirit of the Age* are a new offshoot of these related traditions. But although Hazlitt has chosen representative figures, he does not epitomize them chiefly as kinds of men. And, although he is alert to striking traits, he has on the whole little to say of a man's course of life, and he makes little use of anecdote or appearances. With appropriate differences, matching the occupation of the man, Hazlitt is concerned with the nature of each one's commitment, style of action, and effectiveness.

Thus Bentham, introduced with a fine rhetorical bravado as an architect of constitutions from Paris to Pegu, is seen as limited by his grasp of human feeling (a defect J. S. Mill was later to recognize so poignantly). Godwin, shown in a kindly, reminiscent (but not sentimental) spirit, is said to have "conceived too nobly of his fellows . . . he raised the standard of morality above the reach of humanity, and by directing virtue to the most airy and romantic heights, made her path dangerous, solitary and impracticable" (11.18).

Behind Hazlitt's view of Godwin and Bentham as both, in differing ways, led too far afield by abstract reason, lies his own respect for Burke's emphasis on feeling, a respect as marked as is Hazlitt's scorn for Burke's defense of hereditary power and hereditary privilege. Herschel Baker has wisely observed that both Hazlitt and Burke "distrusted the trim constructions of theorists undisciplined by feeling and experience," and pointed out that Hazlitt, "like Burke, was mindful of the force of time and habitual association in shaping human values."[15]

A related regard for some kind of tact in conversation,

for suppleness of mind, and for clarity in choice of aim governs Hazlitt's exposure of the fixities of Mackintosh's brilliance, the one-sided philanthropy of Wilberforce, or the crudity of Cobbett's use of energy. One of the sharpest passages of antithesis—and *The Spirit of the Age* contains many—occurs in the contrast between the conversation of Mackintosh and of Coleridge:

> The ideas of the one are as formal and tangible as those of the other are shadowy and evanescent. Sir James Mackintosh walks over the ground, Mr. Coleridge is always flying off from it. The first knows all that has been said on a subject; the last has something to say that was never said before. . . . The conversation of Sir James Mackintosh has the effect of reading a well-written book, that of his friend is like hearing a bewildered dream. The one is like an Encyclopedia of Knowledge, the other is a succession of *Sybilline Leaves*! (11.102).

The ability to discriminate and find terms for such differences is a resource that accompanies Hazlitt throughout his search in these varied individuals for the spirit of the age. An assumption of the whole book is the value of good conversation, or of sensitive style in Parliamentary debate. For example, after paying tribute to Brougham's detailed command of his facts, Hazlitt concludes

> With so many resources, with such variety and solidity of information, Mr. Brougham is rather a powerful and alarming, than an effectual debater. In so many details . . . the spirit of the question is lost to others who have not the same voluntary power of attention or the same interest in hearing that he has in speaking . . . if he can,

others *cannot* carry all he knows in their heads at the same time; a rope of circumstantial evidence does not hold well together . . . (11.136).

It is undoubtedly true that, as Herschel Baker has said, the unity of the essays here collected arises from their "subtle exploration of the central problem of the age: the reciprocal relations of convention and revolt, of freedom and restraint."[16] But there is unity also in the perception of each individual's possible pattern of achievement, and frequent falling short by the habit of his own disposition.

In treating Southey and Scott, Hazlitt is unflinching in his opposition to the cowardice he sees implicit in their embrace of legitimacy. Yet he pays Scott the novelist as high a tribute as any might wish; "He is a writer reconciling all the diversities of human nature to the reader . . . he treats of the strength or the infirmity of the human mind, of the virtues or vices of the human breast, as they are to be found blended in the whole race of mankind" (11.65).

He is less inclined here to castigate Coleridge and Wordsworth for political apostasy than in many of the public strictures on them that he had expressed in the past. Now it is the mystery of the deflecting tendencies in Coleridge's genius that he portrays.

He who has seen a mouldering tower by the side of a chrystal lake, hid by the mist, but glittering in the wave below, may conceive the dim, gleaming, uncertain intelligence of his eye: he who has marked the evening clouds uprolled (a world of vapours), has seen the picture of his mind, unearthly, unsubstantial, with gorgeous tints and ever-varying forms . . . (11.29).

But it is in the genius of Wordsworth that Hazlitt finds an emanation of the spirit of the age that may be universal, pointing to a liberation of feeling that will transcend the failures of historic accomplishment. Wordsworth's muse, Hazlitt maintains, is a leveling one in both its avoidance of traditional ornament and its welcoming of elemental human sympathies. Wordsworth

> has . . . neither the gorgeous machinery of mythologic lore, nor the splendid colours of poetic diction. . . . He sees nothing loftier than human hopes; nothing deeper than the human heart. This he probes, this he tampers with, this he poises, with all its incalculable weight of thought and feeling, in his hands. . . .
> . . . so Mr. Wordsworth's unpretending Muse, in russet guise, scales the summits of reflection, while it makes the round earth its footstool, and its home! (11.86, 88).

Hazlitt recognizes here the central identity of the Romantic age, which animates his own best writing.

In this book he had, then, achieved something new. In the first place the potential unity of the central theme is realized in a number of related essays. And these essays achieve a distinct originality in capturing traits of a man's style and temperament that affect his contribution to the ongoing vitality of the time, in success or in failure. Reminding one at times of Clarendon's characters, Hazlitt has nevertheless made something new; we might call it the portrait essay. He can suggest a scene—Bentham walking in his garden, Godwin relaying an anecdote of a "a day passed at John Kemble's in company with Mr. Sheridan, Mr. Curran, Mrs. Wolstonecraft and Mrs. Inchbald, when the conversation took a most animated turn, and the subject was of Love" (11.28). He seldom describes the physical appearances of men—the descriptions of Wordsworth and Southey are exceptions. The unforgettable detail of actual behaviour—a counterpart to Clarendon's Sidney Godolphin timidly turning back from a ride, in bad weather, but fighting in the Civil War with unquestionable gallantry—is not often found in *The Spirit of the Age*. But the separate identities of men emerge in Hazlitt's portrait essays, and the age itself, which had placed the author in a position of proud resistance, is seen overshadowed by reaction as it moves toward the current of reform that Hazlitt did not live to see.

The style of these essays is trenchant and resolute. They exhibit a sureness and rapidity of execution, confirmed by the direct and open tone of the speaker. Elusive qualities of men are conveyed in effective imagery— as in the description of the mind of Coleridge, quoted above. Like Burke's, Hazlitt's imagery is appropriate, relevant, and expansive rather than revelatory of individuality of observation. For the most part his rhythm in these essays is forward-moving and sometimes impetuous. As in his other writings, antithesis often suits his purposely striking contrasts. Here too he sometimes risks an oratorical flourish, as in the essay on Sir Walter Scott, with the long apostrophe beginning "Oh! Wickliff, Luther, Hampden, Sidney, Sommers" and ending "Ye who have produced this change in the face of nature and society, return to earth once more, and beg pardon of Sir Walter and his patrons, who sigh at not being able to undo all that you have done" (11.66-67). This is carried off with a sustained eloquence that Hazlitt can call upon when a genuine need arises. Otherwise, as Coleridge remarked of him, "He sends wellheaded and well-feathered Thoughts straight forwards to the mark with a Twang of the Bowstring."[17]

Few writers have been more articulate on the subject of prose style than Hazlitt. As a major discussion of it occurs in his next book of essays, *The Plain Speaker*, it will be convenient to take some account here of some of his earlier statements.

Hazlitt did not share, as did Coleridge and Lamb, a creative affinity with the seventeenth-century prose writers. He was, however, a sympathetic reader of a number of them. He recognized not only the grandeur of Bacon's imagination but the variety of his style, which he found "equally sharp and sweet, flowing and pithy, condensed and expansive, expressing volumes in a sentence, or amplifying a single thought into pages of rich, glowing and delightful eloquence."[18] Appreciative of Browne, Hazlitt nevertheless obviously regards him as enigmatic, an eccentric who "scoops an antithesis out of fabulous antiquity, and rakes up an epithet from the sweepings of Chaos."[19] This description, as well as his reference to Browne as decking out "contradictions and non-entities" in "the pride and pedantry of words,"[20] shows that Hazlitt did not understand Browne's versatility and the evolution of his different works. It is with Jeremy Taylor that Hazlitt is most at home. He describes him in terms affected by Taylor's own imagery when he says "His style is prismatic. It unfolds the colours of the rainbow; it floats like the bubble through the air; it is like innumerable dew-drops that glitter on the face of morning, and tremble as they glitter."[21] Unaware of Browne's capacity for very individual meditation on universal themes, Hazlitt can more easily admire Taylor's "choral song" because Taylor "took obvious and admitted truths for granted."[22]

In his *Lectures on the English Comic Writers*, there

are further comments by Hazlitt on prose style. Admiring Steele and Addison as periodical essayists, Hazlitt does not pause to describe their language. No one, of course, could have rivaled Dr. Johnson's aptness and eloquence in his commendation of Addison's prose. When it comes to Dr. Johnson himself, Hazlitt is decisive in refusing to place value on his style. It is worth pondering the reasons. The description itself is telling:

> The structure of his sentences, which was his own invention, and which has been generally imitated since his time, is a species of rhyming in prose, where one clause answers to another in measure and quantity, like the tagging of syllables at the end of a verse; the close of the period follows as mechanically as the oscillation of a pendulum, the sense is balanced with the sound; each sentence, revolving round its centre of gravity, is contained within itself like a couplet, and each paragraph forms itself into a stanza (6.102).

I believe that Hazlitt saw that no one could go forward from Johnson's prose, that it was as finished an example of its own kind as was possible to produce. Macaulay's slipping to a coarser version of it is a corroboration. Furthermore, the kind itself, its Corinthian symmetry, was unsuitable to the variations in mood and feeling that a writer like Hazlitt would explore, and Hazlitt would not submit to an alien discipline. "It destroys all shades of difference," he complained, "the association between words and things" (6.102).

The possible coincidence between language and object that Hazlitt finds lacking in Johnson, he gives as one of several reasons for his admiration of Burke. "Burke's execution, like that of all good prose, savours of the texture of what he describes" (12.12). "Burke's style is airy, flighty, adventurous, but it never loses sight of the subject; nay, is always in contact with, and derives its increased or varying impulse from it" (12.19). His preference for Burke's as "the most perfect prose-style, the most powerful, the most dazzling, the most daring" arises partly from the sense of difficulties overcome by a controlled adventurousness.

No aid, Hazlitt maintains, was usually derived from the material, its coming to life is the result of the activity of the writer's mind. Between the *materia poetica* and the order of composition that the poet finds for it, there is to Hazlitt less of a gap (Hazlitt would not say this if he were writing today). In impassioned prose "the general subject and the particular image, are so far incompatible" that to make them coalesce is a greater challenge to the prose writer than to the poet. "Every word should be a blow: every thought should instantly grapple with its fellow. There must be a weight, a precision, a conformity from association in the tropes and figures of animated prose to fit them to their place in the argument, and make them *tell*, which may be dispensed with in poetry, where there is something more congenial between the subject matter and its illustration—" 'Like beauty making beautiful old rime!' " (12.11). Enthusiasm for Burke's prose evokes from Hazlitt some dazzling tropes of his own, like the parallel between the ascent of the chamois and the flight of the eagle. It is perhaps surprising that in an essay of which the general tenor is that the prose style of poets fails in being too far from the conversational, Burke should nevertheless be the central figure. For Burke's is essentially a formal style. Yet to Hazlitt the conversational does not imply merely the colloquial. What he prizes in it is the movement and elasticity corresponding to, and stimulating, the moods of the mind.

The mixture of essays collected in *The Plain Speaker* very much resembles *Table Talk*. There are general discussions of topics such as "Reason and Imagination," or "Whether Genius is conscious of its Powers." Essays like these are chiefly useful in piecing out Hazlitt's aesthetic or his latent epistemology. There are a few on moods and humours, such as "On Envy" or "On the Pleasure of Hating." Abstract topics often evoke a certain irritability from Hazlitt: he seems to imagine an individual whose convictions are the opposite of his own, and move him to an indignant scorn rather than a playful dialectic. Here also, though, are essays that have not only the tone but the reality and structure of conversation, such as the second one "On the Conversation of Authors," a companion piece to the later "On Persons One Would Wish to Have Seen." Hazlitt's congenial terms of praise and his alert discrimination of kind and temperament enliven his "Old English Writers and Speakers." He recaptures some of the richness of his lectures on the English poets and on the comic writers.

There has been less good prose on prose than poetry on poetry, and what we have is precious. Hazlitt contributes further valuable observations on its opportunities in "On the Difference Between Writing and Speaking." Rejecting the oratorical style, the easy currency of the fluent speaker, Hazlitt insists that the writer has time, and that he take time, "to make novel combinations of thought and fancy, to contend with unforeseen difficulties of style and execution . . ." (12.276). This necessary and lovable labour extends to both resources of feeling and awareness of language. The writer is to give the choice and picked results of a whole life of study; what he has struck out in his most felicitous moods. . . . He may turn a period in his head fifty different ways, so that it comes out smooth and round at last. He may have caught a glimpse of a simile, and it may have vanished again: let him be on the watch for it, as the idle boy watches for the lurking place of the adder (12.277).

He could not always achieve this attentiveness, particularly in the essays that belong to the world of discourse and of opinion. Here he too often strikes an attitude, or contends with the commonplace. He knew, however, that the life of language is linked with the life of feeling. The writer's associations

are habitually intense, not vague or shallow; and words occur to him only as *tallies* to certain modifications of feeling. They are links in the chain of thought. . . . Again, the student finds a stimulus to literary exertion, not in the immediate *éclat* of his undertaking, but in the difficulty of his subject, and the progressive nature of his task. He is not wound up to a sudden and extraordinary effort of presence of mind; but is forever awake to the silent influxes of things . . . (12.277, 278).

And there follows one of the rare expressions of pleasure in writing that Hazlitt permits himself; it is none the less genuine for that.

The lines of growth that led upward were to be followed in a number of essays that remained uncollected in Hazlitt's lifetime. Some of them might have been included in *The Plain Speaker*, and it is a puzzle that they were not. Others, like "The Letter Bell," were among the last that he wrote. A number of them deserve to be regarded as a distinct group, for in them Hazlitt is treating the form of the essay differently.

He is, frequently, summoning from the past a scene or scenes, and episodes, that create the effect of a vivid present. Or occasionally, as in "The Fight," an immediate happening occupies the foreground.

The justly famous "My First Acquaintance with Poets" (published in 1823 in *The Liberal*) had its inception in a letter to *The Examiner* in 1817. Exasperated by one of Coleridge's lay sermons, Hazlitt in this letter creates a contrasting portrait, of Coleridge preaching in the Unitarian Church at Shrewsbury on the opposition between the spirit of the world and the spirit of Christianity, in the days before he had embraced *jus divinum*. The description both of the inspired Coleridge and the enraptured youth is so fine a distillation that Hazlitt was able to incorporate it virtually unchanged in the first part of his matured essay. In the latter, after the moving account of the sermon, there is the scene of Coleridge talking at Hazlitt's house in Wem and the description of his appearance, compared with his host the dissenting minister, Hazlitt's father. The next day, as Hazlitt walks six miles with the poet on his road, Coleridge in his talk "appeared to float in air, to slide on ice" (17.113).

The narrative is resumed as Hazlitt sets out later on his journey to visit Coleridge, and to meet Wordsworth at Alfoxden. The back-and-forth of poets visiting each other, the reading new poems outdoors, all the individual excitements of young writers, are resonant with life, youth, hope, and the encounter with genius. It is not the later fame of the two poets that gives this essay its unforgettable vitality, but the joyful unfolding of the narrator's experience. These men were the heralds to him of immortality. If they later abandoned the hopes of freedom they shared with him, he measured the tragedy, and could not forget the loyalty of the first meeting.

A totally different kind of experience is recounted in "The Fight." Once again, Hazlitt casts his essay in a pure narrative form. The ride down in the diligence and then by the mail coach, supper and talk of sport at an inn, the march to the fight in the morning, the bustle at the ring, the bloody contest until the "gas-man's" defeat, the return journey to London—all is accomplished fact by fact, sensation by sensation, with unerring success. "The Fight" gives the reader a central event and its whole ambience, the approach to it, the climax, and the return of an intelligent, surprised witness. A novelty is achieved in the form of the essay.

A different pattern shapes "On a Sun-Dial," opening with its motto *Horas non numero nisi serenas*, and proceeding image by image through human means of reckoning time. The sundial, the hourglass, French watches, castle bells, the busy chimes of Amsterdam, all the means of telling the hour or minute pass before the reader's mind in a haunting progress. Here are no people or episodes; the unity comes from related suggestions and the solitary moods of the observant writer, last seen reclining whole mornings on a bank on Salisbury plain, innocent of duration.

Again, in "The Letter-Bell," Hazlitt showed uncanny skill in writing a new kind of essay. He is now a master of what might be called active recollection—not nostalgic, but challenging a sharpened awareness of the past. And the past has a dimension of colour, a votive quality. This essay is about the summons, at once conditional and universal, sometimes unheeded but often welcome, to correspond with our friends, our older or our contemporary relations. Who can fail to recognize its impetus, or be unmoved by the dramatization of it in the scarlet-coated figure who rang the letter-bell, as Hazlitt either ran to meet its bearer, or sat regretful in his lodging? The structure of this essay rivals symbolism in the novel a century later. But the point is that "The Letter-Bell" is better for its purpose than as an echo in a novel. There is concentration on a channel of experience, all the more real for being single, a possibility in prose that approaches, but is not, fiction.

Thinking of poets of his own age, in comparison with those of the past whom he admired and loved, Hazlitt regretted that his contemporaries found their themes in the "moods of the mind." Poetry lay deep in his own imagination; he is seldom far from it, and his manner of quoting it never depends on topic or superficial relevance; he brings forth lines and stanzas embedded in his very being—and, next to Shakespeare, Wordsworth as often as any, it seems to me. What then, did he regret, in the concern of the romantic poets with "the moods of the mind"? Shakespeare and Milton, he thought, "owe their power over the human mind to their having had a deeper sense than others of what was grand in the objects of nature, or affecting in the incidents of human life," whereas to writers like Wordsworth and Coleridge, "there is nothing interesting, nothing heroical but themselves" (5.53). Without pausing to dispute this verdict, one must point out that Hazlitt's strength as an essayist drew upon and exemplified the strength of his age; and his limitations reflected its limitations, except in politics.

Under Hazlitt's directing hand, the essay became capable of reflecting a "plenary consciousness," such as

he had said the London citizen possessed (12.73). Partly this is the result of the differing purposes he followed:
the speculative essay, such as "Whether Genius is Conscious of its Powers"; the path of personal experience
traced, "On Going a Journey"; the portrait essay as in
*The Spirit of the Age*; the narrative as in "The Fight";
or the essay creating a pattern of free impressions such
as "The Sun-Dial" or "The Letter-Bell." Equally, Hazlitt's extension of the capacity of this form results from
his developed and developing skill as a prose writer.
This is less active in some of the discursive pieces but
comes fully alive in others. Typically he begins without
ado, and then fashions his piece with impetus, pace, attack, stroke on stroke. His alertness turns new corners
with the aid of his powerful illustrative metaphors. At
times, we must admit, there is a lack of organic unity in
proceeding to an end, but he does not dawdle. His critical prose is calm, friendly, authoritative without the
assumption of authority.

In "On the Difference Between Writing and Speaking" he had described the character of an author as re-
quiring that he do justice to his own feelings, and "the
whole of a man's thoughts and feelings cannot lie on the
surface, made up for use; but the whole must be a
greater quantity, a mightier power, if they could be got
at, layer under layer, and brought into play by the levers
of imagination and reflection" (12.279). And it is so, in
his essays taken as a group. To approach the mightier
power implicit in the whole, we may have to discard
some of the layers by the way. The moods summoning
the mind of Hazlitt vary; but the generative ones were
his capacity for admiration, and his unfailing response
to the experience of youth and art.

# The Virtù of De Quincey       5

One day in 1837, the Edinburgh publisher Adam Black saw the sheriff's men conveying a small, genteel although threadbare figure to nearby Calton gaol. Recognizing the victim as Thomas De Quincey, he stopped to ask the reason for the arrest. A debt of £30 was not beyond Black's power to guarantee, and he did so, on condition that De Quincey write the articles on Shakespeare and on Pope for the new (7th) edition of the *Encyclopaedia Britannica*.[1] This incident might be taken as emblematic of De Quincey's writing career. Like many others, he wrote out of the necessity to earn, but unlike them he worked often without plan, providing a vast number of articles on miscellaneous subjects, chiefly for the periodical press. But, in spite of his procrastination, publishers wanted his work, for he had a following among readers—first because of the identity he had established as "The English Opium Eater," then because of his success in meeting the demands of literary journalism by the exercise of his unusual gift.

The editors of *The London Magazine*, of *Blackwood's*, *Tait's*, and finally Hogg's *Instructor* and *Titan* had been his taskmasters. At ten guineas a sheet (sixteen printed pages, in double columns of small type) for Blackwood's "Maga" or at a rate of twenty guineas for *Tait's*,[2] he tried to support a large family. No wonder that he could not always pay the grocer or meet the rent of the various lodging-places for himself, apart from his family, to which he resorted for the privacy and quiet necessary to his projects. Forced at times to take sanctuary at Holyrood, where debtors could escape prison, reduced to pawning his clothes, so that he could not go out for books that he needed, De Quincey never made a comfortable living in his profession until his late years. But in spite of the impairment to his health caused by opium, in spite of his tendency to delay, he wrote about one hundred and fifty articles (as well as two books, *Klosterheim* and *The Logic of Political Economy*, which are of much less interest than his other work). The collection of his writings, first by the American firm of Ticknor and Fields and then by De Quincey himself for his Edinburgh publisher, Hogg, brought him substantial sums. (Shortly before that, his tiny annuity of £100 was increased to £200 when his mother died at the age of ninety-three or ninety-four.) To the Edinburgh "collective" edition (it was not complete) De Quincey gave the title *Selections Grave and Gay*.[3] If it now has a somewhat old-fashioned ring, it is nevertheless an interesting choice because it reflects two moods in De Quincey's writing which were often effectively and sometimes powerfully juxtaposed.

The qualities "grave and gay" may lead us to the virtù of De Quincey, if we may reclaim the Italian sense of the term with its suggestion of strength and even cunning, rather than a mere connoisseurship or general excellence, which De Quincey also possesses. These qualities suggest the underlying courage and courtesy that may be present in writing as well as in behavior. De Quincey's personal courtesy was perhaps the trait most often praised and admired by those who knew him; in his writing it deepens into the sympathy with the child, "the pariah," the outlaw, which is so well-known in him, and at the same time dignifies the object of that sympathy. Courage appears in the manner in which De Quincey adapted and redirected his ambitions to the demands of necessity, with the result that in some pieces of his writing he achieved a new form, moving from the essay to a special kind of narrative.

The likelihood is that if De Quincey had not had to write for money he would either have written badly or not at all. A diary, kept when he was eighteen, shows him an early recruit to the Romantic movement! " 'My imagination flies, like Noah's dove, from the Ark of my mind . . . and finds no place to rest the sole of her foot except Coleridge—Wordsworth and Southey.' "[4] He records a list of the works he hoped to execute: among others "Yermak the rebel, a drama"; "A pathetic tale of which a black man is the hero"; "A life of Julius Caesar"; "An essay on poetry."[5] He describes briefly a scene for a novel he has thought of.[6] But he emphasizes, "I have besides always intended of course that *poems* should form the corner-stones of my fame."⁷ De Quincey had no gift for verse and was never to be a poet. Nevertheless, the latent interests of a writer are there in the diary, and the sensibility; and the uncertainty of aim is natural to a young man.

Nothing occurred to focus these interests. The "wretched opium" had begun its sway by the time he was a student at Oxford. But De Quincey's intellectual incertitude, his susceptibility to German philosophy and to the fascination of Ricardo's theory of economics, no doubt also deflected him. He defended himself to his mother for abandoning the half-hearted study of law, in terms that reveal a vast and vague ambition unlikely to result in any significant literary outcome. He tells her that he had rejected his boyish hope of "high stations and honours in the state" in favour of a desire "that, by long and painful labour combining with such faculties as God had given me, I might become the intellectual benefactor of my species" and "accomplish a great revolution in the intellectual condition of the world . . . and as one effect of that revolution place education upon a new footing, throughout all civilized nations."⁸ The phrasing and the instinctive obeisance to long preparation are Miltonic—but here the resemblance to Milton ends. When he drafted this letter De Quincey was thirty-three, had written nothing substantial, and obviously did not think of his interests as chiefly literary. A second draft of the letter continues, "Marriage brought with it many expenses—we have had two children, . . ."⁹ and the need of supporting them led to his first connection with *Blackwood's Edinburgh Magazine.*

Unlike many writers, De Quincey never had any trouble in securing a publisher or interesting an editor. It is ironic that in spite of the importunate letters of

John Wilson (editor) and William Blackwood (publisher) of "Maga," none of the articles for which De Quincey had his first contract was produced. But not long after this unsuccessful start he went to London and, taking only a few months to write it, published in Taylor and Hessey's *London Magazine* in the fall of 1821, "The Confessions of an English Opium Eater, being extracts from the life of a scholar."[10]

The subtitle is significant. De Quincey had referred to himself as a "gentleman scholar" and in some respects he remained one throughout his life. At this time there is no evidence that he thought of himself as a professional writer—indeed he did not in fact become one for another ten years. The success of the "Confessions" then suggested to him further papers on his own life, leading to the "Autobiographic Sketches," and prompted him to exploit on other occasions the topic of opium. But to fill out the "sheets" for *Blackwood's* and *Tait's* he also had to draw heavily on his vast store of reading for biographical and historical articles as well as for those primarily in the realm of literary criticism. With the bulk of these articles, which range from topics in ancient history to new theories in economics, I shall not be concerned. Most of them are still readable, chiefly for the sake of De Quincey's skilful presentation, but most of them would seldom be read even by scholars if other work of his were not more original. But, both for its own sake and as an aid in understanding those pieces in which he succeeds most remarkably, something must be said of De Quincey's criticism.

## II

One would expect it to be of a high order, and occasionally it is. By criticism of a high order I mean writing by a person to whom literature is an active and unique experience, not possibly to be known in any other part of life, but itself both a part and source of life. The experience so recognized, if truthful and enjoyable language makes it known, may allow us to regard criticism as an art—not to be set beside tragedy or comedy, the lyric or short story, or the novel, but an art that nature helps to make. Some of Dryden's essays, parts of Johnson's, some of Virginia Woolf's and some of T. S. Eliot's, among other examples, might serve. Few of De Quincey's articles belong beside them. Yet he was aware of the value that might be at stake. "Criticism," he wrote, "if it is to be conscientious and profound . . . must be almost as unattainable by any hasty effort as fine poetry itself."[11]

The life of such criticism begins in reading, but it also depends on much that the critic has found out as a writer of a different kind. De Quincey was an omnivorous reader although sometimes an inattentive one. He had some periods and some writers that he used as a system of reference. He was a "good Grecist" but an anti-Hellenist in his preference for literature of the Christian era to that of antiquity.[12] Shakespeare, Milton, Wordsworth were constellations in his sky, by which he measured the brightness of lesser stars. Nevertheless, his essays on individual authors are usually disappointing; the author often becomes merely a topic for him, and he is tempted to wage sham battles over minor controversies of a biographical kind. What retrieves his criticism is the paragraph, the page or pages, in which his active judgment is suddenly liberated, or in which he is able to clarify some major principle, as he seeks to do in his treatment of the play within the play in Hamlet (which I find more stimulating than his better-known discussion of the knocking at the gate in Macbeth).

Although after a period of admiring friendship De Quincey had become estranged from Wordsworth and from Coleridge, he had by natural sympathy grafted onto his own thinking the principles that give his criticism all that it possesses of theoretical strength. From Wordsworth, as he acknowledges, he had absorbed the distinction between the literature of knowledge and the literature of power, while from Coleridge he probably derived the principles of thought incarnate in language, and of nature as an analogy of universal mind. But these principles are fortified by De Quincey's exposition of them, so that it would be unjust to say that we have them in Wordsworth and Coleridge, and can spare their repetition in De Quincey.

To find value in De Quincey's use of such principles is not to suggest that they all have inherent validity. The distinction between the literature of knowledge and that of power is on the one hand too obvious, if merely used to contrast books conveying information with works of a higher sort. On the other hand, it is defective in the very limited concept it implies of knowledge. The real merit in his discussion belongs to his description of "power":

> Now, if it be asked what is meant by communicating power, I, in my turn, would ask by what name a man would designate the case in which I should be made to feel vividly, and with a vital consciousness, emotions which ordinary life rarely or never supplies occasions for exciting, and which has previously lain unawakened, and hardly within the dawn of consciousness—as myriads of modes of feeling are at this moment in every human

mind for want of a poet to organize them? I say, when these inert and sleeping forms *are* organized, when these possibilities *are* actualized, is this conscious and living possession of mine *power*, or what is it? (x, 48).

And he gives *King Lear* as an example of a work of art able to endow the reader with such power. But De Quincey of all critics should have been able to perceive that the coming into consciousness of what was previously unconscious or only dimly known deserves to be thought of as knowledge, too. Rightly rejecting the didactic as an aim of poetry, he fails to see that didacticism is not an inevitable accompaniment of either teaching or knowledge. Without perceiving the conflict of ideas, De Quincey moves to correct his own narrower distinction when he says, "Poetry, or any one of the fine arts . . . can teach only as nature teaches, as forests teach, as the sea teaches, as infancy teaches,—viz. by deep impulse, by hieroglyphic suggestion. Their teaching is not direct or explicit, but lurking, implicit, masked in deep incarnations" (xi, 88-89), or confirms this:

> Gleams of steadier vision that brighten into certainty appearances else doubtful, or that unfold relations else unsuspected, are not less discoveries of truth than the downright revelations of the telescope. . . . It is astonishing how large a harvest of new truths would be reaped simply through the accident of a man's feeling, or being made to feel, more *deeply* than other men. . . . Wordsworth has brought many a truth into life, both for the eye and for the understanding, which previously had slumbered indistinctly for all men (xi, 315).

Here De Quincey's natural ability to discover the sources of his own feeling has emancipated him from the more superficial distinction between books of knowledge and the literature of power. In short, he is not a critic who—like Dryden or T. S. Eliot—excels in the elucidation of a principle, but working from a principle seems to stimulate and fortify him in his report of what has meant most to him as a reader.

When he writes about prose, De Quincey speaks with more authority, more acutely, more specifically, than in most of his judgments of poetry. Perhaps his greatest single contribution as a critic is in the application of the organic theory of style to prose.

Suppose we say briefly that the "organic" theory of literature stresses the reciprocal relations of form and content. (This is better, I think, than to refer to their "unity.") Reciprocal relations approach unity in the best writing that we know, but the unity is won from an interaction, an interinanimation. In his major essay, "Rhetoric," De Quincey is concerned with the absence or appearance of this possible unity. At the outset he seems baffled by the concept *rhetoric*, on which he had chosen to write—but who could deny it to be a perilous venture? Aware of the amplitude of suggestion this term had for the Greeks, but naturally unable to revive these overtones, De Quincey seeks to redefine the word and to strip it of the implications of ostentatious ornament or of sophistry it had acquired in later times. Tentatively he improves on the popular use of the term by suggesting that a man "is held to play the rhetorician when he treats a subject with more than usual gaiety of ornament" (x, 81), and holds that such a writer "is occupied with the general end of the fine arts—that is to say, intellectual pleasure" (x, 82). But then he handicaps his progress by setting up a hurdle between "rhetoric" and "eloquence," declaring that "Where conviction begins, the field of Rhetoric ends; . . . and, as to the passions . . . they are not within the province of Rhetoric but of Eloquence" (x, 82). This distinction has the double disadvantage of confounding a literary quality with a psychological state, and limiting the human response to a special type of utterance.

He moves to better ground when he takes up the relation of style and "the ornamental parts of composition" to rhetoric. At last, although in a parenthesis, he comes to a decision: because *"they are in many cases indispensable to the perfect interpretation of the thoughts,* we may admit arts of style . . . as the ministerial part of Rhetoric" (x, 92, my italics). By means of this vantage point he can look down into the thick forest of seventeenth-century prose writing and identify the towering oaks. He is now compelled to transcend, or at least subdue, the unhelpful opposition he has set up between rhetoric and eloquence. Browne and Jeremy Taylor he praises as "if not absolutely the foremost in the accomplishments of art . . . undoubtedly the richest, the most dazzling, and, *with reference to their matter,* the most captivating, of all rhetoricians" (x, 104, italics added). It does not escape him, as the motion of his own mind impels him forward, that he is approaching a different sense of what prose can do. In Browne and Taylor "are the two opposite forces of eloquent passion and rhetorical fancy brought into an exquisite equilibrium, —approaching, receding,—attracting, repelling, . . . chasing and chased, as in a fugue . . . so as to create a middle species of composition, more various and stimulating to the understanding than pure eloquence, more gratifying to the affections than naked rhetoric" (x, 104-105).

He is on the verge of a discovery about the possibilities of prose, and why these were in a unique state in the seventeeth century. He sees, but does not develop, the fact that there is a relationship between the state of society and the themes available to a writer. Thus he says that the Athenian orator gains strength from the fact that the great topics in the assemblies would be peace or war, vengeance for public wrongs or mercy to penitent offenders, "and every aspect of open appeal to the primal sensibilities of man" (x, 98). In contrast, in modern times "the impoverished condition of civil eloquence" results from the complexity of public business. Likewise, rhetoric and eloquence flourished in England in the late sixteenth and early seventeenth century "when science was unborn as a popular interest, and the commercial activities of aftertimes were but sleeping in their rudiments" (x, 100). Because of the changes in the structure of society there can be no chance for the revival of rhetoric either in public speaking or in written composition. But he does not link this general observation with his sensitiveness to the ease with which in Browne and in Taylor the individual mind gains command of universal themes. He comes close to it, especially in this comment: ". . . where the understanding is all alive with the subtlety of distinctions, . . . the variety and opulence of the rhetoric is apt to be oppressive. But this tendency, in the case of Taylor, was happily checked and balanced by the commanding passion, intensity, and solemnity of his exalted theme, which gave a final unity to the tumultuous motions of his intellect" (x, 108).

This is a good example of De Quincey's use of the organic theory of style to relate the movement of thought and the manner of expression in a particular author. The organic theory also supports his contrast between the prose of Johnson and of Burke. In Burke, "every truth . . . every thesis of a sentence, *grows* in the very act of unfolding it," whereas Dr. Johnson's sentences contain thoughts "fully preconceived." "Hence, whilst a writer of Dr. Johnson's class seems only to look back upon his thoughts, Burke looks forward" . . . (x, 125n.). In both cases—that is, in his comment on Taylor and in his comparison of Burke and Johnson—we see an awareness of chances and opportunities that De Quincey is alert to both in his essays and in his more imaginative writing. In the ordinary essay—biographical or historical, his sense of the subject often "is all alive with the subtlety of distinctions," sometimes at the expense of progress in a uniform direction. And in his longer, imaginative pieces, the interest lies in the movement forward of his themes as well as in the problem of a final unity. The essay, "Rhetoric," also offers clues to the kind of conscious skill required by a writer like De Quincey, with his love of imagery, of variation, "of novelty diffused over truths coeval with human life" (x, 125).

In other essays De Quincey, no doubt by choice, does not enter much into discussion of English prose writers. But in the second of his two pieces on Lamb (the review of Talfourd's *Memorials*), his discussion of the prose of Hazlitt and of Lamb is arresting. (Lamb he admired, as he did not Hazlitt, but found both subject to the same faults, or at least shortcomings.) Hazlitt lacked eloquence because he was not capable of continuity:

> No man can be eloquent whose thoughts are abrupt, insulated, capricious and (to borrow an impressive word from Coleridge) non-sequacious. Eloquence resides . . . in the relations of manifold ideas, and in the mode of

their evolution from each other . . . the main condition lies in the *key* of the evolution, in the *law* of the succession. . . . Now Hazlitt's brilliancy is seen chiefly in separate splinterings of phrase or image which throw upon the eye a vitreous scintillation for a moment, but spread no deep suffusions of colour, and distribute no masses of mighty shadow (v, 231).

After noting that Lamb did not agree with this opinion about Hazlitt, De Quincey expresses a similar disappointment in reading Lamb, who, he says, "by native tendency, shrank from the continuous, from the sustained, from the elaborate" (v, 234). All that he has to say on this point is highly instructive—especially as to his conviction that without the elaborate "much truth and beauty must perish in germ." He then relates Lamb's failure in this respect to his insensitivity to music, and proceeds, "it was a corollary . . . that Lamb had no sense of the rhythmical in prose composition. Rhythmus, or pomp of cadence, or sonorous ascent of clauses, in the structure of sentences, were effects of art as much thrown away upon *him* as the voice of the charmer upon the deaf adder" (v, 235). In these remarks we find a clue to De Quincey's own effort, even under the conditions of working for the periodical press, to develop in his imaginative writing something more continuous than the usual essay. We find a clue also to his reason for ending the "English Mail Coach" with a "Dream Fugue" and the revised edition of the "Confessions" with "The Daughter of Lebanon," and finally a clue to the failure of his "Suspiria." In both the essay on Rhetoric and the discussion of Hazlitt and Lamb, De Quincey not only contributes to our understanding of prose but reveals what he sought for in his own work.

The prefaces included in the various volumes of De Quincey's *Selections Grave and Gay* often contain helpful information about the circumstances of composition of particular works, and occasionally a valuable comment on his intention. But, for his thinking about prose, the General Preface is the only one that greatly matters. Here he divides his articles into three classes. The first, which includes the "Autobiographic Sketches," proposes primarily to amuse the reader, although in some "the amusement passes into an impassioned interest" and at times "the narrative rises into a far higher key," when a degree of abstraction may take place from ordinary events, and there is "nothing on the stage but a solitary infant, and its solitary combat with grief— a mighty darkness, and a sorrow without a voice" (I, 9). It is impossible to doubt that De Quincey refers here to the piece called "Affliction in Childhood." But this poses a problem—for "Affliction in Childhood" originally was published as a part, and is the understructure, of the *third* group of his writings. (The second group, addressed "to the understanding as an isolated faculty," and called simply "Essays" presents no difficult question and does not draw upon De Quincey's essential originality.)

But the third group is brought forward as a "far higher" class of compositions, in virtue of their aim. To this class "The Confessions of an English Opium Eater" belongs, and also ("but more emphatically") the "Suspiria de Profundis." Pointing out that he is about to publish both in a revised form, De Quincey declares that he will then feel entitled to ask for a judgment of "their claims as works of art." He adds that there is singular difficulty in creating in language "the visionary scenes derived from the world of dreams" and that there has been a dearth in literature "in this one department of impassioned prose" (1, 14). Taking these comments together, we see that De Quincey thinks of narrative "in a far higher key," of the creation in language of visionary scenes derived from the world of dreams, and of impassioned prose as the summit of his aims and the quintessence of his accomplishments. These statements show that he did think of some of his prose as being of an experimental kind. My effort in treating further of his work will be to distinguish between those pieces that are mere experiment and those in which he enlarges the capacity of prose.

## III

In its original version, "The Confessions of an English Opium Eater" is one of the great works in English. De Quincey's revision and expansion of it for his collective edition went far to dilute its strength. He added details that have intrinsic interest, and are helpful to his biographers, but ruin the structural economy of the original "Confessions." De Quincey seems to have suspected this. Writing to his daughter Emily in 1855 he says that the enormous labour the revision has cost him should have led to improvement of the work as a whole. "And yet, . . . greatly I doubt whether many readers will not prefer it in its original fragmentary state to its present full-blown development . . . [A]s a book of amusement it is undoubtedly improved; what I doubt is, whether also as a book to impress."[13]

Proceeding on the assumption that the original version is the one that deserves sustained attention, there is still a problem in arriving at the true center of the book, from which life is circulated to the rest of it. De Quincey was, I think, himself uncertain or unaware of this center. Making his début as a magazine writer, he seized upon the sensational appeal that might be counted upon in a "confidential" record of his drug addiction and his struggle to overcome it. This is his emphasis in the note "From the Author to the Reader" with which the "Confessions" begin, and it is confirmed by the apparent plan, divided into four sections: "Preliminary Confessions," "The Pleasures of Opium," "Introduction to the Pains of Opium," "The Pains of Opium." But the intrinsic interest of the "Confessions" does not derive from its account of the doubtful pleasures or indubitable pains of the drug. The account serves chiefly to create a background of struggle that enhances the portrait of the meditative gentleman scholar.

If, as a journalist, De Quincey at the time of first publication emphasized the clinical interest of the "Confessions," he judged differently, but as mistakenly, in giving his later view of the literary value of the work. "The object of ['The Confessions'] was to reveal something of the grandeur which belongs *potentially* to human dreams" (XIII, 334). This statement was made to introduce his "Suspiria" as a "sequel" to the "Confessions," a further development of his descant upon dreaming. Even in the original version, De Quincey had explained that the purpose of the narrative that composes the "Preliminary Confessions" was to furnish a key to the scenery of the dreams and to create an interest in the confessing subject, the gentleman philosopher whose nature made him capable of dreaming. But in fact the narrative, which De Quincey sees as almost utilitarian in purpose, is the heart of the work, the center of its vision upon life.

For De Quincey's unsurpassable gift is not for sequences of revery or dreaming, but for an intense vision of the actual. Why do we reread the "Confessions"? Not for description of the vague architecture or personages of the dreams summarized or commented on at the end, but for the episodes in Wales, London, and Grasmere. From the moment when the schoolboy, whose accomplishments in Greek already make us accept him as a precocious scholar, escapes from the house of his headmaster, the "archididascalus," not only is our sympathy with him aroused but we are ready for humour, suspense, and trial. The pride that drives the youth from his safe lodging to the hardships of wandering and reduces him finally to awful hunger on a diet of blackberries and rose hips, the brief interlude of shelter with the young Welsh people—all these incidents are not merely preparatory but significant in themselves.

De Quincey's "Coming to London" exceeds in interest that of any similar story that I have read. The wonder is that he, who had a liking for pathos, could write this part without pathos—which is a damaging literary quality. Indeed, he tells with the strictest objectivity of his taking refuge in the unfurnished house of the lawyer, his effort to reassure the young child he finds there, a stray like himself, that there are no ghosts, his keeping her warm in his arms when they have no cover. The comradeship with this waif precedes and thereby in some way reinforces the story of his friendship with Ann of Oxford Street. In both cases, but in the second more than in the first, De Quincey succeeds in evoking an extraordinary sense of the solitude of these young people in the crowded city, and of the streets and squares that were more real to them than the human throng:

> Being myself, at that time, of necessity, a peripatetic, or a walker of the streets, I naturally fell in, more frequently, with those female peripatetics, who are technically called street-walkers. Many of these women had occasionally taken my part against watchmen who wished to drive me off the steps of houses where I was sitting. But one amongst them . . . yet no! let me not class thee, oh nobleminded Ann—, with that order of women;—let me find, if it be possible, some gentler name to designate the condition of her to whose bounty and compassion . . .— I owe it that I am at this time alive. For many weeks, I had walked, at night, with this poor friendless girl, up and down Oxford-street, or had rested with her on steps and under the shelter of porticoes . . . (p. 39).[14]
> —One night, when we were pacing slowly . . . after a day when I had felt unusually ill and faint, I requested her to turn off with me into Soho-square. Thither we went; and we sate down on the steps of a house, which, to this hour I never pass without a pang of grief . . . (pp. 40-41).

Ann's rushing off to buy the young scholar a glass of port wine when he is on the point of collapse; the necessary postponement of his plan to find legal redress for her wrongs; his journey away from London and her failure to appear at the appointed rendezvous in Tichfield Street, upon his return—all these happenings are related straightforwardly and in a tone of simple candor, and have a powerful emotional impact. In comparison, the passage at the end of the "Confessions" relating the appearance of Ann's face in his dreams is artificial:

The scene was an oriental one; and there also it was
Easter Sunday. . . . And at a vast distance were visible . . .
the domes and cupolas of a great city—an image or faint
abstraction, caught, perhaps, in childhood, from some
picture of Jerusalem. And not a bow-shot from me, upon
a stone, and shaded by Judaean palms, there sat a woman;
and I looked, and it was—Ann! . . . Her looks were tran-
quil, but with unusual solemnity of expression . . . but
suddenly her countenance grew dim, and, turning to the
mountains, I perceived vapors rolling between us . . . in
the twinkling of an eye I was far away from mountains,
and by lamp-light in Oxford-street, walking again with
Ann—just as we walked seventeen years before, when we
were both children (pp. 122-123).

This has interest as an artfully composed notation of
"the potential grandeur of dreams," but it depends entirely upon the first interest the reader has felt in Ann,
and attempts to revive that with an obvious appeal in
the last sentence to a lingering pathos. The facts, given
to us in the narrative, are deeply moving; the dream
echo lapses into the weakness of sentiment.

"The Confessions" had reached a climax of feeling in
the opening narrative; De Quincey recognized this and
allowed it expression in the great passage with which
the section ends: "So then, Oxford-street, stony-hearted
stepmother, thou that listenests to the sighs of orphans,
and drinkest the tears of children, at length I was dis-
missed from thee!" (p. 59). The final perspective from
Oxford Street is the image of the young scholar gazing
up the roads leading to the north, to Grasmere, and
this links the first with the latter part of the "Confessions." For the following ones, less vivid than the London narrative, owe their interest to the sympathetic

portrait already created of a solitary and contemplative youth, who had endured severe hardship for the sake of his freedom, and had been redeemed by understanding and affection. In the part relating the pleasures of opium, the strength of the composition does not come from the report of how many drops of laudanum the narrator took at one time or another. It comes, again, from the reality of life in London; the Saturday nights spent at the opera admiring the singing of Grassini, or at other times wandering forth with the poor of London among the stalls and markets. Likewise, in the section analyzing the pains of opium, scenes of reality, not phantasmagoria, appeal most to the imagination. The scholar in his mountain retreat confronted by a Malay visitor, to whom he talks in Greek and gives a lump of opium, is a lovable man—and in the visit of the Malay there is the same combination of humour and suspense that marked the boy's departure from the house of the "archididascalus." In both these sections the somewhat tedious report on opium-taking acquires significance not so much as a preparation for the dreams, but as a cause of the "gentleman scholar's" isolation and struggle.

We now have been given "a key to some parts of that tremendous scenery which afterwards peopled the dreams of the opium-eater" (p. 15). De Quincey had to decide: how to end his narrative, that, unlike a voyage or a battle, had no inevitable ending. He chose to add notes relating the reappearance in dreams not only of Ann but of the Malay and of the image of a dead child, of oriental scenes and animals, and general observations upon his habits of dreaming. What De Quincey says *about* dreaming and the value of it is always more convincing than the specimens that he gives of it, however useful they might be to a psychologist. He does not succeed in giving these specimens of dreams an integral relation to earlier events in the "Confessions," nor does he succeed by this means in resolving the sorrow or suffering of the opium eater. One reason for this is that the dreams have a primarily literary or traditional origin. Among those he characterizes (rather than relates) one may find a confirmation of this. He explains that he had been looking over Piranesi's *Antiquities of Rome*, and had then been told by Coleridge of another set of engravings by that artist, his "Dreams," which "represented vast Gothic halls," mysterious engines, endless disconnected staircases, with Piranesi toiling ineffectually to escape (p. 114). Obviously Coleridge described to De Quincey a work of Piranesi which is called not "Dreams" but *Carceri di Invenzione*. Far from being as Coleridge maintained "the scenery of [Piranesi's] own visions during the delirium of a fever," the *Carceri* represent his contribution to the tradition of fantasy in the painting or drawing of architecture—beginning in the baroque period and ending with this late example. It is easy to see how Coleridge's description of it would catch the attention of De Quincey, on whose youthful mind Gothic romances, with similar architectural fantasies, had made such an impression. This incident helps to corroborate Miss Elisabeth Schneider's conclusion that the " 'dream' writing of Coleridge and De Quincey derives far more from the coalescing of individual temperament with literary tradition than from the consumption of opiates."[15] De Quincey at any rate harboured an interest in this tradition for many years; it eventually led him to the writing of his "Suspiria de Profundis."

IV

When the group of papers forming the original set of "Suspiria" began to appear in *Blackwood's* in 1845, De Quincey described them in the title as "Being a Sequel to the Confessions of an English Opium Eater." The sense in which he meant this is explained in the Introductory Notice, where he makes the statement I have already quoted, to the effect that the *purpose* of "The Confessions" was to reveal the potential grandeur of human dreams. The Introductory Notice continues with a striking testimony of De Quincey's interest in the "dreaming faculty," which he believes is declining as a result of social and scientific revolution. He anticipates the theories of Jung in his praise of "the magnificent apparatus which forces the infinite into the chambers of a human brain, and throws dark reflections from eternities below all life upon the mirrors of the sleeping mind" (p. 149).[16] He then ponders the relative importance of his childhood experiences and his enslavement to opium in stimulating the imagery of his dreams, and decides that his experience of death and intense grief in childhood initiated the dream scenery and the variations that "seem likely to have been growths and fructifications from seeds at that time sown" (p. 156).

His first emphasis, then, is on the genetic explanation of dreams, as a clue to the dreams themselves. For this purpose he began the series with "The Affliction of Childhood," intended to serve the same purpose as "Preliminary Confessions" in the earlier work. But in comparison it lacks straightforwardness. In the moment when the boy is alone with his dead sister, and hears a wind like a "vast Aeolian intonation" and sees "the pomps and glory of the heavens outside," he is caught up in a trance, and experiences a vision of flight and pursuit to the throne of God, implying immortality (p. 176). This is the unforgettable climax, but it is succeeded by a mixture of incongruous autobiographical detail and somewhat self-conscious abstract expatiation upon the themes of solitude and grief. It is not surprising that in preparing his collective edition De Quincey transferred this piece to the "Autobiographic Sketches," where it essentially belongs—yet the "Suspiria" cannot be read intelligently without it.

The self-conscious treatment of the abstract themes is the outgrowth of De Quincey's second preoccupation in the "Suspiria," to provide examples of the kind of writing he calls "impassioned prose." The later statement in the General Preface about the high value he attached to them is confirmed by his letter to his friend Professor Lushington, at the time when they were first published, in which he says that they are "the *ne plus ultra*, as regards the feeling and the power to express it, which I can ever hope to attain."[17] It would not be far wrong to argue that the comparative failure of the "Suspiria" results from a divided aim: to give expression to De Quincey's wholly genuine interest in dreams as reappearances of imagery from earlier experience, and to provide specimens of these in set pieces of writing, "pyrotechny" in prose.

At one time De Quincey intended to collect the "Suspiria" into a volume, but he never did so. Quite apart from the fact that some of the accounts of dreams and "noontime visions" were lost, through fire and other causes, De Quincey was obviously unable to work out a unifying conception or structure for a collection of them. This may be seen in the discrepancies and lack of congruity in the set originally published in *Black-wood's*. Although it was announced that these papers would appear in four parts, only two appeared. Part I, in *Blackwood's* of March, April, and June, 1845, includes "The Affliction of Childhood," "The Palimpsest," "Levana and Our Ladies of Sorrow," "The Apparition of the Brocken," and "Savannah-La-Mar." The installment of Part II that came out in July was later given the titles "Vision of Life" and "Memorial Suspiria." The rest of Part II and Parts III and IV did not follow as planned. We have reason to think, however, that "The English Mail Coach" was once intended by De Quincey to form a part of "Suspiria." For reasons I shall shortly discuss, it grew into a work of very different character and both when it was printed in *Blackwood's* in 1849 and in his collective edition De Quincey did not connect it with the "Suspiria," but rightly treated it as an independent work. The only successors to the 1845 group of "Suspiria," then, are the oriental tale with a Christian moral, "The Daughter of Lebanon," added to the "Confessions" in the revised version, and the fragments that were collected in volume 1 of the *Posthumous Works*[18] —fragments so brief and disconnected as to make it likely not merely that we cannot reconstruct a plan for the whole, but that De Quincey himself never achieved one.

The diverse character of the papers in "Suspiria" bear that out. The autobiographical "Affliction of Childhood" is succeeded by "Palimpsest," a skilful but conventional essay in which De Quincey explains the term and makes it an analogy for the deposit of layers of impressions in human consciousness. This essay, as it were, presents the *theory* of De Quincey's dreams. The first piece to be offered, then, as a true example of the vision, and of "impassioned prose," is "Levana and Our Ladies of Sorrow" with its rapid opening "Oftentimes at Oxford I saw Levana in my dreams. I knew her by her Roman symbols" (p. 237). But what follows is again an essay, constructed around a triple personification. De Quincey tells us exactly what he is doing: ". . . I want a term expressing the mighty abstractions that incarnate themselves in all individual sufferings of man's heart; and I wish to have these abstractions presented as impersonations, that is, as clothed with human attributes of life, and with functions pointing to flesh. Let us call them, therefore, *Our Ladies of Sorrow*" (p. 240). The effect of this device is somewhat operatic: one lady with her diadem, one with her "dilapidated turban," one whose head is "turreted like that of Cybèle," conspiring to educate him in affliction. The elaborate pageantry of the personifications of sorrow yields to a last sentence which in its simplicity undoes and atones for all of the rest: " 'And so shall our commission be accomplished which from God we had—to plague his heart until we had unfolded the capacities of his spirit,' " (p. 246).

In "The Apparition of the Brocken" De Quincey has more command of structure, and more seeming purpose. He uses the anecdote of a phantom appearing under certain conditions of weather as an analogy to a figure in his dreams that he calls the Dark Interpreter. He promises further illustrations of this figure in a later stage of his "opium experience." In the so-called Finale of Part 1 of *Suspiria*, "Savannah-La-Mar," the Dark Interpreter views the city submerged beneath tropic waters, and reflects on the finitude of time as known to us, and justifies sorrow and disaster as instruments of God's mysterious ways of raising man. Here, as is often the case, De Quincey's introduction posits a religious theme, but represents no active insight. "Savannah-La-Mar" at least suggests the imagery of a dream, and is less didactic than other parts of the *Suspiria*.

We see then that these "dreams," which at one time De Quincey refers to as "Oxford visions," are not visions at all but relatively abstract musing upon the themes of suffering and loss, with a tendency to personification, and a true visual suggestion of a dream only in "Savannah-La-Mar." In the subsequent part, "Vision of Life," De Quincey outdoes Dickens in his effort to wring pathos from a deathbed scene and in his tracing of future domestic sorrows in the family he sketches. We cannot help being reminded in reading this that De Quincey was now writing in the age of Victoria; perhaps something of the Romantic interest in dream fantasy has given way to a moralistic emphasis.

What we are most likely to remember about the "Suspiria" is a sentence here and there, a picture of a civilized kingdom submerged under sea, and De Quincey's own enthusiasm about these experiments of his. Most critics have acquiesced too easily in his claim that there is something extraordinary about the style of the *Suspiria*. Even if the term "impassioned prose" is rejected, often "prose poetry" is substituted for it. But the texture and rhythm of these pieces expose the fallacy of such descriptions.

We must of course reject both terms. The term "impassioned" connoted to De Quincey associations with music, with the movement of light[19]—but it implies also a performance, an effect of delivery, as one might say "an impassioned aria." De Quincey is often capable of a controlled and subtle cadence, as in the famous sentence, "And her eyes if they were ever seen, would be neither sweet nor subtile; no man could read their story; they would be found filled with perishing dreams, and with wrecks of forgotten delirium" (p. 242). But the desire to achieve the effect of "impassioned" utterance betrays him into bad writing. In the same passage, he continues of Mater Suspiriorum: "She weeps not. She groans not. But she sighs inaudibly at intervals" (p. 243). The inversion in the first two sentences (and De Quincey avails himself of it all too frequently) is an attempt to create an effect which the sense does not support. Likewise, of Our Lady of Sighs: "Murmur she may, but it is in her sleep. Whisper she may, but it is to herself in the twilight. Mutter she does at times, but it is in solitary places that are desolate as she is desolate . . ." (p. 243). Here again the feebleness of meaning makes the deliberate parallelism ridiculous.

Rhythm or musical pattern may be achieved in prose as well as poetry, we know, but it is not in the same degree symmetrical, and does not move from the end forward to the beginning as well as from the beginning to the end. Its path is uni-directional. No absolute contrast can be made between prose and poetry, but their differences work to the advantage of each. One general difference is that even in highly figured, symbolic, and rhythmical prose the circles of thought and association stir out wider than they do in most poetry; the explanatory, the parenthetical, the retrospective or the analytical displace the formal bounds. In spite of the consequent and valuable shift in rhythmic or a-rhythmic emphasis, there are a few compositions in prose that attain not only a structure of ideas but a sustained rhythmic pattern—the best example is the last section of *Urn Burial*. In this respect it is quite misleading to compare De Quincey with Browne, especially if the

"Suspiria" should be chosen as example. For this "impassioned prose" fluctuates between the conversational and the declamatory, with invasions of the preceptorial. Nothing of this kind is comparable to the independent meditative progress natural to Browne, or to the intensity of imagination we encounter in many parts of the sermons of Donne and of Taylor—occasionally in a whole sermon.

One reason for this discrepancy is that the seventeenth-century writers could enter upon and develop universal themes that their hearers or readers accepted as true. Individual experience gave freshness to meditation on such themes, but it was not necessary to conjure them into existence. The "Suspiria" show how hard it was to attempt this two centuries later. They are unsuccessful because De Quincey wavers between experiment in prose and the desire to exploit the personality of the opium eater. They fail collectively because they are monotonous, reiterating the lesson of one aspect of life, unable to relate it to others. De Quincey does not seem able to relate sadness and retrospection to the variety of life, to a sphere which would ennoble them. The "Suspiria" exhibit Whitehead's fallacy of "simple location."[20] The conjunctions of time and place and person should be new but are not. Retrospection governs all. The "Suspiria," if taken together with the "Confessions" and his narrative prose, acquire interest not as examples of a hybrid like "prose poetry" but as partial efforts in the direction of the novel. "Also I shall do away with exact place and time," Virginia Woolf says. "Anything may be out of the window—a ship—a desert—London."[21] What De Quincey almost accidentally reached for, Mrs. Woolf realizes in *Jacob's*

*Room* and *The Waves*. Only in the novel has prose been able to develop an autonomous pattern from within.

## V

The incomplete series of "Suspiria," then, probably owes its existence to the fact that De Quincey misjudged the nature of his success in the *Confessions*, attributing the strength of that work to the link between opium experience and dreaming, rather than to the central narrative. Like the *Confessions*, his two other great works are primarily narrative in form: "The Revolt of the Tartars" (1837) and "The English Mail Coach" (1849). Elton has pointed out that De Quincey's translations and adaptations of German romances, begun in 1827, exercised him in the craft of narrative; but, if so, this exercise only kept in training a skill he already possessed.[22]

The reader of "The Revolt of the Tartars" must be impressed at the outset by De Quincey's command of the structure of the whole: both its embodiment of universal themes and its architectural design. He announces, first, those aspects of the flight of the Nomads that call chiefly upon the imagination:

> The *terminus a quo* of this flight, and the *terminus ad quem*, are equally magnificent; the mightiest of Christian thrones being the one, the mightiest of Pagan the other. And the grandeur of these two terminal objects is harmoniously supported by the romantic circumstances of the flight. In the abruptness of its commencement, and the fierce velocity of its execution, we read the wild barbaric character of those who conducted the movement. In the unity of purpose connecting this myriad of wills, and in the blind but unerring aim at a mark so remote,

there is something which recalls to the mind those almighty instincts that propel the migrations of the swallow and the leeming [*sic*] . . . . Then again, in the gloomy vengeance of Russia and her vast artillery, which hung upon the rear and the skirts of the fugitive vassals, we are reminded of Miltonic images—such, for instance, as that of the solitary hand pursuing through desert spaces and through ancient chaos a rebellious host . . . (vii, 368-369).

These themes unify the whole, but the actual conduct of the narrative is likewise articulated in advance by De Quincey's perception of its chief dramatic elements: that the enterprise was a conspiracy, with important contrasts and conflicts among the leading characters; that it was also a great military expedition comparable to an anabasis; that it was, ultimately, a religious exodus, which carried along with it not only the fighting men but whole families, a whole people, with their herds of sheep and cattle, their horses and their camels.

From his boyhood De Quincey had read widely in books of travel, and he naturally responded to the chance of describing the settlements on the Volga, on the Eurasian steppes, in the outer domains of the Emperor of China. But he understood that the necessarily episodic pattern of accounts of travel, and the miscellany of information necessary to their authenticity, made it virtually impossible that such works should escape from "literature of knowledge," or information. In the flight of the Kalmucks, however, he had a story with a beginning, a middle, and an end; he saw also a connection between the character of the principal actors and the causal chain of events. Therefore, while using with utmost skill and suggestiveness the "scenical situations," "the *steppes*, the camels, the snowy and the sandy deserts," he never exploits them for isolated effect. He seizes every chance to connect the motives of the leading persons with the development and timing of the major episodes. The interplay of rivalry between the Khan, Oubacha, and the Satanic Zebek-Dorchi, his jealous rival, is made the most of in the preparation of the flight. The climax comes when the Khan aids the Russian Weseloff to return to his people, and the latter saves the Khan's life from Zebek-Dorchi's plot against it. This episode, which is both inherently dramatic and helpful in reinforcing the evidence of Zebek-Dorchi's villainy, is not found in the sources De Quincey used. Like other happenings or scenes, it is evidence of De Quincey's power of narrative invention, not for the purpose of embellishment, but to heighten the dramatic effect or support the fundamental structure of his account. Early in the story he emphasizes and gives his own interpretation of the feud between the Russian governor of Astrakhan and the Grand Commissioner Kichinskoi, a conflict which blocked timely discovery by the Russians of the Kalmucks' plan to flee. Similar heightening and selection is shown in De Quincey's treatment of the first great encounter on the flight: the Kalmucks' seizure of the fortress of Koulagina, and the defeat of a substantial portion of them by the Kossacks. And a particularly noteworthy example of the way in which De Quincey makes the timing or content of the episodes reinforce the portrayal of the chief actors comes at the halfway point in the Tartar flight. Bergmann, his principal source,[23] had placed at an earlier stage, on the Irghitch River, his description of the accumulating discontent of the tribe. De Quincey postpones this outbreak until the crossing of the Torgau is completed, when the Khan offers to abandon the flight and return to Russia. It is easy to see what is gained by the coincidence of the people's murmuring and the Khan's reconsideration. De Quincey's change here does not detract from fundamental accuracy but is one of many instances of the selectivity and invention necessary to a work of art.

But of all De Quincey's special choices contributing to the dramatic effect and the coherence of the whole, the most impressive is his working out of the end. All the sources agree that the remainder of the Kalmucks, decimated by the incredible hardships and the fierce attacks of their enemies, were hospitably received in the land of the Emperor Kien Lung. But only De Quincey makes the Emperor a witness of the tribe's arrival in his territory. For this purpose De Quincey imagines the Emperor engaged in hunting in a wild frontier district, on the confines of a desert. Standing at the opening of his tent he perceives at a distance a vast cloudy vapour rolling forward. During the next few hours

> . . . the dusty vapour had developed itself far and wide into the appearance of huge aerial draperies . . . and . . . where the eddies of the breeze acted upon the pendulous skirts of these aerial curtains, rents were perceived, sometimes taking the form of regular arches, portals, and windows, through which began dimly to gleam the heads of camels "indorsed" with human beings—and at intervals the moving of men and horses in tumultuous array—and then through other openings or vistas at far distant points the flashing of polished arms (VII, 411-412).

Here imagery characteristic of De Quincey's "dreams" invests a real event with mysterious meaning, and assists in the comprehension of its vastness and complexity, as well as of the underlying unity of purpose. One is aware also of a corresponding command in the rhythm of the prose—none of the weak exclamatory emphasis so frequent in the "Suspiria," but a measured, calmly directed progress to the climax, "the flashing of polished arms."

From this point to the end of "The Revolt of the Tartars," De Quincey blends material from his sources with matter of his own invention to bring about a resolution of both the individual conflict and the mass migration. Zebek-Dorchi's plot against the Emperor is discovered, and results in his assassination. The evil scheming of the "author" of the Tartar exodus, to whom De Quincey has given a Satanic role, meets with retribution. The remnant of the tribe is restored to prosperity, but De Quincey gives due weight to the ending of their nomadic life and their transfer from a Christian to a pagan civilization. By skilful treatment of the principal characters and the development of events, and by the resolution of both individual and general strands in the action, De Quincey has not only written "the epitaph of nomadism" (as Toynbee calls it),[24] but has given it "the unity of a well laid tragic fable."[25]

The principle of the "objective correlative" is sound. In "The English Mail Coach," as in "The Revolt of the Tartars," De Quincey had what he lacked in the "Suspiria," a sequence of events, of life in action, to support the structure of feeling and emotion. He succeeded in connecting the experience of the young man who is the virtual hero, and the central sensibility, with a large impersonal theme, and he very nearly succeeds in developing the theme itself to a higher stage of meaning. In one of his essays De Quincey expressed his conviction

that "a *public mind* and a common *connecting interest*"
is necessary to a healthy society and to its literature, if it
would surmount "trivial anecdotage" (VII, 103). The
Royal Mail was a symbol of the presence of a central
intellect, the government, that in the midst of danger
"overruled all obstacles into one steady cooperation to
a national result" (pp. 517-518).[26] And it fortified the
common connecting interest by bringing to distant cities
and towns the immediate news of England's victory in
the great battles of the Napoleonic war.[27]

The tremendous speed of the mail coach implies
danger as well as glory, and the imagination of youth
welcomes both. In his humorous description of the Oxford students eager to ride on the box with the coachman, De Quincey skilfully provides a setting for the narrator's joy in the speed of motion, in the mystery of
arrival and departure, and in darkness. These experiences also prepare for the climax and final catastrophe.
While nominally the personality of the opium eater is
drafted into service, and while De Quincey emphasizes
that the narrative is to serve as explanation of the imagery of the "Dream Fugue," its true interest is not autobiographic nor does it fundamentally belong in the
same class of writing as the "Suspiria." In "The English
Mail Coach" we have a new kind of narrative with a
special kind of hero. It comes closer to a book like Melville's *White Jacket* than to anything else. Who but
Melville could equal the feeling conveyed of youth and
defiance and the irony of impending change that is here
introduced:

> The night, however, being yet dark, as the moon had
> scarcely risen, and the streets being at that hour empty . . .
> I lost my way, and did not reach the post-office until it

was considerably past midnight; but, to my great relief
. . . I saw in the huge saucer eyes of the mail, blazing
through the gloom, an evidence that my chance was not
yet lost. . . . I ascended to my seat on the box, where my
cloak was still lying. . . . I had left it there in imitation
of a nautical discoverer, who leaves a bit of bunting on
the shore of his discovery, by way of warning off the
ground the whole human race, and notifying to the
Christian and the heathen world, with his best compli-
ments, that he has hoisted his pocket-handerchief once
and forever on that virgin soil; thenceforward claiming
the *jus dominii* to the top of the atmosphere above it . . .
(pp. 555-556).

Through the excited observation of the narrator the
scenes realize an extraordinary degree of actuality. He
exults in the elegance as well as the power of the Royal
Mail, with its single ornament on a dark ground of
chocolate colour, "the mighty shield of the imperial
arms, but emblazoned in proportions as modest as a
signet ring," in contrast to its vulgar competitor on the
road, "a tawdry thing from Birmingham . . . all flaunt-
ing with green and gold" (p. 529). And when, slipping
the royal horses like cheetahs, the coachman outstrips
the Brummagem tallyho, and the guard blows a "blast
of triumph, that was really too painfully full of deri-
sion," the narrator's own mockery and triumph gave
the edge of veracity to this incident (p. 530). It is
through his prescience, too, that the last part acquires
the force of an almost predetermined series of events:
he sees the superb one-eyed coachman as a Cyclops, and
knows that the lateness of the start from Birmingham
will require extra speed. He learns that the coachman's
reason for being on this route—not his regular one—

has deprived him of sleep, which he will be tempted to make up on the way. De Quincey has made imaginative use of his power of logical development to prepare for the isolation of the helpless youth beside the sleeping coachman, as the King's mail bears down upon the "frail reedy gig."

Not only has each section of "The English Mail Coach" its appropriate minor climax, but the whole is unified by the way the narrator welcomes the experience of victory, national and individual. The first kind of victory is that of youth and "vital experience of the glad animal sensibilities" which find expression in the successful contest with the Brummagem tallyho and the romantic worship of "Fanny of the Bath Road." Youth also loves the larger, public victory, when, before leaving London, "horses, men, carriages, all are dressed in laurels and flowers, oak leaves and ribbons," and all hearts are dilated by "a personal connection with the great news" (p. 541). This brings them into a different relationship with the people they pass on the road or meet in cities and villages, some apprehensive for their kin, all united in a national sympathy in which the beggar forgets his lameness, the charwomen "feel themselves by birthright to be daughters of England" (p. 544). But the last, a personal victory, is not to be won by the narrator: his inability to wrest the reins from the sleeping coachman leads to the "vision of sudden death," and his failure to surmount this trial is compared by De Quincey to a reenactment of the fall of man (p. 554). We may think at this point, also, of *White Jacket* and his fall from the mast.

By choosing to end the narrative part of "The English Mail Coach" here De Quincey fails to provide a dénouement. He avoids the problem of working out further

the conscious feelings of the narrator. Instead, subtract-
ing these from his account, he resorts to the grandiose
imagery of his "Dream Fugue" for a conclusion. As in
his comment on the "Confessions," De Quincey seemingly mistook his powers. We read "The English Mail
Coach" for its vividness, for actuality glorified by excited apprehension. The "Dream Fugue," in its variety,
fantasy, and irrational conjunctions of person and place,
does, it is true, come closer to being a vision created
from the subconscious than any of the "Suspiria" except
"Savannah-La-Mar." But it is too artificially worked out
to simulate a dream. The décor and detail are occasionally vapid ("golden tubes of the organ"), and the resort
to direct emotional appeal is sometimes ludicrous, as in
the exclamation "Oh baby! . . . shalt thou be the ransom
for Waterloo?" (p. 579). The fugue breaks the structure
of the whole and introduces a strident tone inconsistent
with the irony and straightforward dignity of the main
narrative. With its mixture of horror and sentiment,
and its architectural mysteries, the fugue would be an
appropriate episode in a Gothic romance. In "The English Mail Coach" it is chiefly valuable as an effort toward
a more transcendent realization of the theme of victory.

"Hush!" I said, as I bent my ear earthwards to listen—
"hush!—this either is the very anarchy of strife, or else"
—and then I listened more profoundly, and whispered as
I raised my head—"or else, oh heavens! it is *victory* that
is final, victory that swallows up all strife" (p. 576).

The strained and selfconscious writing of this passage
("Hush . . . hush! . . . or else . . . and whispered as
I raised my head—or else, oh heavens!") rises out of
the artificiality of the attempt to resolve the themes
of the narrative by a set piece of writing with a wholly

different context. De Quincey's success in the earlier sections and comparative failure in the "Dream Fugue" reveals something fundamental about the nature of prose writing. His narrative is all the better in that it remains close to actual event and does not venture upon the ground of the novel. His conclusion seeks to capture a universal theme by means of an individual dream fantasy—here we see how little his work resembles, or could resemble, that of a writer like Browne or Taylor.

Where shall we draw the line between the narrative of "The English Mail Coach" and the novel? De Quincey's work is not a documentary, not reporting, for it finds its meaning in the effect of events upon the imagination of an individual, rather than in the events themselves. But neither is it a novel (or, in view of its shortness, a *nouvelle*) for two important reasons. One is that there are no significant relationships between the narrator and other people. There are, we may say, persons but not characters in it. The driver of the Bath mail looks like a crocodile and has a beautiful daughter who waits at dawn to meet the coach. During the brief pause until the horses are changed, when the "crocodile's" back is turned the narrator whispers with Fanny. She later reappears in his dreams—but nowhere else. Or, to take the more important episode, he does not know and never will learn the fate of the young couple in the frail reedy gig which was sideswiped by the Holyhead mail. Although he feels himself to be involved in the outcome because of his failure to stop the coach, they never know who shouts the warning. Now if the young man in the gig, the apparent survivor, were to meet the narrator, and one or both of them were to meet Fanny of the Bath Road in some other place—we should be on our way to fiction. The novel is fiction because it grows out of a multiple hypothesis that the reader understands to be one: "If, then, and then, if . . . ."

The second reason why such narratives as "The English Mail Coach" cannot be placed in the category of fiction (although they may contain invented episodes) is that we expect from the novel the story of a story: not merely what happens, how, and to whom, but the way the creation of characters, the structure and sequence of scenes and the author's view of them become a movement making life more intelligible. The material that De Quincey attempts to use in the "Dream Fugue," mingling events far back in the narrator's past, buried in memory, with his reconciliation to the catastrophe, would require a much larger scale and a real development of character. Short of this, which lay outside his power, De Quincey should have tried to find a way to end the narrative within the framework of the hero's waking consciousness.

## VI

I suggest, then, that in the narrative of the "Confessions," "The Revolt of the Tartar Tribe," and "The English Mail Coach," De Quincey is developing a new capacity of prose, while in the "Suspiria" and the "Dream Fugue" he had unsuccessfully tested another. The first kind of experiment is successful because it stops short of the borderline of the novel. The second fails because only the novel, or the medium of truly meditative prose such as Browne's, would offer the means of realizing the vision of experience implied.

The nineteenth-century prose writer, even one of De Quincey's genius, could not move to impersonal truth by the same route as Browne or Jeremy Taylor. The

impersonal center out of which the most powerful feeling arises, or to which it refers itself, was no longer
available to him. The great themes that radiate from
Christian belief or from the concept of universal law
no longer commanded the interest and conviction of a
whole society. When a writer can assume that the reader
shares certain beliefs with him, he can draw upon reserves of strength. Then, as in Sir Thomas Browne,
personal association, individual insight and observation
may play freely on the theme. Or, if like Emerson and
Thoreau, he is writing out of new conviction and discovery, bringing alive the thought that rises up to him
from the past because it finds a new generation of believers, the writer has great resources. But this was not
De Quincey's situation. Believer as he was, his faith was
dormant; his conservative kind of loyalty checked new
growth of thought. Therefore in his "Suspiria" and
"Dream Fugue" he has to construct the theme itself out
of association and fantasy. The resulting effect is kalei-
doscopic; as with a kaleidoscope, we know we are looking at toy patterns.[28]

De Quincey himself had made a distinction between
"the rhetorical fancy, which is most excited by mere
seeming resemblances" and "the philosophic fancy, or
that which rests upon real analogies" (x, 109n.). In his
less successful experiments, he works through the rhetorical fancy. Yet he does succeed in creating a slice of time,
a pattern of consciousness, that has a certain thickness.
Virginia Woolf was aware of this power. De Quincey,
she noticed, "shifted the value of familiar things. And
this he did in prose, which makes us wonder whether,
then, it is quite so limited as the critics say, and ask further whether the prose writer, the novelist, might not
capture fuller and finer truths than are now his aim if he

ventured into those shadowy regions where De Quincey has been before him?"[29]

But if his writing is suggestive to a novelist, the novel form was not a possible one for De Quincey—in spite of his youthful ambition. His romance, *Klosterheim*, is incredibly stiff and artificial. *The Spanish Military Nun*, although written with zest, and still very readable, is an adaptation. De Quincey could not create character; his figures in these tales are puppets. It is not surprising that his attitude toward novelists expresses an amazing lack of awareness of what was being accomplished. He was apparently indifferent to Jane Austen, disparaged Dickens, disapproved of Thackeray, and appreciated only the poetry, not the novels, of the Brontës.

In his thoughtful book on De Quincey, Mr. Edward Sackville-West has said that De Quincey was a conscious artist "in so far as he regarded style (*i.e.* method of communication) as of vital importance in the conveyance of that kind of matter with which he personally dealt—the literature of Power. But his artistry ends here: he is hardly interested in Form at all."[30] All that I have had to say about the "Confessions," "The Revolt of the Tartars," and "The English Mail Coach" points to an opposite conclusion. Just as, in his criticism, De Quincey's strength lies in his application to prose of the organic theory of style, so in his own writing his chief originality lies in his evolution of a unique kind of narrative, in which the vision seen as the end point of experience casts an intense light upon the actual.

In fact, De Quincey's style cannot be analyzed in separate swatches. To say this is not to deny his tenet that style "ranks amongst the fine arts, and is able therefore to yield a separate intellectual pleasure quite apart from the interest of the subject treated" (x, 260). Yes,

"style" may yield intellectual pleasure apart from the
interest of the subject, when we direct special attention
to it, but it will never deserve this attention unless
vitality in the author's choice and command of his subject has won it first. And this De Quincey has expressed
again and again in stating that style is an organic thing
"in so far as language is connected with thoughts, and
modified by thoughts" (x, 164). The reason that his
own style is distorted if sentences are chosen for scan-
ning or suchlike nonsense, or even for notation of characteristic syntax, is that it is the modification of one
sentence by the preceding or following one which
produces De Quincey's rhythm—and yet this relationship is not periodic or progressive, it is rather a flowing,
an eddying, a confluent pattern. He indicated these qualities himself:

> The two capital secrets in the art of prose composition
> are these: first, the philosophy of transition and con-
> nexion; or the art in which one step in an evolution of
> thought is made to arise out of another; all fluent and
> effective composition depends upon the *connexions*: sec-
> ondly, the way in which sentences are made to modify
> each other; for the most powerful effects in written elo-
> quence arise out of this reverberation; as it were, from
> each other in a rapid succession of sentences (x, 165).

His use of transitions and connections reflects his courtesy toward the reader, lighting the way for him. It may
be seen in any of his essays: De Quincey writes for the
individual, he does not address a public. His aim is to
conduct, to divert, to enlighten, to reveal, rarely to persuade or conquer conviction.

The mood suggested by the title *Selections Grave and
Gay* is the key not only to the tone of De Quincey's

prose but even his rhythm. His belief that humour and pathos are *idem in alio*, antagonistic truths confirming each other, governs his "gay rhetoric," which he said is "an art rejoicing in its own energies" (x, 109). It is this mood, rather than "prose poetry," that leads De Quincey to his metered parody of lines from Gray's "Elegy" in "Murder Considered as One of the Fine Arts": "Toad-in-the-hole was no more seen in any public resort. 'Nor up the lawn, nor at the wood was he.' By the side of the main conduit his listless length at noontide he would stretch, and pore upon the filth that muddled by" (xiii, 57).[31]

The play of humour upon a subject of pathetic or even potentially tragic character is conspicuous in "The English Mail Coach," also, and sometimes leads to some forcing of effect. The most persistent sign of this is his beginning the sentence with a marked and artificial inversion of the word order: "*Us*, our talk and impetus charmed against peril in any collision" (p. 563). (The resort to italics is another frequent symptom of artificial emphasis.) This tendency became more marked in the revisions of the original texts as De Quincey prepared them for his *Selections Grave and Gay*.

Since almost all De Quincey's writing for periodicals was subject to the pressure of time it might be supposed that, good as it was, it might benefit from some revision. He did improve the paragraphing, and he makes the punctuation more deliberate. In other respects the earlier version is often to be preferred. Apart from the fact that the new material introduced into the *Confessions* dilutes the intensity and blurs the outline of the first version, the rewriting of particular passages causes a loss of simplicity. For example, take the way in which De Quincey first introduced Ann of Oxford Street:

> This person was a young woman, and one of that un-
> happy class who subsist upon the wages of prostitution.
> I feel no shame, nor have any reason to feel it, in avow-
> ing, that I was then on familiar and friendly terms with
> many women in that unfortunate condition. The reader
> needs neither smile at this avowal, nor frown . . . (p. 38).

In recasting this passage he altered the first sentence to
read ". . . one of that unhappy class who belong to the
outcasts and pariahs of our female population"; and he
substituted for the third sentence "Smile not, reader
too carelessly facile! Frown not, reader too unseason-
ably austere! Little call was there here either for smiles
or frowns" (iii, 359).

Again, in the description of Ann (after her disappearance), De Quincey tampered with his faultless earlier
language: "I should know her again amongst a thousand, if I saw her for a moment; for, though not handsome, she had a sweet expression of countenance, and a
peculiar and graceful carriage of her head" (p. 59). This
became: "I should know her again amongst a thousand,
and if seen but for a moment. Handsome she was not;
but she had a sweet expression of countenance, and a
peculiarly graceful carriage of the head" (iii, 375). The
combination of impressions in the one perfectly governed sentence is broken apart; "if seen but," instead
of "if I saw her," replaces a concrete by a generalized
expression; "Handsome she was not" is falsely emphatic,
and again is removed from the tone of observation; and
finally, "a peculiar and graceful carriage of the head"
suggests something memorable and more distinct than
the phrase "peculiarly graceful." Where it is possible
to observe such changes, the rhythm as well as the tone
of the earlier version usually seems more authentic.

The indivisibility of rhythm from other possibilities of configuration was pointed out by De Quincey in his statement that "Mysterious is the life that connects all modes of passion with rhythmus" and that "imagery, cadence and length of grammatical clauses are related."[32] The vast majority of his articles, being dependent chiefly on information, created no opportunity for such symmetries. Even there, however, an occasional sentence reminds us of the author's power—as, for example, this explanation of Christ's knowledge of men:

> Christ, during his ministry in Palestine, is brought as if by special arrangement into contact with all known orders of men: Scribes and Doctors, Pharisees and Sadducees . . . Roman officers insolent with authority . . . Galileans the most undervalued of the Jews . . . rich men clothed in purple and poor men fishing for their daily bread, the happy and those that sat in darkness, wedding parties and funeral parties, solitudes amongst hills or sea-shores and multitudes that could not be counted, mighty cities and hamlets the most obscure, golden sanhedrins and the glorious temple where he spoke to myriads of worshippers, and solitary corners where he stood in conference with a single contrite heart (VII, 115).

Even the digressions—which are frequently mentioned as one of De Quincey's faults, leading to prolixity—at their best may have the effect of a rhythmic shaping in the essay as a whole, as turning to a new direction or a shift of feeling to a different key. But logical habits of mind and the accuracy that tempted him to introduce everywhere into his prose small modifications of the main idea of a statement tend to dilute the strength of the phrase or the force of language.

The interest of De Quincey's best writing, if I am

correct, is not in its separable qualities but in the *control* of language, imagery, cadence in the service of a rhythmic conception. Although he does not treat any such possibility in his essay on rhetoric, his criticism of Wordsworth's "Excursion" shows his informed awareness of the relation of theme to overall structure. This comment of his is so instructive that I must give the major part of it here:

> In the very scheme and movement of the "Excursion" there are two defects which interfere greatly with its power to act upon the mind with any vital effect of unity. . . . One of these defects is the *undulatory* character of the course pursued by the poem,—which does not ascend uniformly, or even keep one steady level, but trespasses . . . into topics yielding a very humble inspiration, and not always closely connected with the presiding theme. In part this arises from the accident that a slight tissue of narrative connects the different sections . . . Yet, as the narrative is not of a nature to be moulded by any determinate principle of controlling passion, but bends easily to the caprices of chance and the moment, unavoidably it stamps, by reaction, a desultory or even incoherent character upon the train of the philosophic discussions. You know not what is coming next as regards the succession of the incidents; and, when the next movement *does* come, you do not always know *why* it comes. This has the effect of crumbling the poem into separate segments, and causes the whole (when looked at *as* a whole) to appear a rope of sand (XI, 313).

Substitute some relevant phrase like "insight into experience" for "philosophic discussions," and we may apply a number of the discriminations expressed here not only to De Quincey's own prose but to that of many other writers. Viewed with these expectations, the short-comings of some parts of the "Confessions" stand out, even while we acknowledge that unity is achieved through the sensibility of the "gentleman scholar." Similar reasons justify De Quincey in regarding his accounts of his Lake District and London life and friends as "Autobiographic Sketches" rather than autobiography. The misjudged decision to detach the theme from its substructure drained life from the "Suspiria," and encouraged their self-conscious sighing and palpitating rhythms. But in the best part of the "Confessions" and supremely in "The Revolt of the Tartar Tribe" and "The English Mail Coach" De Quincey evolves an appropriate form in which he is able simultaneously to narrate, to interpret and to intensify. This is prose that does not stop with itself: it should have descendants.

Emerson                                 6

and the Freedom of the Reader

Even before he had chosen and later abandoned
the ministry as his profession Emerson thought of himself as a writer and set down his aims with an unusual
degree of foresight. As early as 1824 (when he was twen-
ty-one), he wrote in his journal that every few centuries
books appeared which embodied the wisdom of their
times—such as "the Proverbs of Solomon, the Essays of
Montaigne, and eminently the Essays of Bacon." And
he added: "I should like to add another volume to this
valuable work. . . . [T]here are some reasons that induce
me to suppose that the undertaking of this enterprise
does not imply any censurable arrogance . . . there may
be the Wisdom of an Age, independent of and above

the Wisdom of any individual whose life is numbered in its years" (J i, 392-393).[1]

As he thought again of his future writing, a few months later, his emphasis was different. He dreamed of providing for America moral counsel such as Addison had once given England. But since in America the Third Estate had "righted itself by God's aid" the writer would be sponsored by a different muse. Thus fortified, he would emulate Addison in appealing to a large number of readers. "I shall therefore attempt in a series of papers to discuss, in a popular manner, some of those practical questions of daily recurrence, moral, political and literary, which best deserve the attention of my countrymen" (J ii, 15). The two aims, to be the representative of the times and its counsellor, to speak for and to speak to his countrymen, did not collide only because a powerful leaven of idealism, in both the metaphysical and the ethical sense, worked on the spirit of the age in the nineteenth century. Counteracting forces, the fierce pursuit of material interests, or the forms of determinism favoured by the advance of science, Emerson would have to reckon with. As a student of moral initiative he would at times have not merely to acknowledge these forces but to confront them directly. He succeeded because both his life and his writing took root in a conviction that favoured experiment in the purest sense: a circle of belief, but a refusal to close the circle.

This conviction, which is the center of energy in all his writing, from his first book, *Nature*, to his final essays, was formulated most tellingly in a late journal entry. "Imagination," he wrote, "is the nomination of the causal facts, the laws of the soul, by the physical facts. All physical facts are words for spiritual facts, and

Imagination, by naming them, is the Interpreter, showing us the unity of the world" (J IX, 127). But can the
essayist—and Emerson is first and last an essayist, though
one of a new kind—afford to sacrifice detail and the
multiplicity of things so absolutely? In Emerson's case
he could, for two reaons. In the first place, not only his
belief in analogy, but his unconquerable expressiveness,
opened jets of individuality in his writing everywhere.
In the second place, he became a prophet of evolution,
a celebrant of development and change.

In his youthful choice of models—Bacon, Montaigne,
Addison (to whom he often added Plutarch as a major
predecessor)—Emerson could hardly have been expected to ponder the limits at which the essay strains.
Bacon called his Essays "Counsels Civil and Moral," but
these counsels are offered not so much to instruct us as
to invite our observation. Montaigne's essays move from
reflections on conduct to a highly individual moral self-
portrait. Yet there is implicit in the tradition Emerson
chose (essayists like Hazlitt and Lamb lie outside it) an
element of instruction that carries with it the hazards of
intrusiveness. There are times when in periods of reflection we would sit down willingly to measure our
understanding with the moral essayist, but as ordinary
readers we look for the ever-varying flow of experience
to be given its freedom in language.

Emerson's practice of distilling his essays from his
lectures (which in turn are expansions and regroupings
of passages from his journals) worked both for and
against his progress as a writer. The practice of lecturing gave him the advantage of testing his central ideas
over a period of time and in a variety of contexts. The
subsequent selection from the lectures of paragraphs
and sentences as well as themes, and the detailed revi-

sion and pruning for compression, increase in many essays the element of challenge and intensity. This accounts for the paradox that the lectures are often exploratory in tone, whereas some essays have more markedly the effect of conscious address to a public.

Lecturing, on which Emerson's living partly depended for many years, was not in itself uncongenial to him. He did not mind making an effort, as far as sincerity permitted, to suit the needs of the audience. But on no conditions would he sacrifice his own freedom of expression. He responded severely to an invitation in which it was suggested that he should avoid any reference to religious controversy "or other exciting topics upon which the public mind is honestly divided." He replied on the same day, "I am really sorry that any person in Salem should think me capable of accepting an invitation so incumbered" (J IV, 293). It was not in this sense that he felt the press of "thinking for the market," but rather that lectures did not sufficiently allow for "what is private, and yours, and essential" (J VIII, 365). Fortunately, however, his own interest in natural history and biography was shared by the lyceum-goers and the hearers in, say, The Academy for the Diffusion of Useful Knowledge. If he converted the stuff of these topics into things new and strange, at least in some stretches, he nevertheless was able to go in a natural direction. He did not criticize the limitations of his audiences, as Thoreau, far less successful as a lecturer, was tempted to do.

It even seemed to him that the lecture might be a new literary form. "Why not write as variously as we dress and think?" he asked himself. "A lecture is a new literature, which leaves aside all tradition, time, place, circumstance, and addresses an assembly as mere human beings, no more" (J v, 233-234). Yet inevitably, and healthily for his growth as a writer, he felt dissatisfied with the form and its occasion.

> In these golden days it behooves me once more to make my annual inventory of the world. For the last five years I have read each winter a course of lectures in Boston, and each was my creed and confession of faith. . . . Yet my objecton is not to the thing, but with the form, and the concatenation of errors called *society* to which I still consent, until my plumes be grown, makes even a duty of this concession also (J v, 287-288).

Overleaping the limitations he saw, he comes in the same passage to a transcendental aim for his lectures. He declared that "the form is neither here nor there. What shall be the substance of my shrift? Adam in the garden, I am to new name all the beasts in the field and all the gods in the sky. I am to invite men drenched in Time to recover themselves, and come out of time, and taste their native immortal air" (*ibid.*, p. 288). On the surface, this is an aim directed to others, but so pure in essence that it could only be seen or expressed for itself alone. This glimpse of it, and attempt to justify it for the sake of his listeners, explains the tension and true polarity of Emerson's essays—not the movement between mind and matter, or fate and freedom, but between the admonition and the vision, between the spirit of the age and the unending evolution of spirit.

To Emerson perhaps more than to any other imaginative writer of his time the spirit of the age meant science. As Stephen Whicher and Robert Spiller have pointed out, science "was perhaps the principal agent in his shift from a theological to a secular base for his moral philosophy."[2] As an "idealist," he benefited from the

remote influence of Kant, the closer speaking of Coleridge, and his lifelong communication with Plato and
all his congeners from Plotinus to the "divine" Thomas
Taylor; but Emerson's originality finally appears in the
bridge he built between Platonism and evolution. Although he is obviously not and did not seek to be a
systematic thinker, his instinct and imagination led him
in the direction that Whitehead pursued to a wider
passage. But in the early essays this insight of Emerson
is only implicit. He had been powerfully stimulated by
his visit to the Jardin des Plantes in 1833, where he had
seen the series of forms arranged in an ascending order
of classification, leading him to exclaim, "I feel the
centipede in me,—cayman, carp, eagle, and fox" (J III,
163). More explicitly, in his early lecture, "The Relation of Man to the Globe," he told his hearers that:

> Man . . . has been prophesied in nature for a thousand
> ages before he appeared; that . . . there has been a pro-
> gressive preparation for him; an effort . . . to produce
> him; the meaner creatures, the primeval sauri, containing
> the elements of his structure . . . whilst the world was . . .
> preparing to be habitable by him. He was not made
> sooner, because his house was not ready (*Early Lectures*
> I, 29).

But this conception falls into the pattern of a scale of
being, reinforcing Emerson's faith in a correspondence
between inner and outer, between the spiritual fact and
the physical fact, and is not incompatible with the early
equilibrium of his convictions in *Nature*.[3]

This little book is Emerson's own charter of emanci-
pation from all that seemed to him limiting in eighteenth-century thought, in Unitarianism, in merely em-
pirical investigations. In the better-known essays that

follow it his chief function is in the encouragement of independent purpose. Whether in his sacrament of "Self-Reliance" or his faith in the scholar as man thinking, a function of humanity itself, that immortalizes "The American Scholar," Emerson speaks as a liberator. If the reader has made his own entry on this territory of freedom, there still is novelty for him in the account of a hardier explorer. Further, there comes back to him a waft of evidence from a territory he may not enter. Perhaps it has not been given to him to know his mind as a part of the universal mind. But this sensation Emerson has not only felt but assimilated, and he can convey if not inevitably impart it:

> Who can set bounds to the possibilities of man? Once inhale the upper air, being admitted to behold the absolute natures of justice and truth, and we learn that man has access to the entire mind of the Creator, is himself the creator in the finite (W I, 64).

This illumination he recorded even more boldly in his journal: "I behold with awe and delight many illustrations of the One Universal Mind. I see my being embedded in it; as a plant in the earth so I grow in God. I am only a form of him. He is the soul of me" (J IV, 247). He is candid, furthermore, when a duality of mood divides him from the channel of his highest perception, and the passage just quoted continues: "Yet why not always so? How came the Individual . . . to parricide thus murderously inclined, ever to traverse and kill the Divine Life? Ah, wicked Manichee! Into that dim problem I cannot enter. A believer in Unity, a seer of Unity, I yet behold two" (J IV, 247-248).

He is willing, then, if the level of the barometer falls, to look down to read it. He does this in "Experience."

This essay does not seem to me so much an expression of pessimism, as Stephen Whicher holds, but rather one of many varied reports on the "moods of the mind"—a report from which, if he will, the frustrated transcendentalist may learn that air is not all rarefaction. If "Nature, as we know her, is no saint," and her darlings "do not come out of the Sunday School, . . . nor punctually keep the commandments," still even after this warier reckoning Emerson banks on the virtue of self-trust (W III, 64). The purpose of this essay does not seem to be primarily to convince or to engender a conviction, but to chart some bearings of the inner life. As we ponder the inherent possibilities of Emerson's prose in these essays, we see a contrast between those like "Self-Reliance" and "Compensation," in which the annunciatory and declarative conviction is urged upon us, and those like "Experience," "Circles," and "The Over-Soul," in which there is a more meditative disclosure. F. O. Matthiessen found that "The Over-Soul" today "proves generally unreadable."[4] On the contrary, it seems to me that if we read it not as doctrine, but with an unfettered interest in the state of awareness in which "the present moment and the mere trifle [have] become porous to thought and bibulous of the sea of light" we are on the track of Emerson's true originality (W II, 290).

No writer could hope to maintain continuous access to this level of contemplation without risking dullness, drift, and repetition. Fortunately Emerson has an intermediate vein. In his Journal he takes account of his liking for facts, providing they are not unadulterated: "I notice that I value nothing so much as the threads that spin from a thought to a fact, and from one fact to another fact, making both experiences valuable and presentable, which were insignificant before, and weaving together into rich webs all solitary observations" (J VIII, 504). This vigour of apprehension and even shrewd sense of reality give force to parts of *Representative Men*, to *English Traits*, and to portraits such as his "Thoreau." The description of the power of steam in *English Traits* furnishes a good example of this range:

> The wise, versatile, all-giving machinery makes chisels, roads, locomotives, telegraphs. Whitworth divides a bar to a millionth of an inch. Steam twines huge cannon into wreaths, as easily as it braids straw, and vies with the volcanic forces which twisted the strata. It can clothe shingle mountains with ship-oaks, make sword-blades that will cut gun-barrels in two (W v, 160-161).

Other equally forceful examples might be chosen from various parts of *Representative Men*. These two books represent an interval, an exercise of variety making new uses for Emerson's liveliness of statement. Yet they do not win us to reread them as the best writing of their kind: the symbolic portraits in *Representative Men* do not overtake Carlyle's finest biographical essays, or even Macaulay's—not to speak of Clarendon. Nor does *English Traits*, readable and likeable as it is, belong in the company of *Democracy in America*. A clue to the nature of Emerson's interest and to the unfulfilled possibility in both books lies in one of his statements of self-appraisal: "A great tendency I like better than a small revelation, and I hate to be imprisoned in premature theories. I have no appetite such as Sir Thomas Browne avows for difficultest mysteries, that my faith may have exercise; but I had rather not understand in God's world than understand through and through in Bentham's and Spurzheim's" (J III, 531). Emerson was a sure student of the great tendency if it was of sky colour, mind colour, but there is much unease when he tries to connect this with the historical current or Bentham's world. That is one of the principal reasons why in neither of these books is the sum more than the equal of its parts.

When the pursuit of large tendency led Emerson to range all phenomena under one law, attempting to make the ethical-historical track consistent with the revolving atom, his prose bends under the weight of a chiefly assertive reconciliation. This seems to me to take the life out of *The Conduct of Life*. Robert Spiller believes that this sequence is "the culmination of Emerson's work," in which a diminution of romantic fervour is more than balanced by "a positive gain in firmness of texture."[5] A respectful disagreement arises out of one's conception of what Emerson as a prose writer was uniquely given to do, and what he sometimes volunteered for as spokesman of the Spirit of the Age. In the opening chapter, "Fate," he beats with his hand on the drum of determinism. There are moments of superb insight: "Fate then is a name for facts not yet passed under the fire of thought; for causes which are unpenetrated" (W VI, 31). But he (most unlike himself) cannot sit quiet by this reserve. We have noticed his love of facts; this disposition makes for the decisiveness and animation of many passages in "Power" and "Wealth." But equally and often in *The Conduct of Life* it brings him to something almost like apology. The optative mood, when generalized, betrays a want of grasp:

> Let us build altars to the Blessed Unity which holds nature and souls in perfect solution, and compels every atom to serve an universal end. . . .
> Let us build altars to the Beautiful Necessity.[6] If we thought men were free in the sense that in a single exception one fantastical will could prevail over the law of

things, it were all one as if a child's hand could pull down the sun (W VI, 48-49).

Emerson is weak when he would explain to us what cannot be so simply explained. In *The Conduct of Life* he attempts, by contrasting power with fate, culture with wealth, to make later chapters correct the one-sided emphasis of earlier ones; but it is a performance on an abacus. There is the true Emersonian note, often: "The revelation of Thought takes man out of servitude into freedom. We rightly say of ourselves, we were born and afterward we were born again, and many times" (W VI, 25). But the effort to synthesize the influences of Oriental thought, or in this instance a somewhat mechanical concept of evolution, and nineteenth-century ideas of the supremacy of will, fails to convince. We feel that Emerson confuses the putting of a case justifying the actual with the contemplation of an ideal order.[7]

The practice of slowly revising lectures for publication in books, and resorting to passages widely separated in the journals, meant that work of different periods overlaps. This has, I think, disguised a conflict and a climax in Emerson's development as a writer that must have taken place between 1848 and 1851. The lectures that ten years later, after the usual revision, were published as *The Conduct of Life* had been first delivered in Pittsburgh in 1850. Four years after this series, Emerson gave a lecture in New York City on the Fugitive Slave Law. This great discourse, which should be included in every selection from his work, marks the apex of his recovery from the inferior concept of Fate as representing a unity in nature and history. Not being a systematic thinker, Emerson did not observe his return to freedom as dominant—he did not amend the assumptions of *The Conduct of Life*. But "The Fugitive Slave Law" offsets it. For Webster, in a sense, represents fate. As Emerson wrote in his journal in his agony at Webster's part in the passage of this infamous law, "Webster truly represents the American people just as they are, with their vast material interests, materialized intellect, and low morals" (J vIII, 216). And almost seeing the change within himself, he added shortly:

> The use made of Fate in society is babyish. . . . It should rather be to bring up our conduct to the loftiness of Nature. . . . Let [the scholar] empty his breast of all that is superfluous and traditional, of all dependence on the accidental, on money, on false fame, on falsehood of any kind; and speak wild truth, . . . let him be instead of God to men, full of God, new and astonishing (J vIII, 218).

But when *use* is made of "fate" its sway is ended, and this accounts for the "new and astonishing," the recovered vigor of tone, in the address on the Fugitive Slave Law.

As every student of him knows, one of Emerson's deepest convictions, deepest instincts, was that he must not confuse his function with that of the reformer. His refusal to join the Brook Farm community was only one of many occasions impelling him to record his adherence to the prompting of his own self-knowledge. At the outset of "The Fugitive Slave Law" he boldly avows his indisposition to debate political issues:

> I do not often speak to public questions;—they are odious and hurtful, and it seems like meddling or leaving your work. . . . And then I see what havoc it makes with any good mind, a dissipated philanthropy. . . .

My own habitual view is to the well-being of students or scholars (W xi, 217).

This very recoil of the opening gun allows Emerson to find a true trajectory. It is to students and scholars he will speak, for "It is to these I am beforehand related and engaged, in this audience and out of it—to them and not to others." Now he shapes his word not *for* the American Scholar but to him, or rather *them*, the American Scholars.

> . . . when I say the class of scholars or students,—that is a class which comprises in some sort all mankind, comprises every man in the best hours of his life; and in these days not only virtually but actually. For who are the readers and thinkers of 1854? Owing to the silent revolution which the newspaper has wrought, this class has come in this country to take in all classes (W xi, 218).

In his penetrating study, *Freedom and Fate*, Stephen Whicher has pointed out the change in Emerson's audience from the plain, quiet, even "mystical" young people who listened to his early lectures to "the great literary and fashionable army" who would have heard *The Conduct of Life*.[8] It is almost as if, in "The Fugitive Slave Law," Emerson had recovered for himself the sense of a new American mind, which, as he had felt in his youth, offered the writer a different muse. It is to hearers and readers of that third estate "which had righted itself by God's aid" that "The Fugitive Slave Law" is directed.

Many entries in Emerson's Journal show that for years he had brooded over the mystery of Webster's powers as an American phenomenon: the genius of the advocate, implacable will, matchless presence on public occasions, bulk of influence, and defect of sensibility. The dramatic portrait given in "The Fugitive Slave Law," with its marked shading and contrast between the Adamitic quality, his eloquence, offset by a fatal lack of heart, is worthy to be set beside Clarendon's characters. And the relentless attack on the "Slave Institution" and its defenders is a historic portrait in which Emerson surpasses Hazlitt in characterizing the spirit of an age:

> It was the question whether man shall be treated as leather? whether the Negro shall be, as the Indians were in Spanish America, a piece of money? Whether this system, which is a kind of mill or factory for converting men into monkeys, shall be upheld and enlarged? And Mr. Webster and the country went for the application to these poor men of quadruped law (W XI, 227).

"The Fugitive Slave Law" exhibits a recovery from the comparative crudities of *The Conduct of Life* through a finer modulation of some of Emerson's major themes. Self-reliance, "the height and perfection of man," now becomes reliance on God (W XI, 236). Compensation is here, in the assertion that "What is useful will last, whilst that which is hurtful to the world will sink beneath all the opposing forces which it must exasperate" (W XI, 237). But we are not to wait for the impersonal avenging forces; something more is demanded of us than a naive trust in the forces of history. And at the end of this essay-address the gods cast off their disguise more convincingly than in "Illusions." Now it is Emerson's hope that "we have reached the end of our unbelief, have come to the belief that there is a divine Providence in the world, which will not save us but through our own coöperation" (W xi, 244). The return to the elixir of freedom has emancipated the writing itself; Emerson does not stop to exhort or to suggest resolves; he unswervingly follows a track of conviction and positive illumination.

Yet, for all its merits, it is not "The Fugitive Slave Law" that I think of as an example of the "new and astonishing" in Emerson's later prose, but passages from a group of lectures that preceded it, and were revised for subsequent delivery with new material added, although never published by Emerson himself. A composite essay drawn from them was prepared for the press by Emerson's friend and biographer, James E. Cabot, and appears in the last volume of the Riverside edition of Emerson's *Works*.[9] The tenor of the writing on themes nourished in his imagination over a long period of time invites the reader to place it beside another essay of the later period, "Works and Days."

Two months before the beginning of the lectures in London in June 1848, Emerson had written to his wife, "My newest writing . . . is a kind of 'Natural History of the Intellect' very unpromising title is it not? and you will say,—the better it is the worse."[10] The title if not unpromising is deceptive, at the same time that it is characteristic. Natural history, in the sense of concrete observation of living things, had always mattered to Emerson but it had never magnetized his powers as it had Thoreau's. But in a more general sense it had frequently been an abstract theme or had furnished illustrations to his essays. It was never absent from his mind as one term in the conviction pervading all his work from his first book, *Nature*, to these experimental lectures, in which he reasserts his belief that "Every object in Nature is a word to signify some fact in the mind"

(W XII, 5). The whole group delivered in "the Literary and Scientific Institution" in Portman Square included some on quite different topics; but the passages I refer to originated in the three he grouped as "Natural History of the Intellect" or in his later versions of these lectures. It is significant that he was working on them in a year when he had renewed and deepened his acquaintance with English science and scientists, visiting the Hunterian Museum in the company of its curator Richard Owen, listening to Faraday lecture, attending the Geological Club. And he had dined in Edinburgh with Robert Chambers whose *Vestiges of Creation*, read a few years before, had contributed to his interest in evolution.

With this background of circumstances it is not surprising that Emerson began his 1848 lecture-essays by comparing his undertaking, preliminary as it might be, with that of Owen or Faraday. He dreams as Bacon did of a *prima philosophia* comprising universal laws common to all the sciences and to intellect as well. We might suppose that an early effort in the direction of psychology, tinctured by philosophy, was to be attempted. But this would be to mistake the character of Emerson's writing and the climax of expression attained here. He quickly leads us in a truer direction. We see that what he seeks is the nucleus of life in an individual consciousness: "what we really want is . . . a certain piety towards the source of action and knowledge. . . . What is life but the angle of vision? A man is measured by the angle at which he looks at objects" (W XII, 9-10).

Emerson in his approach to a unity of mind and emotion in the moment of experience is a precursor of much that is exploratory in the modern novel or modern poetry. It is for the sake of clarity and intensity that he distrusts (for his purpose) the systematic form, completeness, sought by the metaphysician. He states this quietly in a much later version of this lecture. "I write anecdotes of the intellect; a sort of Farmer's Almanac of mental moods," he says, and suggests that "he who contents himself with dotting a fragmentary curve, recording only what facts he has observed, without attempting to arrange them within one outline, follows a system also . . . " (W xii, 11). This economy controls an effort to pursue truth of impression by isolating what can be reported, without substructure of explanation. It parallels the effort of the Impressionists and the "récherches" of Cézanne.

As meditation on the "Natural History of Intellect" continued it offered scope to Emerson as an imaginative writer in the deepest sense. After many years of practice, he has reshaped his way of composing, and his purpose has been refined so as to eliminate the hortatory or monitory note. He touches on matter of philosophy, only to reconvert it into activity of wonder. One might say that philosophy (with notable exceptions such as Plato) presents the result of ideas; Emerson, a literary as well as philosophical son of Plato, creates the experience of ideas. More generally he is an innovator in discovering how to incorporate the new level of experience in these essay-lectures. How is this to be done without telling directly of yourself and your habits, as Montaigne does, or describing happenings in your life or someone else's, as Hazlitt and De Quincey do? Emerson has found the possibility of presenting moments of awareness directly. It is impossible not to sense the joy in the knowledge of being that possesses him: "To Be is the unsolved, unsolvable wonder. . . . Who are we, and what is Nature, have one answer in the life that rushes into us" (W XII, 16). He imagines that the source of all vitality is a higher life of mind, and this leads him to the most suggestive, most mature statement of his central idea:

> . . . I believe the mind is the creator of the world, and is ever creating;—that at last Matter is dead Mind; that mind makes the senses it sees with; that the genius of man is a continuation of the power that made him and that has not done making him (W XII, 17).

Here the concept of evolution, which in many of Emerson's earlier essays appears as a witness of the spirit of the age, is transformed into direct experience of a creativity that sustains itself infinitely, of mind evolving to a higher form of itself. And this contemplation brings with it an appropriate reserve:

> I dare not deal with the element in its pure essence. It is too rare for the wings of words. . . .
> Every just thinker has attempted to indicate these degrees, these steps on the heavenly stair, until he comes to light where language fails him. Above the thought is the higher truth,—truth as yet undomesticated and therefore unformulated (W XII, 17).

Whether our convictions parallel Emerson's or meet his somewhere in some nonparallel conjunction becomes irrelevant. We no longer have to ask ourselves, as we might have in reading earlier essays like "Self-Reliance" or "Compensation," how much of the appeal to our assent may be accepted. Emerson now has achieved a mode of expression in which he speaks as a character might speak in a novel—but as he could not speak in a novel. Here is an immediate record of the mind's sensations, more explicit than fiction could carry. And how extraordinary in its unimpeded movement, its purity of tone, its naturalness of metaphor is Emerson's prose as he reformulates ideas that had visited him in his youth.

> Each man is a new power in Nature. He holds the keys of the world in his hands. No quality in Nature's vast magazines he cannot touch, no truth he cannot see. Silent, passive, even sulkily, Nature offers every morning her wealth to man. She is immensely rich; he is welcome to her entire goods, but she speaks no word, will not so much as beckon or cough; only this, she is careful to leave all her doors ajar,—towers, hall, storeroom and cellar (W xii, 28).

> My percipiency affirms the presence and perfection of law, as much as all the martyrs. A perception, it is of a necessity older than the sun and moon, and the Father of the Gods. . . . It is impatient to put on its sandals and be gone on its errand, which is to lead to a larger perception, and so to new action (W xii, 41).

These essay-lectures, evolved through a period of time, and never wholly composed as a sequence, have nevertheless a particular interest when the question of Emerson's form, or want of it, is raised. Many—even among the most sympathetic—of Emerson's critics have allied themselves with Carlyle's adverse reflection on the atomicity of his prose. (Carlyle, as many will remember, had said that his sentences "did not, sometimes, rightly stick to their foregoers and their followers: the paragraph not as a beaten *ingot,* but as a beautiful square *bag of duck-shot* held together by canvas!")[11] Apart from the fact that we would not expect Carlyle to appreciate Emerson's selectivity, we need not deny the force of his comment as applied to the *Essays* of 1844. Others, however, with good ground have defended the coherence of an essay like "Experience." An older critic

of his style, W. C. Brownell—well worth reading today—recognized in the essays

> . . . the way in which in spite of *lacunae* of rhetorical
> connection the relations of things are elicited, their re-
> lations to each other, to the cosmos, to the individual.
> . . . Everything means something additional. To take it
> in you must go beyond it. The very appreciation of an
> essay automatically constructs a web of thought in the
> weaving of which the reader shares.[12]

Brownell also discerned a higher unity than that of the
sentence in Emerson's structure: "No writer ever had
in more opulent measure the unusual power of main-
taining throughout varied thematic modulation a single
tone, a central thought, until the expression of its strict
implications was complete, and one after another of its
phrasings apt for echo in eloquent unison."[13] Nevertheless Brownell did not see how far he had gone in discovering a new form in Emerson, and he subordinates
these valuable observations to a dissatisfaction with
Emerson's "lack of continuity" and failure to reinforce
the theme by the treatment.

Emerson was up against this problem and he knew
it. But what recourse had he? For his purpose he could
not, like De Quincey, avail himself of a suggested narrative controlled by dominant themes—a device that
Thoreau also laid hold of in his different manner, in *A
Week on the Concord and Merrimack Rivers* and parts
of *Cape Cod* and *The Maine Woods*. Emerson is frank
in acknowledging his handicap, even when he is on the
way to overcoming it:

> It is much to write sentences; it is more to add method
> and write out the spirit of your life symmetrically. But to

arrange general reflections in their natural order, so that I shall have one homogeneous piece,—a Lycidas, an Allegro, a Hamlet, a Midsummer Night's Dream,—this continuity is for the great. . . .

But what we want is consecutiveness. 'T is with us a flash of light, then a long darkness, then a flash again. Ah! could we turn these fugitive sparkles into an astronomy of Copernican worlds (W XII, 52-53).

Anyone who supposes Emerson to be merely a writer of sentences need only compare his best essays with Bacon's, with Browne's *Christian Morals*, or Traherne's *Centuries of Meditation*. A symmetry of design he lacks, or a progress to a climax (so that there is nothing of his comparable to *Urn Burial*). Yet even in the more overtly purposeful earlier essays it is because nothing unnecessary is added for the sake of explanation that the flash of light against the dark of what is unknown made the most appropriate rhythm for Emerson. The use of juxtaposition, the absence of discursiveness and digression, make for a fusion of idea and feeling that is new. And as he composed the later essays he began to find more place for symbol, for congenial myths in his prose as well as his poetry. "Illusions," which does much to overcome the intractability of *The Conduct of Life*, ends with the rescue of the young mortal from his fancies of being swept on by the vast crowd, insignificant amid a shower of deceptions. "And when, by and by, for an instant, the air clears and the cloud lifts a little, there are the gods still sitting around him on their thrones—they alone with him alone" (W VI, 325). But in the "Natural History of Intellect" Nature itself is lifted from abstraction to myth so unerringly that all obtrusiveness falls off, and "she speaks no word, and will not so much as beckon or cough. . . ." There is a real difference between this sentence and the entry in a journal in 1836, where "it seems in what we call tempting opportunities, as if the old dumb power did beckon and cough."[14] The young man's observation of himself is amusing; but the older writer will not annotate the mystery.

Myth and symbol are the scaffolding for "Works and Days." Opinion has tended to dismiss the book in which it appeared, *Society and Solitude,* as evidence of a diminution of Emerson's power, but this central essay at least says otherwise. In the structure of its first half, "Works and Days" resembles his remarkable tour de force, "Napoleon" (in *Representative Men*). Speaking as if in that mood when most responsive—it might seem at first naively responsive—to the spirit of the age, he shows us a gleaming wall of facts: science, industry, invention, trade, fused by their own interlinkings and the track of success.

> What of this dapper caoutchouc and gutta percha, which makes water-pipes and stomach pumps, belting for mill-wheels, and diving bells, and rain-proof coats for all climates, which teach us to defy the wet, and put every man on a footing with the beaver and the crocodile? What of the grand tools with which we engineer, like kobolds and enchanters, tunneling Alps, canalling the American Isthmus, piercing the Arabian desert? (W VII, 160).

The spirit of his age seems to grip Emerson strongly as he notes invention breeding invention. He builds his wall of facts so well that a succeeding age can stand upon it. But having done so he moves it with his crowbar so that we can see beyond it. The first movement is by the satiric use of myth: "Tantalus . . . has been seen again lately. He is in Paris, in New York, in Boston. He . . . thinks he shall reach it yet; thinks he shall bottle the wave." And then the essay rushes swiftly to its turning point. "It appears that we have not made a judicious investment. Works and days were offered us, and we took works" (W vii, 163, 166).

And as the wall is moved (it is not thrown down) an opening into a different space shows us days, and the day is as a god: "The new study of the Sanskrit has shown us the origin of the old names of God,—Dyaus, Deus, Zeus, Zeu pater, Jupiter,—names of the sun . . . importing that the Day is the Divine Power and Manifestation, and indicating that those ancient men, in their attempts to express the Supreme Power of the universe, called him the Day . . ." (W vii, 166-167).

No other essay gives finer evidence of Emerson's tact, his charm. Pausing only occasionally to address the reader directly, he seems to go ahead of us lightly yet visibly on the path of his enchantment. He makes use of ideas we recognize as familiar signs to him—of illusions, of deities disguised. But, as in the "Natural History of Intellect" lectures, he seems emancipated from the weight of argument entirely; he has attained a free state of consciousness and can afford largesse of homage.

Reading such pages one cannot agree with Henry James that Emerson never achieved a style, or found his form. James begins his brilliant "partial portrait" by stating that Emerson had his message, but he was a good while looking for his form—the form that, as he himself would have said, he never completely found.[15] James's conclusion makes the point even more sharply. Emerson, he maintains,

is a striking exception to the general rule that writings live in the last resort by their form; that they owe a large

part of their fortune to the art with which they have
been composed. It is hardly too much . . . to say of Emerson's writings in general that they were not composed
at all . . . he differs from most men of letters of the same
degree of credit in failing to strike us as having achieved
a style.[16]

If only we could ask James what essayist had in his
judgment succeeded, where Emerson had failed! No
essay can achieve a form comparable to fiction, for without characters and action there cannot be the same
inner mobility. Emerson had from his youth thought a
great deal on the examples from which he might learn
and that might favour his endeavour. Plutarch, Montaigne, Bacon, even Landor stimulated an explicit consideration of form. (And what unerring instinct compelled him to observe, in spite of his great pleasure in
reading Landor, that the latter lacked abandon?) The
journals are full of arresting observations on the writer's
task; whether his responsiveness to the "vascular" in
language ("Cut these words and they would bleed"
[J v, 420]) or his awareness that the opportunities of
composition, of structure, are Phoenix-like. As F. O.
Matthiessen has pointed out, in Emerson's early essays
the residue of his previous writing of sermons and his
typical American interest in oratory is discoverable. But
before he could himself attain it, Emerson had foreseen
the possibility of a subtler arrangement. As early as 1835
he wrote:

> Shun manufacture, or the introducing an artificial ar-
> rangement in your thoughts—it will surely crack and
> come to nothing,—but let alone tinkering, and wait for
> the natural arrangement of your treasures; that shall be
> chemical affinity. . . .

A meek self-reliance I believe to be the law and constitution of good *writing* (J III, 550).

If "The American Scholar" is perhaps the finest example of his early work, in which logic helps to expand the theme, the composition of "chemical affinity" is tested in "Circles" and perfected in passages of the "Natural History of Intellect" and "Works and Days." We are familiar with Emerson's admission, in reply to one of Carlyle's strictures, that his sentences lacked cohesion. But this statement comes early. The following passage from "Works and Days" is an example of that modulation of each sentence by the others that De Quincey defined as the art of composition. The miracle of days

> is hurled into every beggar's hands. The blue sky is a covering for a market and for the cherubim and seraphim. The sky is the varnish or glory with which the Artist has washed the whole work,—the verge or confines of matter and spirit. Nature could no farther go. Could our happiest dreams come to pass in solid fact,—could a power open our eyes to behold "millions of spiritual creatures walk the earth,"—I believe I should find that mid-plain on which they moved floored beneath and arched above with the same web of blue depth which weaves itself over me now, as I trudge the streets on my affairs (W VII, 171).

Such a passage is an example of "natural arrangement" or "chemical affinity." The congruity and progress of the imagery rather than a series of connectives gives it order. Henry James is probably right that Emerson at a certain point could go no further, but this is not because he had not, but because he had, found his form. The conditions for a natural arrangement of impressions arising from the moods of the mind cannot, even by a disciplined writer, be summoned at will. The task of transmuting into lectures material from the journals, and revising the lectures, became increasingly hard for him and after 1870 he could no longer attempt it. Inevitably much of his writing falls below his best work, and could be discarded, save for the fact that anything conceived by such a phenomenal mind has a special import.

The journals possess much more than that actual if minimum value. They are more a seedbed than a savings bank. And the seedbed has plants set down beside each other in a different order from that of the nursery, the orchard, or the cutting garden. The journals are readable in many hours when we might be unready for the essays. This happens not merely because the order of ideas is more varied, and the circumstances of their recording more immediate. Nor is it only because the journals present the writer in his own milieu—talking with Alcott or Margaret Fuller, riding home from a lecture with Elizabeth Hoar, enjoying the Saturday Club, walking with Thoreau or Ellery Channing. No, the fascination of the journals lies in their generosity; we may be at home with a mind in growth, we observe its forward motion, its returns upon itself, its frustrations, its renewals. Above all we see that a man may write truly on the first try; we see what openings his meditation brings him, not wholly to be surpassed by any later selection, revision, or expansion in either the lectures or the published essays.

The publication now underway of a complete edition, the *Journals and Miscellaneous Notebooks,* and of the remaining volumes of recoverable lectures will make possible a more refined comparison of the evolving stages of Emerson's writing. But these are tools for the specialist. The ordinary reader may be overwhelmed by the inclusion in the complete journals of so much that reappears in the well-known essays. If he does follow through the separate stages, he will observe the greater compression, perfecting of syntax, solicitude for clarity and cadence, and more deliberate order in the version Emerson prepared for publication.

All this may be acknowledged. Yet the journals deserve to be regarded as an *oeuvre*, to be valued for themselves. They both prepare us for the essays and emancipate us from them. The journals have not the same verve and éclat. They do not allow us to feel the collective strength of Emerson's meditation on a single theme as many of the essays do. But they let us immerse ourselves in the stream of his observation and his reading more spontaneously. They confer even more unstintingly his bounty and beneficence. Since in the tone of the journals we are not confronted with an unspoken demand for assent, the reader advances more swiftly to the freedom that is Emerson's gift.

In both the journals and the essays the generosity of the writer appears in many forms. Emerson's way of linking himself with earlier writers is one of the most appealing. F. O. Matthiessen has best interpreted Emerson's alliance with "The Metaphysical Strain"; but he brings many other writers alive. With respect to prose, I know no one who more truly confirms Eliot's principle that the best writing of the present alters, possibly for the better, the tradition we have inherited from the past. He was well aware of this union and reunion of minds. In his journal in 1850 he noted, "I once interpreted the law of Adrastia, 'that he who had any truth should be safe from harm until another period,' as pronounced of originators. But I have discovered that the profound satisfactions—which I take to be the sentence of Adrastia itself—belong to the truth received from another soul; come to us in reading, as well as in thinking" (J VIII, 456). By summoning, in his meditations and experiments, the aid of equal or superior, Montaigne or Plato, Plutarch or Bacon, he verifies his principle that "No book has worth by itself; but by the relation to what you have from many other books, it weighs" (J VIII, 490). In this sense Emerson and the writers who favoured his enterprise are reciprocally related.

By allowing him to place his relationship to past and present, to neo-Platonism and antislavery, to Asia and to England and to Concord, the journals underwrite the veracity of the essays. They chart the way to Emerson's growing understanding of himself as a writer. He had begun by hoping to embody the wisdom of the age. In an objective sense he does this—that is, in Matthiessen's terms, when he says that Emerson "has left us the best intellectual history [of his time] that we have."[17] He does so also in the more profound sense that he—however dimly at first—intended. Like Wordsworth or Coleridge or Goethe, he cut new channels for the expression of feelings that lie deep in human nature. To do this he had to launch his first bark, the valiant book, *Nature*, followed by the supporting affirmations and intensities of the early essays. But we should have only half of Emerson, should miss the full savour of his originality, if he had not found how to move on to greater freedom for himself as a writer. Increasingly, as time went on—with the puzzling exception of *The Conduct of Life*—he knew how to remove the extraneous emphasis, left from the early sermon writing and the practice of lecturing, from the poured metal of the essays.

He did not stall half way in his early fervour: "People came, it seems, to my lectures with expectation that I was to realize the Republic I described, and ceased to come when they found this reality no nearer. They mistook me. I am and always was a painter. I paint still with might and main, and describe the best subjects I can" (J VI, 470). He is, even in a special address like "The Fugitive Slave Law," given the power to paint moral forces and ideas so that they live beyond their generation. And in "Works and Days," or the unfinished "Natural History of Intellect," Emerson wrote meditative prose worthy of its descent from Browne. If it lacks ordonnance, architectural design; it has, like the end of *The Garden of Cyrus,* unforced inner cohesion. Without any limiting circumference of dogma, Emerson rediscovers a way to the intersection of eternity with time, through the partnership of the mind in the directions of change, and through "the quality of the moment." In faithfully pursuing a writer's route to freedom, Emerson makes room for the reader. He does not wink or nod, coax or bully, scold or pontificate. Of how many of the best prose writers of the nineteenth century can that be said? "Some books leave us free and some books make us free" (J V, 359). Emerson does both. In his best essays, composed from the font of his faithful journals, he has left us on our own.

# Thoreau: 7

## The Concrete Vision

Although Thoreau says much in his journal about writing, he does not seem openly to ponder the question of what kind would suit him. Whereas Emerson had consciously aimed to be an essayist, Thoreau drifted into his beginning efforts in this direction. Lacking any easily available market for his initial work, with the aid of friends he sought publication in periodicals, and simultaneously prepared some lectures for reading in a lyceum. He did not plainly confront the problem of form for the linking of his unique perceptions into something independent, and articulate as a whole.

Emerson, who probably suggested to Thoreau that he keep a journal, encouraged his younger friend to

submit manuscripts to the *Dial* when it was founded
by the transcendentalists in 1840. By this time Thoreau
had delivered some lectures in Concord, woven from
his journal entries. Margaret Fuller, the *Dial*'s first
editor, published some of his poems and one short piece
on Persius that had been recommended by Emerson.
She rejected two other essays as well as some of Thoreau's poems. When Emerson took over as editor in
1842, he gave Thoreau the chance to prepare his first
substantial prose composition, "The Natural History
of Massachusetts," published in that year.

Thoreau made the best of the assignment Emerson
had given him, in effect to assess and comment on some
official reports of wild life in the state. Because he drew
freely on his own knowledge, this article is readable
still, in spite of its inevitable dependence upon an extraneous task. Much of the material at hand is delivered
in descriptive batches varied by laconic statements of
fact ("the bear, wolf, lynx, wildcat, deer, beaver and
marten, have disappeared; the otter is rarely if ever seen
here at present; and the mink is less common than
formerly").[1] The reader's attention comes alive in other
passages, where Thoreau permits himself to follow what
he later calls the path to perception, moving from the
separate observation to some wider possibility of feeling:

> In the winter, I stop short in the path to admire how
> the trees grow up without forethought, regardless of time
> and circumstances. They do not wait as a man does, but
> now is the golden age of the sapling. . . . With cheerful
> heart one could be a sojourner in the wilderness, if he
> were sure to find there the catkins of the willow or the
> alder. When I read of them in the accounts of northern
> adventurers, by Baffin's Bay or Mackenzie's river, I see

how even there too I could dwell. . . . They are worthy
to have had a greater than Minerva or Ceres for their
inventor. . . .

Nature is mythical and mystical always, and works
with the license and extravagance of genius.[2]

When Thoreau presents directly the way he saw the
trees, and proceeds in imagination to a wilderness he
knew in travel books, he arrives at the formulation of
one of his procreative themes. But the progress has as it
were *happened,* even though an inevitable outcome of
his gift; the reader does not feel that this writer knows
how to construct the vessel for it. Nevertheless, Emerson
had used his judgment on Thoreau's early writing to
the latter's advantage. Choosing not to publish two
earlier manuscripts, "The Service" and "Sir Walter
Raleigh," both submitted to the *Dial* and still, after
Margaret Fuller's rejection of them, in his possession,
Emerson preferred to sponsor "The Natural History
of Massachusetts" as the first writing to allow Thoreau's
"work & fame [to] go out into all lands."[3] "The Service"
and "Sir Walter Raleigh" both suffer from an artificial
posture leading to a false rhetorical tone. The contrast
between them and "The Natural History" is epitomized
in a sentence Thoreau used in his conclusion, a statement which is at the heart of his most genuine writing
in his journal; its purport was in varying ways to set
the problem of composition for him in his later books:
"Let us not underrate the value of a fact; it will one day
flower in a truth."[4] In this awareness he stands on common ground with Sir Thomas Browne, although for
other reasons he was to use and appraise this knowledge
in a different way.

Another early essay, "A Winter Walk," has met with

praise, but it is too much a set-piece of description. The author writes in a somewhat self-conscious impersonal manner, as if instructing the reader. "See yonder thin column of smoke curling up through the woods. . . . There must be a warmer and more genial spot there below, as where we detect the vapor from a spring forming a cloud above the trees. What fine relations are established between the traveller who discovers this airy column from some eminence in the forest, and him who sits below."[5] Such writing gives the reader the impression of being conducted through the woods by a sensitive and expert guide; it lacks the vigor of an active, first-hand report.

In comparison, "A Walk to Wachusett," although slight, and not so obviously an expression of the transcendentalism that Thoreau followed in his early route to speculation, is a more promising composition. In it Thoreau sustains a real narrative, making his transit through the rural scenes and up the mountain equally present with his reading and his imagined self. "At length, like Rasselas . . . we resolved to scale the blue wall which bound the western horizon. . . . But we will not leap at once to our journey's end, but imitate Homer, who conducts his reader over the plain, and along the resounding sea, though it be but to the tent of Achilles. In the spaces of thought are the reaches of land and water, where men go and come."[6] The pattern of this essay sets a precedent for *A Week on the Concord and Merrimack Rivers*; the account of the actual going forth and the return of the travellers opens into spaces of his, the narrator's thought—though here it is much less deeply sounded. The rhythmical progression of time from the beginning of the journey to its end, the different kinds of awareness at dawn or noon or night, are skilfully used—again an experiment in form that anticipates *A Week*.

By the time the man of almost thirty sat down in his hut by the pond to work on two books, first about the voyage on the Concord and the Merrimack, then *Walden*, he must have known that he faced a new task. If he had published little, uneasily adapting his material to the scarce opportunities, he was nevertheless an experienced writer. For almost ten years he had kept his journal; and in it not only had he gained practice in ways of observing and of writing, he had also won freedom to write for himself rather than the unprepared reader. He had stored up riches worthy of a larger setting. He needed the size of a book to allow a matching in proportion of the topography of experience to the route travelled by the perceiving mind.

In *A Week*, his solution is triumphant. He has for the ground of his design two parallel patterns. One is time's own passage, with certain special intervals like that of awakening before dawn, "nooning," the making of camp at night, and the ideal week (only actual by a fiction) of the whole journey. The other is the life of the river, measured by the effort of rowing up it, but as much by its invariable flow and its likeness with other streams. The temporal and spatial symmetry of this ever-present parallel design frees the narrator to incorporate in the voyage the accompanying forays of his thought.

The abstract themes of Thoreau's meditation in *A Week* are sometimes referred to as "digressions,"[7] but to view them so is to slight the dimensions of the book. Thoreau could have written separate essays on these themes (which were to find in whole or in part many other channels of expression in his writings: antiquity, myth, the Indian, nature, genius, the poet). In *A Week*, however, he creates an atmosphere that *evokes* thought on these topics. Although we notice some clumsy steps from the narrative of the river journey to the narrative of the mind's music, there are significant moments that bind the two together.

Let us look first at the here and now in the book, some of the events that make the journey of these modest "voyageurs" memorable for its own sake. We might call this the encounter with experience. It begins with awareness of people in relation to the river's teeming life, a composition of a man fishing accompanied by his dog, speculations on fishermen's lives and the recollection of a very old one:

> A straight old man he was who took his way in silence through the meadows, having passed the period of communication with his fellows; his old experienced coat, hanging long and straight and brown as the yellow pine bark, glittering with so much smothered sunlight, if you stood near enough, no work of art but naturalized at length. I often discovered him unexpectedly amid the pads and the gray willows when he moved, fishing in some old country method,—for youth and age then went a fishing together,—full of incommunicable thoughts, perchance about his own Tyne and Northumberland. He was always to be seen in serene afternoons haunting the river . . . so many sunny hours in an old man's life, entrapping silly fish . . . what need had he of hat or raiment any, having served out his time, and seen through such thin disguises? (pp. 30-31).[8]

The reader of this passage knows that a reverent master of language is at work here. The sharply seen figure, his coat smothered in sunlight, standing "amid the pads and the gray willows," becomes a legendary person too, local in his provenance, yet of all time, until, in the last sentence, we are ready to believe that "His fishing was not a sport, nor solely a means of subsistence, but a sort of solemn sacrament and withdrawal from the world, just as the aged read their Bibles."

Thoreau has created this figure in the landscape, he is seen there, and with his "incommunicable thoughts" prepares the reader's mind for the many communicated meditations that travel the time of the travelling—not because they necessarily or even probably were first considered then, but because in this artful *relation de voyage* they find their form.

Thus it should come as no surprise to learn that Thoreau incorporated into his "account" of a journey that took place in 1839 passages written earlier in his journal, and passages written later. This is as it should be, for, although he kept a notebook during the voyage, it gave him only part of the material for the work of art composed at Walden six to seven years later.

We never forget the sliding past of the river itself, its concealment in fog, its shallows and rapids, locks, canal boats and boatmen, shores and the seldom-seen farms, creatures that live in the stream or on its banks— fish and frogs, muskrats, the bittern. It is worth pausing to examine episodes that recount a meeting of the young rowers with other river habitants. The first of these is an image of other boatmen:

> Two men in a skiff, whom we passed hereabouts, float-
> ing buoyantly amid the reflections of the trees, like a
> feather in mid-air, or a leaf which is wafted gently from
> its twig to the water without turning over, seemed still
> in their element, and to have very delicately availed
> themselves of the natural laws. Their floating there was

a beautiful and successful experiment in natural philosophy . . . for as birds fly and fishes swim, so these men
sailed. It reminded us how much fairer and nobler all the
actions of man might be, and that our life in its whole
economy might be as beautiful as the fairest works of art
or nature (p. 56).

The economy of life in the sense of our disposition of
our times and energies is not overtly the theme of *A
Week* as it is of *Walden*, but it has a place there. (Another and longer part having to do with life's own economy is the episode of Rice and the mountain farm.) But
we notice in this passage how skilfully conjoined is the
visual presentation of an event with the reflex thought
it encourages.

The actual conduct of the river voyage follows the
form of its prototype, *the relation de voyage* to the
Orient or South Seas, or of river explorers in North
America, by a careful logging of positions observed,
other parties sighted, supplies available, and the transit
of night and day. But the scale here is so absolutely
different that these notations in themselves create the
effect of an imaginary world. Instead of loading of stores
—salt beef and biscuit, wines for the officers, live animals for future consumption—there is the careful
record of melons and potatoes, meals of bread and sugar,
the landing to get water or occasionally milk from a
farm. The scrupulous description of making camp on
land at night and the morning's embarkation, usually in
the concealment of fog, secures the reality, the brevity
and the length of a week. On the first night out, an oc-
currence after landing conveys the slim margin of it all:

For the most part, there was no recognition of human
life in the night, no human breathing was heard, only

the breathing of the wind. As we sat up, kept awake by the novelty of our situation, we heard at intervals foxes stepping about over the dead leaves, and brushing the dewy grass close to our tent, and once a musquash fumbling among the potatoes and melons in our boat, but when we hastened to the shore we could detect only a ripple in the water ruffling the disk of a star (p. 47).

The exactitude and simplicity of this passage was gained by the practice of art. As Carl F. Hovde has shown,[9] it stems from a longer, more diffuse passage in Thoreau's journal, then a revision in a "workbook" he used, and finally the succinct, briefer yet more powerful version in *A Week*, as quoted here. Take only the dreamlike end of the final sentence: it originally read, "But on the river side I can see only the stars reflected in the water—and now by some ripple in the water—ruffling the disk of a star, I discover him" [a muskrat]. In revising, Thoreau changed this to read: "we could see only the stars reflected in the water scarcely disturbed by a ripple on its surface." But not too easily satisfied with the greater generality of this, Thoreau recaptured his metaphor of the disk, yet avoided the literalness of discovering the musquash in the ripple, the final statement "we could detect only a ripple in the water ruffling the disk of a star" wonderfully coupling the seen and the unseen. In the first version, too, the musquash was "taking toll" of the "melons and potatoes"; in both revisions he is "fumbling among the melons and potatoes."[10] The final version as Thoreau wrote it in *A Week* hauntingly combines the vulnerability of the young sailors with their faith.

One final example will suffice for the actuality of things, creatures, events encountered, and their compatibility with the more contemplative strains of the

book. Here Thoreau himself elicits a deliberate coun-
terpointing of both levels. The passage must be given
almost in full, starting as it does with a real moment
of the voyage:

> As we shoved away from this rocky coast, before sun-
> rise, the smaller bittern, the genius of the shore, was
> moping along its edge, or stood probing the mud for its
> food, with ever an eye on us, though so demurely at
> work. . . . Now away he goes, with a limping flight . . .
> until a rod of clear sand amid the alders invites his feet,
> . . . It is a bird of the oldest Thalesian school, and no
> doubt believes in the priority of water to the other ele-
> ments; the relic of a twilight antediluvian age which yet
> inhabits these bright American rivers with us Yankees.
> There is something venerable in this melancholy and
> contemplative race of birds, which may have trodden the
> earth while it was yet in a slimy and imperfect state. . . .
> One wonders if, by its patient study by rocks and sandy
> capes, it has wrested the whole of her secret from Nature
> yet. . . . What could it tell of stagnant pools and reeds
> and dank night-fogs! It would be worth the while to look
> closely into the eye which has been open and seeing at
> such hours, and in such solitudes, its dull, yellowish,
> greenish eye. Me thinks my own soul must be a bright
> invisible green (pp. 251-252).

Nothing more specific, undeniable a fact than noticing
the least bittern as they re-embarked, nothing more in-
contestable than Thoreau's discerning in it the genius
of the element they are submitting to and learning from,
nothing more characteristic than his sense of an ever-
present past from which there has been an evolution, but
which survives to be known, nothing more like him than
his awareness of the two voyagers as "us Yankees" link-

ing new and old. Once more, the precision of the writing lends an unforgettable vitality to this episode.

We can see now that this happening and others that occurred on the voyage, or were remembered within its framework, prepare for the more abstract meditations, developed at some length, which give body to this slender narrative. The reason why they should not be regarded as digressions is that they develop the implications of the specific happenings and are, furthermore, essentially related to each other, with the exception of the disquisition on friendship, which I should agree to call a digression.

The major themes all have some bearing on the way an individual places his knowledge and finds a true identity for himself. Wildness, mythology, antiquity, nature and art, genius and the poet, man's place in time ramify into each other. Thoreau has no argument to advance, even when he deliberately challenges familiar values. And the crux of the difference between his prose and the seventeenth-century writers he often resembles is that he does not write within Christian belief, but makes it also an object of speculation. In comparison with Emerson, to whom he was of course so much indebted, there is in his speculations more of absolute wonder than of hopeful endeavour (though that exists, too).

Let us follow on the track of his speculations to observe the free network he creates. His admission of a disposition to love wildness stems from a sense of time dating "from an older than the agricultural. . . . There is in my nature, methinks, a singular yearning toward all wildness" (p. 62). Within a page he brings to mind the Indian, for whom "civilization" might be no improvement. But the quality that Thoreau respects is not what we might ordinarily regard as "primitive." "By the wary independence and aloofness of his dim forest life [the Indian] preserves his intercourse with his native Gods, and is admitted from time to time to a rare and peculiar society with Nature" (p. 63). As the writer's thoughts circle he soon moves to Greek myths, and his belief that "the dullest posterity slowly add some trait to the Mythus" (p. 67). He has laid a foundation of idea for the extracts later inserted from Hindu mythology, and his comparison of it to the Christian moral way. But it is important to recognize that myth for Thoreau is not a means of memory, or cycle of repetition, still less the tool of classification into which it has dwindled in the use of some literary scholars today. "Tradition is a more interrupted and feebler memory. . . . The past is only so heroic as we see it. It is the canvas on which our idea of heroism is painted, and so, in one sense, the *dim prospectus of our future field*" (p. 309, my italics). The mythic story is to be created, not merely recollected.

This view is an aspect of, tangential to, Thoreau's search for a center of experience in time. All his writings, the journals, *Walden*, contribute to this. It is striking that in *A Week*, as he announces the intended voyage up the stream, with new scenes and men to be found, ducks flying, gulls wheeling, muskrats swimming, cranberries tossing on the waves, he suddenly sees this as "such healthy natural tumult as proves the last day is not yet at hand" (p. 11). Again, his mood reveals a significant difference between him and his seventeenth-century predecessors, for whom the "last day" was potentially at hand, for whom the time was late. Thoreau with his consanguineous but different sensibility can deal with creative novelty as they could not, except in

matters of detail. For him the first Sunday morning of
his voyage, with more of the "auroral rosy and white
than of the yellow light in it" is "as if it dated from earlier than the fall of man" (p. 51). Even if this freshness and
"heathenish integrity" cannot be consistently maintained, it has been realized on occasion and is the intended spirit of the whole. And it leads to the most
unifying perception of all, the concrescence of eternity
in the present. Hearing a strain of music, by a drummer
in the night:

> I see, smell, taste, hear, feel that everlasting Something
> to which we are allied, at once our maker, our abode, our
> destiny, our very Selves; the one historic truth, the most
> remarkable fact which can become the distinct and un-
> invited subject of our thought, the actual glory of the
> universe; the only fact which a human being cannot avoid
> recognizing, or in some way forget or dispense with (p.
> 183).

The bridge between the writer encouraged by the hopes
of the Romantic period, and later discoverers like Henry
James or Virginia Woolf, is that this liberation of attention and concentration of feeling is based not upon
a predetermined doctrine, but upon fidelity to varied
moments of experience.

Such a fidelity, the preparation for it and inevitable
wonder at its source, is the clue to Thoreau's musings
upon nature and art, poetry and the poet. As Milton had
written of "mercy colleague with justice," so Thoreau
sees nature and art, not as antinomy, but as coeval forces
deriving from each other. Modifying, at the same time
that he echoes, Sir Thomas Browne, Thoreau found
"Nature . . . a greater and more perfect art, the art of

God; though, referred to herself, she is genius; and there is a similarity between her operations and man's art even in the details and trifles" (p. 337). An interesting light is cast upon his sense of "wildness" when he says, "Art is not tame, and Nature is not wild, in the ordinary sense. A perfect work of man's art would also be wild or natural in a good sense. Man tames Nature only that he may at last make her more free even than he found her, though he may never yet have succeeded" (p. 335). Thoreau links his concept of wildness with both art and nature as belonging to what is undiluted by custom or routine, and though it may be the outcome of the most highly civilized faculty, is unpredictable and procreative in its energies. Finally, near the end of *A Week* Thoreau makes an important and it may seem surprising declaration: "May we not *see* God? Are we to be put off and amused in this life, as it were with a mere allegory? Is not Nature, rightly read, that of which she is commonly taken to be the symbol merely?" (p. 403). The form of the questions delivers his answer to them, respectfully.

In his study of "formal elements" in *A Week* Mr. Drake expresses his belief that Thoreau's conviction here that nature is not mere symbol or mere allegory was only a temporary belief and is superseded in *Walden*.[11] On the contrary, I believe it to be confirmed by the lasting evidence of his journal, as well as this passage in *A Week*. While at times Thoreau sincerely speaks the language of correspondences that links transcendentalism with its seventeenth-century forebears, he is also capable of an insight less derivative: in the process of studying and knowing what seems to be symbol or allegory, we may encounter the heart of reality, and in knowing nature as art, we may know the source of being.

In fitting himself by his river meditations to approach this knowledge, Thoreau accomplishes some of his best writing, and we cannot therefore discount *A Week* even when admiring the subtler skill of the composition of *Walden.*

Finally, we see in Thoreau's treatment of the poet and the genius a related development of the ideas we have been tracing in *A Week.* The poet's sometimes necessary hibernation frees him from the quotidian to know the day anew.

> We love to think in winter, as we walk over the snowy pastures, of these happy dreamers that lie under the sod, of dormice and all that race of dormant creatures, which have such a superfluity of life enveloped in thick folds of fur, impervious to cold. Alas, the poet too is, in one sense, a sort of dormouse gone into winter quarters of deep and serene thoughts, insensible to surrounding circumstances; his words are the relation of his oldest and finest memory, a wisdom drawn from the remotest experience. Other men lead a starved existence, meanwhile, like hawks, that would fain keep on the wing, and trust to pick up a sparrow now and then (p. 106).

But as it is part of Thoreau's conviction that the poet cannot be tracked, he does not embark on this perilous theme for long, or revert to it often. He has no such developed concept of the poet as detector and speaker of symbols as Emerson does, in his essay "The Poet." Here again Thoreau escapes the equations Emerson resorts to. His beliefs are not opposed, but have a somewhat different foundation. Poetry "is not recoverable thought, but a hue caught from a vaster receding thought" (p. 347). Although, like Emerson, he tends to ignore or minimize the ingredients of writing, he knows that "The talent of composition is very dangerous,—the striking out of the heart of life at a blow . . ." (p. 348).

Perhaps one of his most surprising statements is that "Great prose, of equal elevation, commands our respect more than great verse, since it implies a more permanent and level height, a life more pervaded with the grandeur of the thought" (p. 363). If not a view that can consistently enlighten us, it reveals the difference in command of the sources of literary art known to Thoreau himself. On the whole, his making the poet, poetry, genius, and art a field of his attention in the meditations of *A Week* is related to what he says about the wild, antiquity, time, as part of a brooding upon mysteries we may encounter if graced by reverence and the knack of the occasion.

This is the counterpoint of *A Week*, the occasional and the meditative; each gives life to the other. I have tried to show that the essay-like pages regarded by some as digressions are in fact a flowing current of feeling and thought, to which the river journey gives direction. From discussions such as I have noticed, or the more specific ones on Goethe or Persius, we are recalled to a specific time of youth in New England by the sighting of an island or a canal boat, the rattling of the oars, the passage through Arcadian scenes. *A Week on the Concord and Merrimack Rivers* is an experimental book. Its texture is uneven, threads pulled out by the too frequent quotations and the insertion of Thoreau's own verses. But he has made his own model for the conjunction of what he saw and what therefore, or otherwise, occupied his mind and feelings. He has room for a new resolution of the wonderings to which the imaginative prose of Donne or Browne invites us; he has freed these themes from a context limited by certain traditional religious expectations. If its surface is less finished, its profundities more possible than fathomed, *A Week* is nevertheless a tenderer, more open-hearted book than *Walden*.

In contrast to the linear narrative of *A Week*, with recesses and avenues of speculation, *Walden* has a circular pattern. As a self-portrait of a young man revealing his beliefs, it is closer to *Religio Medici* than any other book, but unlike it in that it enacts a parable.

The opening section, "Economy," might almost stand alone (and it is no accident that some of the most frequently quoted passages occur in this chapter). Reading it, bear in mind that Thoreau's original title for his book included the phrase "to my townsmen." He makes it clear that a partial incentive for his book was to answer their frequent questions about his life in the woods. But the function of this opening section is to shape for them a question they did not have vision to ask, as to the nature of the choice he made in going there. Here he records the definitive blast of his will by which he separated himself from a commitment to the life of trade and commerce that made men "tools of their tools."

Studies of *Walden* have helpfully pointed out the presence in it of the year's cycle, moving to the renewal of spring and morning in its last chapter.[12] But this pattern is in the background, not the foreground. The opening chapters turn on the meaning of a chosen life and a chosen place. Once the compatibility of home-made circumstances, of voluntary poverty, has been established in "Economy," the writer proceeds instantly, in "Where I Lived and What I Lived For," "Reading," and "Solitude," to a direct revelation of contemplative awareness of varying kinds. Other chapters such as "The Bean Field" return to the action that endorses such a life. There is a counterpoint throughout of fact—the cost of tools and timber, the building of a chimney— and idea or dream:

> Sometimes, in a summer morning, having taken my accustomed bath, I sat in my sunny doorway from sunrise till noon, rapt in a revery . . . until by the sun falling in at my west window, or the noise of some traveller's wagon on the distant highway, I was reminded of the lapse of time. I grew in those seasons like corn in the night, and they were far better than any work of the hands would have been. They were not time subtracted from my life, but so much over and above my usual allowance. I realized what the Orientals mean by contemplation and the forsaking of works. For the most part, I minded not how the hours went. . . . My days were not the days of the week, bearing the stamp of any heathen deity . . . for I lived like the Puri Indians, of whom it is said that 'for yesterday, to-day and to-morrow they have only one word, and they express the variety of meaning by pointing backward for yesterday, forward for to-morrow, and overhead for the passing day.' This was sheer idleness to my fellow-townsmen, no doubt; but if the birds and flowers had tried me by their standard, I should not have been found wanting. A man must find his occasions in himself, it is true (pp. 122-123).[13]

*Walden* is a book about the finding of occasions. Some are times of work, like the hoeing of rows of beans that end to end would stretch miles; some are times of surmounting hardship; some are times of amusement and pleasure, like the meeting with Therien, or conversations with visitors. But all are steadied in respect to a new knowledge of the man's self as keenly related to the place and its natural phenomena.

J. Lyndon Shanley's indispensable study, *The Making of Walden*,[14] with its account of manuscript versions and its publication of the first draft, shows that Thoreau had the plan of the whole from the beginning. Certainly he improved it—certainly must have known himself that the first draft was a sketch. But the procedure is there. Even in this version, for example, the essence of the chapters "Where I Lived and What I Lived For," "Reading," and "Sounds" immediately follows the opening "Economy." These early chapters are not narrative, although they contain some vivid details of things as they happen. Primarily, they open room for contemplation, and present its fruits. The narrow view of *Walden* as description of a primitive life overlooks the significance of a chapter like "Reading." Allowing that incessant labour in the first summer kept him from his books, Thoreau says the prospect of reading in the future sustained him through such labour. For reading is a worthy outcome:

> The student may read Homer or Aeschylus in the Greek without danger of dissipation or luxuriousness, for it implies that he in some measure emulate their heroes, and consecrate morning hours to their pages. The heroic books, even if printed in the character of our mother tongue, will always be in a language dead to degenerate times; and we must laboriously seek the meaning of each word and line, conjecturing a larger sense than common use permits out of what wisdom and valor and generosity we have (p. 109).

> To read well, that is, to read true books in a true spirit, is a noble exercise. . . . It requires a training such as the athletes underwent, the steady intention almost of the whole life to this object. Books must be read as deliberately and reservedly as they were written (p. 110).

Reading, then, and the resolution of the mind and feelings in the experience of classic works, is an act as remarkable as fishing or chasing a fox in winter, but calls upon the different faculties that keep one alive while engaged in more ordinary tasks. Like the metaphysical poets, especially Donne, Thoreau brings reading into the compass of the most vivid experience.

"Economy," with its high-spirited satire to underline a departure from one kind of society, prepares for the whole of *Walden*. The chapters that follow it immediately create his livelihood in the fullest sense. It is only after Thoreau has revealed the private individual's joy that he reports in a more matter-of-fact way on the circumstances of the seasons by the pond. The opening chapters build a causeway leading us onto the cantilever suspended from "The Ponds" to "Spring." The bridge travels across middle chapters full of anecdote and incident.

"The Ponds" gathers together the strands of the preceding meditative sections and unifies them. Its beginning with the word "Sometimes" is disarming, for in this chapter Thoreau makes visible a general theme he had announced early in his book. There he had written: "In any weather, at any hour of the day or night, I have been anxious to improve the nick of time, and notch it on my stick too; to stand on the meeting of two eternities, the past and future, which is precisely the present moment; to toe that line" (p. 20). By gentle means he has led us to the "sometimes" at the ponds where he met these dimensions intentionally and unintentionally. On some occasions Walden is the scene of immediate and largely accidental events—an axe falling through a hole in the ice, one kind of insect sliding over its surface faster than another. Yet it has an undefiled unfathomable past.

Perhaps on that spring morning when Adam and Eve were driven out of Eden Walden Pond was already in existence, and even then breaking up in a gentle spring rain accompanied with mist and a southerly wind, and covered with myriads of ducks and geese, which had not heard of the fall, when still such pure lakes sufficed them. Even then it had commenced to rise and fall, and had clarified its waters and colored them of the hue they now wear, and obtained a patent of heaven to be the only Walden Pond in the world and distiller of celestial dews. Who knows in how many unremembered nations' literatures this has been the Castalian Fountain? or what nymphs presided over it in the Golden Age? It is a gem of the first water which Concord wears in her coronet (p. 195).

Walden is not only earlier than the "fall" of man, as early as a golden age, but independent of them, surviving to give *them* memory. The paragraph ends in the first tense, Concord *wears* in her coronet this pond. The book that bears the pond's name hinges on no historical, but an ever-present redemption.

The differing shores of the pond, the changing colour of the water, the land seen looking up from it or aside from it, fish living in it, trees bordering it, invaders seeming to infringe upon it, only attest the immortality of this vision:

Nevertheless, of all the characters I have known, perhaps Walden wears best, and best preserves its purity. Many men have been likened to it, but few deserve that honor. Though the woodchoppers have laid bare first this shore and then that, and the Irish have built their sties by it, and the railroad has infringed on its border, and the ice-men have skimmed it once, it is itself unchanged, the same water which my youthful eyes fell on; all the change is in me (p. 209).

Walden, and the other related ponds, Flint's, Goose, and White's, "earth's eyes," are beyond change in essence however misprized in transience. If they represent knowledgeable indolence, there is also the depth of an encounter with the incorruptible event.

> . . . sometimes dragging sixty feet of line about the pond as I drifted in the gentle night breeze, now and then feeling a slight vibration along it, indicative of some life prowling about its extremity, of dull uncertain blundering purpose there. . . . At length you slowly raise . . . some horned pout squeaking and squirming to the upper air. It was very queer, especially in dark nights, when your thoughts had wandered to vast and cosmogonal themes in other spheres, to feel this faint jerk, which came to interrupt your dreams and *link you to Nature again* (p. 190, italics added).

Nature is not hieroglyphic, has not led the speaker to his cosmogonal theme, but recalls him to herself by an indubitable fact—a fish biting. And the passage ends "Thus I caught two fishes as it were with one hook." Complexity of thought and feeling is realized by a simple occasion. In imagination this represents an advance over the traditional correspondences treasured by writers of the seventeenth century. The equation of idea and fact, each term giving the other its value, is the tenor of *Walden* even more centrally than of *A Week*.

The pond is the heart of the vision, but the chosen place, the hut beside it, its environs, arrivals there, departures from it, call for the realization of the local. I have said that the middle chapters of the book are full of anecdote and incident, details aptly chosen, although not inherently inevitable. This is further evidence of Thoreau's accomplishment as a new kind of writer in prose—to be neither overpraised, nor underestimated. Many circumstances he describes might be otherwise, but happen to be real—the stones around the pond, the paths to and from it, the particular people who come to see the "hermit" even in winter, the animals he pursues or tames. By all these details the incidental is encouraged to generate interests that lie beyond it. In the kind of imaginative prose Thoreau succeeded in writing, the incidental has the part that invention and coincidence do in fiction. In either case, there is an arbitrary element, to which the writer must win our consent. The events and circumstances of life by the pond with their sometimes even trivial moments are the arbitrary element in that book. Chapters like "Brute Neighbors" or "Winter Visitors" are not encompassed by any unifying metaphor or theme. Instead they have a different function. Celebrating the wild, the writer adapts our imagination to it by his candor in detail. We are disarmed by the careful sighting of a red squirrel or a blue jay where we might have expected a bear or a panther. Thoreau tells us himself, speaking in a question, of the purport of this new composition. "Why do precisely these objects which we behold make a world? Why has man just these species of animals for his neighbors; as if nothing but a mouse could have filled this crevice?" (p. 242).

The different ways in which "these objects which we behold make a world" and the kinds of objects, including a man's self as well as his visitors or brute neighbours, give animation and variety to the writing of *Walden*. There is the sheer fun of it, from the writer's own humour of address in "Economy" to episodes like the conversation with Therien or the jokes between young poet and young hermit that made the hut ring with laughter. (The sense of an antic youth is stronger in the first version than in the completed book; the briefer, more staccato paragraphs deliver a more direct humour.) The movement from sections embodying revery and contemplation to the brisk report of other parts creates a sense of movement in the book as a whole. The writer knows how to do different things, not only hoeing beans or plastering a wall, but different kinds of composition.

It is interesting that Thoreau himself at the very beginning makes a point of the fact that this is a book in the first person:

> In most books, the *I*, or first person, is omitted; in this it will be retained; that, in respect to egotism, is the main difference. We commonly do not remember that it is, after all, always the first person that is speaking. I should not talk so much about myself if there were any body else whom I knew as well. Unfortunately, I am confined to this theme by the narrowness of my experience. Moreover, I, on my side, require of every writer, first or last, a simple and sincere account of his own life . . . some such account as he would send to his kindred from a distant land; for if he has lived sincerely, it must have been in a distant land to me (pp. 5-6).

Thus there is more than one reason why the book should be in the first person (and there is a noticeable difference between the "I" of *Walden* and the "we" or occasional third-person references to the travellers in *A Week*). In the passage I have cited above, the first person is indispensable to a book about self-knowledge;

it is also an aid to veracity in an account or report, the sign of a speaking witness to events, inner or outer.

At the beginning and the end of *Walden*, however, Thoreau takes the risk of resorting to the imperative mood and the direct question that Felltham chiefly avoided in *Resolves*. This mood had also governed Browne's *Christian Morals*. But Browne's gentle commands ("Sit soft in the showers of Providence") seem to be addressed by the speaker to himself, and to represent another form of meditation. In *Walden*, as I have pointed out, the commands and questions of "Economy" speak in part Thoreau's own preparation for the experience of *Walden*, in part his ironic communication to his townsmen of the discovery of what is cost in living. He does, however, permit himself to exhort as well as to suggest, and avails himself of this liberty, although with less rhetorical flourish, in "Conclusion." But if the center of *Walden* is the relation of actions and states of mind that constitute an extended parable, "Conclusion" is its application to more of life, as its final aphoristic salute to the dawn indicates. Because he had been, and exults in being "extravagant, extra-vagant" in his summons to his readers, he could conclude with an affirmation of the creative novelty in time, the perpetual achievement of Cosmos out of Chaos, verified by spring.

First in *A Week on the Concord and Merrimack Rivers*, then in *Walden*, Thoreau had broken new ground as a writer of imaginative prose. In the two books published after his death, *The Maine Woods* and *Cape Cod*,[15] he tested his resources as a writer in a different way, but he did not equal the achievement of *A Week* or *Walden*. Neither of the later books is conceived as a whole. The three excursions described in

*The Maine Woods* gave him the opportunity to explore more deeply a theme of significance to him in all his writing, that of the wild. Sherman Paul has skilfully and sensitively elucidated the way in which Thoreau here confronts a wilderness that can defeat man's aspirations,[16] where "Vast, Titanic, inhuman Nature has got him at disadvantage . . . and pilfers him of some of his divine faculty" (p. 64). The ascent of Ktaadn, and failure to reach the summit, evokes from Thoreau a dramatic comparison of his journey with Satan's voyage through Chaos (p. 60). One might say that Thoreau in this section of *The Maine Woods* speaks as Adam performing Satan's voyage. Such is the nakedness, and firstness, of his encounter with this unimagined wild (different from his own instinct for it as a part of essential self) that he again calls on the image of primeval things: "This was that Earth of which we have heard, made out of Chaos and Old Night. Here was no man's garden, but the unhandselled globe. It was not lawn, nor pasture, nor mead, nor woodland . . . Man was not to be associated with it. It was Matter, vast, terrific,—not his Mother Earth that we have heard of . . . the home, this, of Necessity and Fate" (p. 70).

As "Ktaadn" leads to this climax of the wild as an unfathomable dimension in Nature, "Chesunkook" brings a recognition of the wild in man as also a potentially destructive force. The climax here, the killing of the moose, prompts the writer to a more direct comment on an experience than he usually resorts to:

> But, on more accounts than one, I had had enough of moose-hunting. I had not come to the woods for this purpose, nor had I foreseen it, though I had been willing to learn how the Indian manoeuvred. . . . The afternoon's

tragedy, and my share in it, as it affected the innocence, destroyed the pleasure of my adventure. It is true, I came as near as is possible to come to being a hunter and miss it, myself; and as it is, I think that I could spend a year in the woods, fishing and hunting, just enough to sustain myself, with satisfaction. This would be next to living like a philosopher on the fruits of the earth which you had raised, which also attracts me (pp. 121-122).

The last two sentences suggest a relation with *Walden* (and Thoreau was writing the final draft of that book as he produced this section of *The Maine Woods*). But there is no symmetrical linking and potential contrast of themes, as there had been in Browne's *Urn Burial* and *Garden of Cyrus*.

The third section of *The Maine Woods*, "The Allegash and East Branch," complements the two preceding ones only in that the wild is here represented by Thoreau's closest association with an Indian, his guide Joe Polis. But the portrait that emerges is an incidental one, conveyed by unrelated episodes that disclose the Indian's skill in his milieu. Perhaps also in this section the reader becomes more aware of the threat that man's indifference to the wilderness will destroy its meaning (a subject that was to recur with increasing frequency in the journal). Observing the chopper's preference for the log or carcass over the living tree, Thoreau exclaims:

> The Anglo-American can indeed cut down, and grub up all this waving forest . . . but he cannot converse with the spirit of the tree he fells, he cannot read the poetry and mythology which retire as he advances. He ignorantly erases mythological tablets in order to print his handbills. . . .

> Before he has learned his a b c in the beautiful but
> mystic lore of the wilderness which Spenser and Dante
> had just begun to read, he cuts it down, coins a *pine-tree
> shilling* . . . (p. 235).

Here as in his other writing Thoreau does not depend
upon a substructure of myth for any kind of narrative
pattern; he evokes the quality of myth as a perspective
upon experience.

The three studies comprising *The Maine Woods*,
then, fall short of *A Week* and *Walden* by their lack of
a pattern for the whole as well as their less continuous
weaving of experience into idea. The writing is chiefly
episodic, the rapidly moving narrative parts alternate
with pauses allowing description of the seen and the
unseen in the woods of Maine. The cumulative effect
of the book as a whole steeps us in the life of an earlier
world, an older world in time, but younger in the primacy of growing things, in the sensual truth of the In-
dians or the animals at home there.

Like *The Maine Woods, Cape Cod* is a book that
brings into focus the sharp impressions and the human
questions stored up in Thoreau's imagination on three
separate journeys (1849, 1850, and 1855).[17] The new
edition of his writings will undoubtedly make clearer
the way that Thoreau used his first journey to provide a
line for the whole narrative. He brings out in the opening chapter the fact that this book does not tell of a
single pilgrimage. As the essay-narrative continues, we
begin to understand the shuttling back and forth from
the first sighting (the aftermath of the shipwreck at
Cohasset) to the departure by ship from Provincetown
in the last chapter. A comparison with some character-
istics of Melville's prose would be easy but unenlighten-

ing. There are twentieth-century novels that take many more pages to bring the stages of life and the conflicting vitalities of different kinds of people before us simultaneously.

*The Maine Woods* has a profound unity of theme in an interrupted sequence. In *Cape Cod* Thoreau adopts a more sophisticated device by keeping before us the personality of a man older than the explorer of *A Week*, but as brave and open-hearted. Freely giving rein to a mood of sport and fancy, this narrator has looked upon the changes and chances of life too honestly to permit himself the whimsey affected at times by De Quincey's opium eater. The sailors and townspeople take their place with other characters created by Thoreau from real people and are comparable to Melvin or John Goodman in the journal. His encounters with them are sportsman's sketches livened with instinctive humour. Yet the chapter called "The Shipwreck" is set in a different key, by the charitable impersonality with which Thoreau regards violence and suffering. Like Dylan Thomas, Thoreau concluded that "after the first death, there is no other." But consider his description of the old man and his son collecting seaweed cast up by the storm. They were "as serenely employed as if there had never been a wreck in the world, though they were within sight of the Grampus Rock, on which the St. John had struck."[18] It is worthy of a reflection made by Edgar looking down from the coast of Kent on "one that gathers samphire, dreadful trade."

The deservedly famous Wellfleet oysterman entertains Thoreau and his companion, and we are in the world of comedy. Yet the oysterman's virtue was that he had "a sense of his own nothingness" (p. 75). *Cape Cod* gives the reader the enjoyment of a particularly

American kind of comedy, but that is not lost or under-
cut by pages where Thoreau writes with the undeceived
humanity of Swift. Perhaps only readers who have
walked on the outermost beach from Nauset light to
Provincetown can quickly grasp the raciness of Thoreau's humour, his puns, his control of passages where
keen but relaxed attention develops an almost musical
quality in his prose. But then, after the long hard walk,
the travellers look for the "Charity-House" or "Humane
house," meant to succour the shipwrecked sailor.
Neither Swift nor Sterne could excel these few pages,
when first the travellers put their eyes to a knothole in
the door to obtain "the long wished-for insight." They
saw stones and wads of wool, an empty fireplace, "but
it was not supplied with matches . . ." (p. 69). We recall
*Walden*. But Thoreau does not repeat himself. There
is no loss; yet there has been a gain:

> Turning our backs on the outward world, we thus looked
> through the knot-hole into the Humane house . . . and
> for bread we found a stone. It was literally a great cry
> (of sea-mews outside) and a little wool. However, we were
> glad to sit outside, under the lee of the Humane house,
> to escape the piercing wind; and there we thought how
> cold is charity! how inhumane humanity. . . . Virtues
> antique and far away with ever a rusty nail over the latch,
> and very difficult to keep in repair, withal, it is so un-
> certain whether any will gain the beach near you (p. 70).

More than metaphor can do, more than any poem alone
could do, such writing creates the imagination that we
need in order to understand its meaning.

Both *The Maine Woods* and *Cape Cod* record many
present actions of men either as invasions of a truer
state of feeling or as signals of danger challenging hope

or innocence. The humour of the narrator or of the natives of these regions offers restoration. The incorporation into his narrative of voyages from Europe to America suggests possibilities of arrangement in *Cape Cod* that might have been different from his use of other travel accounts in earlier books.[19] It is evident that Thoreau did not have time to effect this in the last chapter. But he had decisively indicated one meaning of the voyage in his opening chapter, where he meditates on the shipwrecked emigrants from Galway, who within a mile of the American shore "emigrated to a newer world than Columbus ever dreamed of," yet of whose existence "we believe there is far more universal and convincing evidence ..." (p. 10). It is an expression of faith in immortality worthy of the underestimated humour in the book of Jonah. Although Thoreau did not altogether successfully relate the oldest explorations of the Cape to the book as a whole, I believe that the point of this section is given by the amusing description of "the greenness of the Pilgrims" (p. 235). Sailing back from Provincetown he appreciates the Captain's skill in docking the ship. The fog is so dense that the narrator cannot see the wharves, nevertheless, "we were to be blown to a crevice amid them." We are back in the familiar world of fact, of barrels, of blocks of granite, and crates and hogheads, "and that is Boston" (p. 248). Our guide returns us to the shore.

In *A Week*, in *Walden*, and to a lesser degree in *Cape Cod* and *The Maine Woods* Thoreau was fulfilling a possibility he had foreseen as he kept his journal: "my own writing may inspire me and at last I may make wholes of parts" (J iii, 217).[20] He had drawn from, and revised sentences and pages in, the journal to make these books, he had rearranged material from various years and times, in the context of an overriding pattern: the river, the pond, the wilderness, the sea and the desert, to make a whole. Yet not only did the writing of the journal precede and follow that of his books, not only does it contain much that does not appear elsewhere, it is, above all, a kind of writing in itself, a kind that repeatedly rises to the height of imaginative intensity, a kind in which Thoreau, though preceded and inspired by Emerson, is in his different way unexcelled.

In the year that he graduated from Harvard (1837), Thoreau began to enter into "the big Red Journal" the fruit of his meditations and observations, and by 1840 this journal contained 546 pages; in the following six months another, of 396 pages, was completed (J VIII, 66). Until a short time before his death, writing in the journal was Thoreau's almost daily occupation. Various entries show that he realized this kind of composition to be different in nature.

> Each thought that is welcomed and recorded is a nest egg, by the side of which more will be laid. Thoughts accidentally thrown together become a frame in which more may be developed and exhibited. Perhaps this is the main value of a habit of writing, of keeping a journal,—that so we remember our best hours and stimulate ourselves. . . . Having by chance recorded a few disconnected thoughts and then brought them into juxtaposition, they suggest a whole new field in which it was possible to labour and to think. Thought begat thought (J III, 217).

And a few days later it occurred to him more clearly that the journal has a value different from the book or essay shaped to a pattern:

I do not know but thoughts written down thus in a journal might be printed in the same form with greater advantage than if the related ones were brought together into separate essays. *They are now allied to life,* and are seen by the reader not to be far-fetched. . . . I feel that in the other case I should have no proper frame for my sketches (J III, 239).

In a sense this comment on the inherent nearness to life of the journal resembles Virginia Woolf's search for a form of the novel that would have a similar intensity and intrinsic unity. What Thoreau sought to do, and achieved, was to see the phenomena of experience in their own place.

But what phenomena? Here the parts of the journal vary considerably—yet it is all one current. The early volumes contain more experiments in essay-like topics, the writer's own reflection on a theme often suggested to him by his reading, or by the inner moral weather of a young man measuring his will and belief. The later volumes, mistakenly undervalued by some scholars, depend more on the plain facts of Thoreau's walks about Concord. Thus the relation of fact to meditation varies in different parts of the journal. This was an issue in Thoreau's own mind. In one of the middle volumes of the journal he noted

I have a commonplace-book for facts and another for poetry, but I find it difficult always to preserve the vague distinction which I had in my mind, for the most interesting and beautiful facts are so much the more poetry and that is their success. They are *translated* from earth to heaven. I see that if my facts were sufficiently vital and significant,—perhaps transmuted more into the sub-

stance of the human mind,—I should need but one book
of poetry to contain them all (J III, 311).

The journal is as noteworthy for what it omits as for
what it sometimes awkwardly includes. In no usual sense
autobiographical, it seldom describes directly the ordinary happenings of Thoreau's life or his relationships
with people. Instead, by the willing discipline of observation, especially, as the work progresses, on his daily,
mostly solitary walks Thoreau transmutes fact into the
substance of the human mind. Here his procedure resembles Browne's translation to the universal from his
reading, notebooks, and collections of rarities, Thoreau
seems to advance the range and release of contemplative
attention. Taken first and last, including even the bare
recordings and measurements that in the later journals
deter some readers, the whole work is devoted to a principle affirmed by Thoreau in 1850: "All matter, indeed,
is capable of entertaining thought." If this is at the center of Emerson's *Nature*, nevertheless Thoreau exemplifies it newly in his concrete vision.

The unpredictable sequences of the journal are like
life itself in their strange variety. Again and again we
see the progress (from the labour of surveying or the
determined walk through rough winter field or swamp,
as well as the summer saunterings), to the moments of
ecstasy and purest joy. As Sherman Paul has said, Thoreau was concerned "with telling how ecstasy was
earned, how life was got, how, in the absence of these
necessities, one deliberately remade his life."[21] To see
these re-entries of the "unconsciousness that is the consciousness of God" (*A Week*, p. 348), we must travel with
the writer through some hard as well as smooth terrain.

If the early volumes (and some that we hope will be

first printed in the new edition of the journal) are the seedbed of his published books, the later volumes present all we have of the envisioned book on Concord that might have crowned them all. As early as 1841 Thoreau had imagined it.

> I think I could write a poem to be called "Concord." For argument I should have the River, the Woods, the Ponds, the Hills, the Fields, the Swamps and Meadows, the Streets and Buildings, and the Villagers. Then Morning, Noon, and Evening, Spring, Summer, Autumn and Winter, Night, Indian Summer, and the Mountains in the Horizon (J 1, 282).

This book, not encompassed wholly by *Walden* or any other, exists potentially in the journal. I have written elsewhere of the exploration of relatedness, of river level to musquash, musquash to hunter, pond to the passing mythological figure of Melvin and his dog, unknown fish first seen by its old contemporary the writer, as probable ingredients of the Concord book.[22] But even had these journal entries been its seedbed too, the journal remains a unique literary achievement in its free spiral form. Again and again even in ordinary moments it suggests to the reader a connection of events of which we are mostly unaware—like the clamshell in the stump of a log, put there, Thoreau says, by a muskrat. The current of life flows throughout, known by grasses, the colour of leaves, the droppings of an owl, the tracks of field mice, as well as by anything else. One is always immersed in a season, one is living a separate day. Hence there is unavoidable repetition, there are isolated anecdotes. The particular detail may be meaningless to the reader who does not know, for example, the botanical names of plants. What is pontederia, and what does it make the shore look like, remaining late in the fall? My dictionary does not tell me, and I have lost my father's copy of Gray's *Botany*. Do I care how high the snow lay on such a January day, as compared with the year before? Not necessarily, but the seemingly incidental opens unforgettably into reaches of mind and emotion.

Here is one bare November landscape where the very bareness is the stimulus to a transcendent vision. The substance of the passage must be given as a crowning example of finding the extra-ordinary in a common scene.

> Standing there, though in this *bare* November landscape, I am reminded of the incredible phenomenon of small birds in winter,—that ere long, amid the cold powdery snow . . . will come twittering a flock of crimson-tinged birds, lesser redpolls, to sport and feed on the seeds and buds now just ripe for them. . . . These crimson aerial creatures have wings which would bear them quickly to the regions of summer, but here is all the summer they want. What a rich contrast! tropical colours, crimson breasts, on cold white snow! Such etherealness, such delicacy in their forms . . . their Maker gave them the last touch and launched them forth the day of the Great Snow. He made this bitter imprisoning cold before which man quails, but He made at the same time these warm and twittering creatures to twitter and be at home in it. He said not only, Let there be linnets in winter, but linnets of rich plumage and pleasing twitter, bearing summer in their natures. . . .
>
> I saw this familiar—too *familiar*—fact at a different angle, and I was charmed and haunted by it. . . . I had seen into paradisaic regions, with their air and sky, and I was no longer wholly or merely a denizen of this vulgar

earth. Yet I had hardly a foothold there. . . . It is only necessary to behold thus the least fact or phenomenon, however familiar, from a point a hair's breadth aside from our habitual path or routine, to be overcome, enchanted by its beauty and significance (J VIII, 42-43, 44).

The whole passage exemplifies Thoreau's triumph, as a writer of imaginative prose, in the generation of the universal from the particular. As Albert Schweitzer said of Goethe, "he does not invent an image to express a thought; instead of that pictures of what he has seen and experienced wait within him for the thought which is ordained to take form in them."[23] Thoreau innocently records the arrival of the form itself, when the ability "to behold the phenomenon from a point a hair's breadth aside from our habitual path" confers an unforeseen glory.

The power to try out the least experience even on bare ground confers its initiatory strength upon the journal. Sherman Paul has remarked that both *A Week* and *Walden* are works of recollection.[24] In the sense that in each of these books the writer relates (in his chosen sequence) a voyage and a space of his life, that judgment must stand. And we have seen how, in *The Maine Woods* and *Cape Cod*, Thoreau proceeded to somewhat different patterns of narrative. For the most part, the journal, the origin of all these more consciously shaped works, is written in the present tense, where the life of the instant is celebrated, and the seeds of growth are winnowed from the obtrusive ambition, inert sentiment, or unjust refusals of men in historical time.

"I now descend the hill," Thoreau notes in his journal, or, "I sit at my ease and look out from under my lichen-clad rocky roof." A person must have walked the same path many times to recognize what is new in it. Because he writes the report for himself, he gains reserve and can afford spontaneous delight in common and uncommon things.

Throughout, in its less interesting stretches as well as the openings of an intensified consciousness, the journal exemplifies Virginia Woolf's distinction between the inert fact and "the fertile fact, the fact that engenders." Both have to be there for the second to be honestly arrived at. The whole has the colour of experience, where "Rain is of the process."

Meditating on the invisible seeds of things, on trees, and shadows, led Browne to his conclusion that "Light that makes things seen, makes some things invisible." Thoreau might almost have written that sentence, but not with the measured cadence. The sermons of Donne and the meditative structures of Browne achieve an ordonnance and an architecture of rhythm that has never been equalled and would be untrue for later writers such as Hazlitt, Emerson, and Thoreau. Thoreau goes forward from Emerson to enter new ground by a differently elected, open circle. For this the journal is a compass, the observations a continuum of vision.

# T. S. Eliot:   8

## The Dialogue of the Writer

A knowledge of philosophy may be a costly thing to a creative writer; its charming cup or "Apollo's lute" may claim days and hours of experience that might otherwise be spent; his command of language is called to service he cannot ultimately fulfill, and that may defer for him finding ways of more concrete expression. Nevertheless without this effort some poets and some critics would never have related, or seen the interest in relating, actuality to transcendent modes of being. It is unnecessary to name the poets who had no direct need of philosophy. To fathom why Milton, or Coleridge, or T. S. Eliot knew the need and exemplify its cost, and why each in his different way obtained insight that entered both his poetry and prose, is beyond the scope of my discussion. It was not necessary to await the publication of Eliot's dissertation on Bradley to be aware of this weightlifting and choice in his early prose. The fascination lies rather in the exigencies of writing to sustain himself, the years of the perhaps now vanished lectures and the still unreclaimed reviews, that accompany his early writing of poetry and emergence as a critic.

Valerie Eliot, in her invaluable introduction to the facsimile of the original drafts of *The Waste Land*,[1] gives a portrait of Eliot's struggle to make ends meet by reviewing and lecturing (concurrently with the publication of his first mature poems). In a letter to Conrad Aiken he reports that he had been reviewing books good and bad, for philosophical journals as well as for the *New Statesman* and the *Manchester Guardian*. Whereas he later said that F. H. Bradley had formed his style, in this letter he admits to the lesson the young reviewer learns, for better or for worse: "Composing on the typewriter, I find that I am sloughing off all my long sentences which I used to dote upon. Short, staccato, like modern French prose. The typewriter makes for lucidity, but I am not sure that it encourages subtlety."[2]

Meanwhile Eliot had another reason to test his power to epitomize ideas, in lectures given to a tutorial class for working people. In two evening lectures a week, at first on topics in political economy, later on a wide range of Victorian writers including "Carlyle, Mill, Arnold, Huxley, Spencer, Ruskin, Morris—then the poets, and then the novelists,"[3] he must have practiced his power to analyze simply and economically. Given the chance in the following year to teach Elizabethan literature, he expressed his pleasure, because he wanted to "write some essays on the dramatists who have never been properly criticized."[4] This confirms the fact that his major early essays were not merely a by-product of teaching and journalism, but a voluntary effort to present some profound aspects of his thought and feeling in prose as well as poetry.

Several periodicals, especially the *Egoist*, the *New Statesman*, and the *Athenaeum* gave him a chance to formulate positions on some of the important questions any intelligent writer has lurking in his mind. I should like to single out a few of the articles and reviews he wrote in these early years for the light they shed on his beginnings as a writer of imaginative prose. A few examples may challenge or even dispel some misconceptions about his apprenticeship, purpose, and achievement in this realm. We need not be limited by Eliot's carefully informal assessment of his essays in the lecture "To Criticize the Critic." Coming toward the end of a long career in the world of letters, a man might feel himself entitled to shape a retrospective view, and to peel off some of the labels his journalistic verve had provided for quick effect in the climate of literary discussion, but others had used as currency that he must be prepared to redeem.

Readers should not, then, be too ready to accept Eliot's statement, "I have written best about writers who have influenced my own poetry."[5] He was entitled to say this; and anyone familiar with his work could instantly recall what essays he had in mind. But such a statement hardly does justice to the kind of imagination that connects the prose and the poetry, or to some of the hitherto uncollected essays and the letters that are in the course of being published. In expressing a justified but perhaps temporary view of his own criticism, Eliot was not primarily thinking about some of his most interesting prose.

If we look further into these early essays and reviews, we will have to recognize that a man's intellectual development, important as that is, differs from his development as an imaginative writer. Of course F. H. Bradley mattered, both for the quality of his thinking and the calmly provocative truthfulness of his manner of statement. And clearly Eliot had a hard time shaking off the fetters of Babbitt.[6] But the Bible probably nourished his mind more deeply (as we might say of nearly every writer considered here). And if Eliot had the wisdom not to attempt a central essay on Shakespeare, to learn all he could about blank verse from other Elizabethan and Jacobean dramatists, that does not mean that Shakespeare was any less alive than Middleton or Marlowe to the poet who wrote "Marina" or could incorporate " 'this music crept by me upon the waters' " in a poem of his own.

In 1917, when Richard Aldington went to serve in France, Eliot became assistant editor of the *Egoist*. The editor and publisher of this now famous "little mag" was Harriet Shaw Weaver, who in defiance of censorship had published Joyce. She also, in 1917, published Eliot's first book of poems, *Prufrock and Other Observations*, in an edition of 500 copies of which 375 were sold by 1921. As Aldington's successor (at a salary of £9 a quarter) Eliot acquired a new group of readers for his review-essays. Only that year two major statements of his thinking about literature had appeared in the *New Statesman* ("Reflections on Vers Libre" and "The Borderline of Prose"). These were quickly followed in the *Egoist* with short articles on contemporary poetry designed to prepare readers for the kind he and Pound and Marianne Moore were already writing, however different each of them was from the others. Likewise— and this is part of the reason why we must think of Eliot not only as a poet and a critic, but as a true writer of imaginative prose—he published in these years some pieces that show conscious reflection on the nature of prose writing.

Two of these appeared within a year, one in the *Egoist* and the other in the *Athenaeum*. Writing first on Henry James, then on Henry Adams, Eliot announced convictions that underlie both his best critical prose and his experience as a poet. He saw James's subject as essentially "a social entity of which men and women are constituents," and "a situation in which several memorable scenes are merely timeless parts, only occurring necessarily in succession." He described James's genius as born of "a mind so fine that no idea could violate it" (as I suggested earlier, an observation that might equally well apply to Sir Thomas Browne). Then Eliot took a position later affirmed in his writings on the metaphysical poets. In England, he said, "ideas run wild and pasture on the emotions; instead of thinking with our feelings (a very different thing) we corrupt our feelings with ideas."[7]

When reviewing *The Education of Henry Adams* for the *Athenaeum*, Eliot had placed his chief emphasis on the American mind or "that fragment of it" Adams represented. Anticipating some of his future statements on scepticism, Eliot here presented "the Boston doubt" as an outgrowth of Unitarianism. In this respect he placed Adams in the company of Emerson—and it is clear that he had given thought to Emerson's life and writing.[8] The whole piece deserves attention; here I wish chiefly to point out that its climax again demonstrates the equation we have noted in the brief essay on Henry James. Expressing his belief that probably "men ripen best through experiences which are at once sensuous and intellectual," that "their keenest ideas have come to them with the quality of a sense-perception; and that their keenest sensuous experience has been 'as if the body thought,'" Eliot found Adams immature in comparison with Henry James.[9]

These two pieces were published earlier than the leading *TLS* article reviewing Grierson's *Metaphysical Poems and Lyrics of the Seventeenth Century*, containing the now well-known phrases such as a "sensuous apprehension of thought." The emphasis on this phrase is not what matters. What matters is that Eliot first conceived it as a phenomenon of great *prose* writing. I shall not try to point out this undercurrent in specific examples of his own prose. Yet, guarded by the logical structure, the "I submit that" or "I infer," "I do not imply," in Eliot's best essays "the sensuous contributor to the intelligence makes the difference."[10]

Two articles, appearing respectively in the *New Statesman* and the *Chapbook*, were born of the controversies of the time with respect to so-called "prose poems." "The Borderline of Prose" is a fine example of the dancing humour to be enjoyed in some of these uncollected essays, where a sequence of names of authors and bits of their real or legendary careers are distilled into fantasy. This permits Eliot subsequently to release a major premise and some telling comparisons. The major premise follows upon a comparison of Rimbaud's *Illuminations* and Aldington's prose poems.

> There is a prose arbitrariness and a verse arbitrariness;
> whichever we are writing, there are moments when we

simply have to conform to the limitations of the medium we have chosen . . . . [S]uccess in either verse or prose consists in the most skilful variations of music, all the while we never allow [the] ground-monotone to become entirely inaudible.[11]

And he proceeds to group F. H. Bradley, Ruskin, and Newman as masters of the English language who achieved in their prose qualities which might be called "poetic," but without trespassing across the borderline.

A few years later the essay "Prose and Verse" in the *Chapbook* explored the problem more fully. This and the associated pieces I am discussing here are related to "Reflections on Vers Libre" and "The Music of Poetry," and must eventually be brought out in future volumes of Eliot's hitherto uncollected writings. Without attempting to analyze or abbreviate the argument of the essay "Prose and Verse," it is important to note that Eliot had been reading Browne, Jeremy Taylor, De Quincey, Poe and others with attention to the phenomena of cadence and imagery. I agree with the general position that he takes in this essay, without stopping to comment on some of its oddities (such as the preference for De Quincey's "Dream Fugue" over *Urn Burial*). Once more linking the faculties of feeling and of thought, Eliot proposes an idea that deserves further exploration. Verse, he maintains, "is always struggling, while remaining verse, to take up to itself more and more of what is prose, to take something more from life and turn it into 'play.' "

And, on the other hand, prose, not being cut off by the barrier of verse which must at the same time be affirmed and diminished, can transmute life in its own way by raising it to the condition of 'play,' *precisely because it is not verse.*"[12]

The insight offered here could lead to a discussion of great interest were it directed to the writing of novelists who approach yet respect the borderline of verse, such as Virginia Woolf, Elizabeth Bowen, and Eudora Welty. It is curious that Eliot did not clearly see how his own conception of the borderline of prose, and the fact that prose as well as poetry could in its different element take life from "play," is verified by the prose of Donne. His brief review of Logan Pearsall Smith's selection of passages from the sermons shows that the reviewer had read the sermons earlier, and given thought to their accomplishment. "As a writer of sermons," he finds "Donne is superior to Latimer, and more mature in style, if not more original . . . than Andrewes. His style is nearer to Taylor or Browne than to either of these."[13] He goes on to suggest that Donne could be as terse or direct as Hakluyt or Raleigh, but that he could not develop his introspective faculty sufficiently because English prose had not developed "in the right direction." This short review is as tantalizing for what it says as for what it does not say. In any case, it provides abundant evidence that Eliot had read a good deal of Elizabethan and of seventeenth-century prose, and had pondered its strength from a writer's as well as a reader's point of view.

When Bruce Richmond, editor of the *Times Literary Supplement,* invited Eliot to contribute leading articles on Elizabethan and Jacobean poetry, especially dramatic poetry, Eliot gained a wider circle of readers. He felt that he had "reached the top rung of the ladder of literary journalism," and many years later paid tribute to

Richmond's training in the responsibility to "write in a temperate and impartial way" when the articles were unsigned.[14] Thinking back on the literary choices made —the elected circle—of several of the writers discussed here, we see that the structure and kind of prose created was in part a function of the chance to get it published, and where it might be published, even of whether it might be paid for. (True, all will admit, of Hazlitt and De Quincey, in a different way of Emerson and Thoreau.) Their best writing was born of love and the need for genius to find its passage out. But none of them would have disowned the imperative to earn his bread, and this sometimes affected the length, emphasis, or tone of a given article or lecture. It accounts in Emerson and Thoreau for the difference between the published prose and the journals. We can see, as we follow Eliot's increasing skill as a prose writer, the difference between some of these *TLS* articles and the review articles written both earlier and later for other periodicals. The publication of his letters is bound to set this work in a new perspective.

He began to put together a book, and *The Sacred Wood* (1920) appeared while he was simultaneously composing *The Waste Land* in his inward mind. The titles of these two works show their affinity (as, later, *For Lancelot Andrewes* and *Ash Wednesday* were to do). Eliot had discovered by himself what no one could have told him about the way the poetry of some of the Elizabethan and Jacobean dramatists worked in their plays. We can see in *The Waste Land* and "Gerontion" an intensity, a simultaneous capture and release of reverberations of experience not possible in Eliot's earlier poems, when he was more under the influence of Laforgue. It is natural that he should have made these interests predominate in *The Sacred Wood*.

Nevertheless, it is equally important that Eliot placed at the beginning of *The Sacred Wood* several articles about critics, in which he is in part at least concerned with the critic's prose as an index to his literary sensibility and analytical power. He does not refuse praise to Swinburne's criticism—ultimately he finds him lacking in penetration. And what is the test? It is Swinburne's inability to detect in Chapman a quality akin to Donne. That is the "quality of sensuous thought, or of thinking through the senses . . ."[15] possessed, Eliot believed, also by Shakespeare, Marlowe, Webster. One is struck by the fact that these now deceptively glossed-over terms were evolved by Eliot in his criticism of *prose* writers, not of poets alone. Indeed, in such language not only had he contrasted Henry Adams and Henry James, but placed favorably in a surprising trio James, F. H. Bradley, and Sir James Frazer.[16]

The reappearance of this concept in *The Sacred Wood* is a clue to Eliot's appraisal of prose writers as well as poets. But it remains, as it were, a thread in the evolving pattern. More impressive is the manifest desire to provide a theoretical foundation to his criticism in the three essays, "Tradition and the Individual Talent," "The Perfect Critic," and "The Function of Criticism." Two of these were included in his book, the third in one of the early years of the *Criterion* (1923). They all show the strength of his philosophical training, and the brevity of statement compelled by reviewing or one kind of lecturing.

"Tradition and the Individual Talent" evolves out of mutually related, but not mutually dependent, propositions. This essay is well known but will never seem familiar. There is the positing of a tradition in which works of art exist in a simultaneous order, such that the addition of a new work of art not only endows it with a significant relationship with those of the past, but alters the existing order, and "the relations, proportions, values of each work of art towards the whole are readjusted" (p. 5). Then there is the conception that the poet's awareness of this whole is, first, an awareness of the mind of his country and of the European mind; it is, second, "what makes a writer most acutely conscious of his place in time, of his own contemporaneity"; third, this sense of tradition implies a kind of "depersonalization" by the poet and a consequent purification of attention by the reader (p. 4).

The positions taken in this profound and beneficent discourse, announced with a kind of starkness that has caused some of them to be misunderstood, underlie all Eliot's criticism, although he has considerably modified his use of the principle of depersonalization.

By it he is chiefly concerned to deny any one-to-one correspondence between the personal experience of the writer and the feelings or emotions given life in a poem (or presumably any imaginative work). The principle is at the heart of what later came to be called the New Criticism; it is the refutation of the biographical fallacy, just as the conception of tradition as a simultaneous order sets aside the historical fallacy. In this respect Eliot progressed far beyond Arnold. Together these principles attest the uniqueness and integrity of the individual work of art, and its living relationship to, its sustenance by, other works of art. Yet Eliot never is deflected to any of the flyovers that claim authority for criticism above the writing that gives it reason for being.

One notices also in this early essay the prevalence of

examples from Dante, who, together with Shakespeare, is to form a polar reference in Eliot's thought. Also in "Tradition and the Individual Talent," there is suggested and emphasized the possible unity of apparently disparate feelings and images, which Eliot is later to explore significantly in his discussion of the metaphysical poets, as well as to create in both *The Waste Land* and *Four Quartets.*

In the manner (although not, I believe, in the purpose) of announcing "depersonalization" as a value there is a reflection of the spirit in Eliot that denies. (We are often aware of it, paradoxically, in some of his pronouncements about religion.) It is even more apparent in "The Perfect Critic," where it leads him to the deliberate and distorting assertion that "a literary critic should have no emotions except those immediately provoked by a work of art."[17] But in this somewhat eccentric and irritable essay there is pure nutriment, nevertheless. It is to be found in his description of Aristotle as one who, in the *Poetics,* "provides an eternal example—not of laws, or even of method, for there is no method except to be very intelligent, but of intelligence itself swiftly operating the analysis of sensation to the point of principle and definition."[18] This and two other statements make the essay occupy an essential place in Eliot's criticism (even though he did not reprint it in his *Selected Essays*). One is the recognition that in the experience of works of art "An impression needs to be constantly refreshed by new impressions in order that it may persist at all; it needs to take its place in a system of impressions."[19] The other is a related principle, that "the perceptions do not, in a really appreciative mind, accumulate as a mass, but form themselves as a structure; and criticism is the statement in language of this structure; it is a development of sensibility."[20] These constructive formulations quite surpass the scattered but not unilluminating references in this essay to the criticism of Coleridge and Swinburne, Arnold and Arthur Symons.

Certain strains and stresses of the writer for the periodical press appear in the third of the important early theoretical essays by Eliot, "The Function of Criticism," published in the *Criterion* in 1923. These faults mark many of the pieces he wrote for that magazine, as well as one of his books that I shall not discuss, *After Strange Gods*.[21] These are principally an attitude of seeming superiority to people whose faults the writer deplores, and an attempt to borrow virtue from symbolic authority. Were these Eliot's essential rather than his transitory qualities, I could not praise him. For instance, in "The Function of Criticism" he imagines that "the possessors of the inner voice ride ten in a compartment to a football match at Swansea, listening to the inner voice, which breathes the eternal message of vanity, fear, and lust" (p. 16). A condemnation understandably spoken by the author of *The Waste Land*, but more ephemerally than in his poetry. But the title and some of the commentaries in the *Criterion* fail to do justice to the editor's hospitality to the individual talents of men whose ideas he opposed—such as Hugh McDiarmuid or W. H. Auden.

Allowing for some of these less significant asides, "The Function of Criticism" is valuable for two affirmations. One is that art, including literature, is autotelic (a word that does not appear in most dictionaries, including the *OED*). The second position that Eliot takes in this essay is never openly enough stated: that is, that there are literary facts that may be shown in the interpretation of a literary work, and can perhaps best be shown by the practitioner. Eliot perhaps goes too far in acknowledging the value of facts disclosed by historical research when he says, "And any book, any essay, any note in *Notes and Queries*, which produces a fact even of the lowest order about a work of art is a better piece of work than nine-tenths of the most pretentious critical journalism, in journals or in books" (p. 21). This pronouncement comes from a failure to point out the difference between facts *in* literature and facts *about* literature.

Facts in literature inhere in its autotelic character—if autotelic is a suitable word. I should prefer to say that literature is a notation of experience in language, constituting a unique mode of thought and feeling. When we read with our best response to language and the shape of experience, and their interaction, we consciously or unconsciously observe the facts *in* literature.

I shall leave comment on Eliot's statement about autotelism for a discussion later in this chapter of his position on poetry and belief. Here I am concerned first with his writing about the facts *in* literature, as it appears in several distinct groups of essays.

The essays on Elizabethan and Jacobean drama appearing chiefly in the *Times Literary Supplement*, over a period ranging from 1919 to 1931, are different in tone from the early theoretical articles I have been concerned with. The theoretical articles are addressed, in a sense, to the world of the man of letters. They are part of the dialogue of the writer with the writer, an appeal for an examination of purpose and assumptions, an appeal also to the committed reader who is willing to make distinctions. Hence their somewhat oracular tone—and there is also a certain amount of fencing with other men of letters like J. Middleton Murry, editor of the *Athenaeum*, for which one of these articles was written. In the *TLS* articles on dramatists, there is a simpler introduction of leading ideas. Like Virginia Woolf's reviews for the *TLS*, Eliot's are addressed to the common reader, although he does offer that reader the free play of imagination that Mrs. Woolf excels in, or the individuality of rhythm in sentence and paragraph, or the haunting quality of an image:

> Death, oblivion, and rest lap round your songs with their dark wave. And then, incongrously, a sound of scurrying and laughter is heard. There is the patter of animals' feet and the odd guttural notes of rooks and the snufflings of obtuse furry animals grunting and nosing. For you were not a pure saint by any means.[22]

In the essays on the dramatists, Eliot is concerned both with what may be called experiential structure and with the rhythm of blank verse, which is of course an aspect of language. The reader is bound to be stimulated by Eliot's awareness of the variety inherent in drama as a literary form. What critic before him had seen this as clearly? Replying to those who feel some inadequacy in Ben Jonson's characters, Eliot distinguishes successfully between Jonson and Beaumont and Fletcher. The appeal of the latter to "emotions and associations which they have not themselves grasped" is hollow. "It is superficial with a vacuum behind it; the superficies of Jonson is solid. . . . a man cannot be accused of dealing superficially with the world which he himself has created; the superficies *is* the world. Jonson's characters conform to the logic of the emotions of their world" (p. 135). This announcement comes with special interest from the man who was later to write *The Cocktail*

*Party* and *The Confidential Clerk*. It implies a judgment as to the scope of the area of human life on which the dramatist's (or novelist's) work depends.

Thus, although Eliot selects his ground carefully—a necessary skill in the composition of articles of this length—he is no disembodied critic. Neither does he assume a tone of superiority to the dramatists with whom he deals. If he acknowledges an imperfection or disappointment, it is in relation to what might reasonably be done by that kind of talent, in relation also to what has been successfully accomplished, to the conditions too of staging and the taste of the audience. If Middleton provides the audience with the expected Italianate horrors, "yet underneath we feel always a quiet and undisturbed vision of things as they are and not 'another thing.' . . . Middleton was a great observer of human nature, without fear, without sentiment, without prejudice" (pp. 145, 147). In essay after essay of this group, a new willingness from the reader is called upon —the reader whose interest without this dialogue might flag from the sheer detail of convention and attitude in a bygone age of the theater.

Whatever a poet may lack, he has to have a good ear; Eliot has a fine one, and makes uncommon use of it in his criticism. Any of his observations in this realm are worth pondering. I cannot remember any historian of literature before him who linked Spenser with Marlowe; Eliot does so surprisingly and unforgettably when he says "There had been no great blank verse before Marlowe; but there was the powerful presence of this great master of melody immediately precedent; and the combination produced results which could not be repeated" (p. 102). The poet of "Gerontion" has full authority to point out that "Every writer who has writ-

ten any blank verse worth saving has produced particular tones which his verse and no other's is capable of
rendering" ( p. 101). This fact, and others related to it,
claim Eliot's willing attention in these essays on the
dramatists. But his interest is never limited to the technical, he is concerned above all to show that "blank
verse within Shakespeare's lifetime was more highly developed, . . . became the vehicle of more varied and
intense feeling than it has ever conveyed since" (p. 100).
He always unites the technical with what it exists to
serve, as when he sees that "in Middleton's tragedy
there is a strain of realism underneath, *which is one with
the poetry. . .*" (p. 146).

The lines that connect expression to feeling, emotion
and idea, and these latter to each other, led Eliot to his
admiration of the metaphysical poets, and are well illustrated in his central essay on them. If some of his
formulations have been overworked by others, and
therefore called into question by such a historian as
Miss Rosemond Tuve, the formulations in my opinion
are nevertheless telling and the essay remains a classic.
"Tradition and the Individual Talent" should have
made it clear that we are not restricted to discussing
poets in the vocabulary of their own time, revealing as
that may be. In placing Milton among the other poets
of his age or offering reasons for the disappearance of
the unified sensibility attributed to Donne and his
school, Eliot has confessed his own inaccuracy. But in
illustrating a "direct sensuous apprehension of thought"
in the different forms it takes with the differing poets
of this nevertheless natural grouping, Eliot is bound
to waken sensibility in all who read him for the first
time on Donne or Herbert, Herbert of Cherbury or
Marvell. Granted all the refinements and sophistications

that have followed in articles and books, the first insight is cast like the dry fly by an expert, to catch a trout, not harpoon a trout as if it were a whale.

These essays we have been considering, both those on the dramatists and others on poets, are shaped appropriately for publication in the weeklies and monthlies where they appeared. A few clear formulations mark each, there are linked ideas but no larger pattern, nor is there an overt relationship to an audience. Meanwhile some very short pieces, many deserving to be reprinted, were the products of talks Eliot gave for the BBC. One of them was "The Genesis of Philosophic Prose,"[23] which deserves attention for its place in the discussion of prose as a literary medium. Several talks preceded it, on Elizabethan prose translations, travel narratives, the lively Grub Street writing of Nashe or Deloney, the "pulpit oratory" of Donne. In these, but most firmly in "Bacon and Hooker," Eliot resumed the examination of questions raised in articles almost ten years earlier. We see his continuing interest in the problem, as he weighs the accomplishment of notable prose writers at the end of the Elizabethan age and in the early seventeenth century.

Formidable as the subject of Bacon and Hooker might seem for a broadcast talk, Eliot quickly indicates why an attentive listener could make sense of it. Catching hold of points he had previously emphasized about the variety and vitality of Elizabethan writing, he introduces an all-too-brief comment on the prose of the great dramatists. There is "the heightened style of Jonson . . . the most intelligent man of his time." This typically challenging judgment is made more acceptable by the just observation that "There is no finer prose than Shakespeare's," which Eliot rightly terms unique.[24]

But after these tributes and acknowledgment of the virtues of Browne or Burton or Taylor, it becomes clear that Eliot prefers to regard himself as one of the sons of Bacon and Hooker. He remarks in the satirists a certain "boyishness," and in other prose writers of these days (looking back to the Tudors or forward to Hobbes and Clarendon) a "stiffness" resulting from the fact that their intellectual antecedents were in Latin, not English prose. What separates all these writers from Bacon or Hooker is a difference of *mind*, he argues. This hinges upon a quality he was to look for in other writers, maturity in the whole tenor of the prose: "in Bacon you find the very mature virtue of concision and spareness."[25] He, and Hooker, are "the fathers of the modern abstract style," the prose style for philosophy or law or any subject "in which exact reasoning, classification and exposition of ideas is the first thing; of prose which is truly prose, not merely prose aspiring after the condition of poetry."[26]

Now we have come to a description that suits Eliot's own style in his strongest essays—although this description is not here related to the possibility that a writer's keenest ideas may come to him "with the quality of a sense-perception . . . 'as if the body thought.' "[27] This factor, however controlled, provides the undercurrent of vitality in the essays of Eliot that will long continue to be read. The "influence" of Bradley upon Eliot is not all-important. What matters more is that Eliot's ability to think philosophically was a source of strength to him even if he wisely let it remain a latent strength, at the service of "the sensuous contributor to the intelligence."

By 1929, then, Eliot had a number of papers that might have been revised and grouped for a book on "The Use of Prose and the Uses of Language." Or it might have been called "Kinds of Thinking and Kinds of Prose." Instead, he published *For Lancelot Andrewes* and a few years later returned to America to give the lectures contained in *The Use of Poetry and The Use of Criticism.*[28] Enough has now been said of Eliot's theoretical interest in prose to make it unnecessary to comment on the essays on Lancelot Andrewes or John Bramhall. But, since Eliot's famous preface to *For Lancelot Andrewes* has caused that book to be seen from the point of view of his Anglo-Catholicism, "classicism," and "royalism," we should note the preoccupation in many of the essays with the qualities of prose itself. The subtitle of the book, *Essays on Style and Order,* perhaps identifies it better than the exclamatory dedication *For Lancelot Andrewes.* Not only in the Andrewes essay, or the Bramhall, but equally in the "Niccolò Machiavelli" and the "F. H. Bradley" ones, Eliot is concerned with style as a way of achieving order (not rule, but a kind of clarity). When we read of Andrewes' "passion for order"[29] we think of the "rage for order" that is the climax of a well-known poem by Wallace Stevens. We can see why Eliot's command of the "modern abstract style" could be consonant with the power of feeling. It is really the equilibrium of these two that is his special contribution to the development of imaginative prose.

The Harvard lectures that furnish the text of *The Use of Poetry and the Use of Criticism* show a change from the BBC lectures and from the essays written for periodicals. There was less need to explain or to refute, less need for the provocative phrase. In future years Eliot, now accepted as the representative man of letters of his century, was to lecture widely, in Wales and Ireland and in Paris and Hamburg, to the Virgil Society, to students in American as well as British universities. Lectures of this nature are brought together in a major book, *On Poetry and Poets*, and will also be found to differ in style from the periodical essays and reviews. There appears in *The Use of Poetry and the Use of Criticism* a willingness to account for the judgments made, an element of intellectual autobiography, that is even more noticeable in *On Poetry and Poets*, leading to what Marianne Moore has called "T. S. Eliot's reticent candor."[30]

*The Use of Poetry and the Use of Criticism* brings into relationship the greater and the lesser but no less real art. "Our talking about poetry," Eliot holds, and exemplifies, "is a part of, an extension of, our experience of it; and as a good deal of thinking has gone to the making of poetry, so a good deal may well go to the study of it" (p. 18). Further, the nature and aims of poetry and criticism arise from a similar chance and a similar need. Poetry "takes life from the people's speech and in turn gives life to it; and represents its highest point of consciousness" (p. 15). It follows that changing direction in the development of poetry is a symptom of social change. Criticism, in its turn, is "a process of readjustment between poetry and the world in and for which it is produced" (p. 27).

From fundamentals such as these Eliot conducts his discourse on poet-critics ranging from Sidney to Matthew Arnold, establishing more firmly his place among them. Throughout he is aware of the need for each age to make a reappraisal of the past, and this awareness leads him to a more adequate understanding of, for example, Wordsworth, than might have been expected of one of Eliot's temperament. He openly admits the connection between Wordsworth's greatness and what he thought—the beginning of his greatness stemming, one knows, from revolutionary ideas uncongenial to Eliot. (About Wordsworth, incidentally, he remarks that the revolutionary and the reactionary are not necessarily far apart—a remark we may be tempted to apply sadly to Eliot himself.)[31]

Throughout this book there are scattered seminal observations, ranging from the poet's right to borrow inventively, to the nature of auditory imagination, to the recurrence of images in the poet's mind, or the interaction of prose and verse. I choose for the moment, however, to focus attention on two important aspects. One is Eliot's attitude toward the means of entry into the writer's work of his own experience. The second is the question interdependent with the first, of poetry and belief.

Although from passages in "Tradition and the Individual Talent" it would appear that Eliot's attitude toward the writer's experience is an almost ascetic one, this—as I tried to intimate in the discussion of that essay—is not the whole truth. The attitude toward experience there conveyed is governed chiefly by the desire to avoid, or better to challenge, the biographic fallacy, the tendency to interpret a writer's work in terms of his life. Or even worse, to fictionalize his life by shredding and reprocessing, attempting to corner the words, lines, allusions of the poem. But at various points in the essays on the dramatists and on other poets, Eliot does recognize the true impact of experience upon the work of art. For example, in his essay on John Ford he wrote, "it is suggested, then, that a dramatic poet cannot create characters of the greatest intensity of life unless his personages in their reciprocal actions and behaviour in their story, are somehow dramatizing, but in no obvious form, an action or struggle for harmony in the soul of the poet" (pp. 172-173). In the important introduction to the *Selcted Poems of Ezra Pound*[32] Eliot gives his best account of the separate channels taken by the accumulation of experience and the mastery of form, until the one meets the other in a perfected work. This, in my opinion, is an improvement upon the metaphor of the catalytic filament of platinum in "Tradition and the Individual Talent." Later, in *The Use of Poetry and the Use of Criticism*, Eliot gives one of his clearest explanations of this problem:

> And what is the experience that the poet is so bursting to communicate? By the time it has settled down into a poem it may be so different from the original experience as to be hardly recognizable. The "experience" in question may be the result of a fusion of feelings so numerous, and ultimately so obscure in their origins, that even if there be communication of them, the poet may hardly be aware of what he is communicating; and *what is there to be communicated was not in existence before the poem was completed* (p. 138, italics added).

There follows from (and precedes) this view the principle that the meaning of the poem is the poem itself; and therefore attempts to elucidate the poem by pointing to its language, structure, or scale of reference can never be exhaustive, final, or complete.

> *If* poetry is a form of 'communication,' yet that which is to be communicated is the poem itself. . . . The poem's existence is somewhere between the writer and the reader . . . (p. 30).
> . . . what a poem means is as much what it means to others as what it means to the author . . . (p. 130).

From this must be derived a doctrine of intellectual freedom that Eliot, at this time in his life at least, was unable to articulate.[33] But he does see, I think, that a kind of pluralism in literary interpretation is valid.

What, then, of the interlinked problem of "poetry and belief"? Eliot had first grappled with this problem in his little book on Dante (1929). He was no doubt trying to assist readers like myself who cannot read the *Inferno* without admiring the poetry and being repelled by the denials of love and valour therein ranked—Ulysses in hell? Eliot takes what seems on first consideration the only tenable view, that we can, we must undertake the willing suspension of disbelief; that to enjoy the poetry it is not necessary to subscribe as a private individual to the philosophic or religious tenets that give the poem substance. In the note to chapter two of his Dante, Eliot characterizes his view of the general problem involved as embryonic. While denying that the reader must share the beliefs of the poet to enjoy the poetry, at a further point in his discussion he admits that "it is possible, and sometimes necessary, to argue that full understanding must identify itself with full belief."[34] The seeming opposition between these two positions is reconciled by the view that "Each is true only within a limited field of discourse" and that "unless you limit fields of discourse, you can have no discourse at all." He rejects Richards' term "pseudo-statement" for statements affirming a value or belief.

Presumably if we understand literature as entering into two or more fields of discourse, in one it would still be "autotelic" while in another it might be esteemed or questioned by the understanding we have through revealed other experience. Such a choice is clearly indicated by the initial position of Eliot's "Religion and

Literature" (1935): "Literary criticism should be completed by criticism from a definite ethical and theological standpoint. . . . The 'greatness' of literature cannot
be determined solely by literary standards; though we
must remember that whether it is literature or not can
be determined only by literary standards."[35] But for
many writers—say Chaucer or Henry James—the poised
terms "poetry and belief" present a strained or irrelevant framework. The whole question is more satisfac-
torily presented by Eliot in *The Use of Poetry*:

> When the doctrine, theory, belief or 'view of life' pre-
> sented in a poem is one which the mind of the reader
> can accept as coherent, mature, and founded on the facts
> of experience, it interposes no obstacle to the reader's
> enjoyment, whether it be one that he accept or deny,
> approve or deprecate (p. 96).

And here we may for the moment let the matter
rest. If Eliot had been guided by the wisdom of this
principle, he would have spared himself the writing of
his next brief set of lectures, *After Strange Gods*, in
which he castigates some of the finest modern writers
for what he deems their heresies. Since I am concerned
chiefly with Eliot's achievement in making literary criticism a channel for imaginative prose, I shall not discuss this book, which is an attempt at ex cathedra pronouncement, neither imaginative nor in the true sense
critical.

Fundamentally, Eliot is generous, in spite of the tone
of severity he assumes when advancing against literary
or other supposed Philistines. Generosity, and the "reticent candor" mark *On Poetry and Poets*.[36] The essays
in this volume (many of them, as I have pointed out,
delivered as lectures) are freely composed. The readiness

to parry a possible opponent, or to deliver a sharp point to the resistant reader that is natural in essays for the periodical press are absent here. Instead, the tone of dialogue more openly prevails.

The dialogues are about the resources of individual poets, and the resources of poetry, and the reader's means of discovering these. Most of these essays bear the pattern of an exchange of ideas with the audience, or potential reader-listener. There underlies them an attempt to clarify and persuade, different from the more plainly declarative or even authoritative tone of Eliot's early criticism.

The newness of these later essays partly consist in the purpose of simultaneously locating and formulating an enlightening question. For example, generations of readers and critics were content to consider some poetry "minor," without asking what the decision implied. Eliot's title "What is Minor Poetry?" itself stimulates a reconsideration. Yet, as in other crucial questions raised in this book, no one had asked this question, or asked it as simply and relevantly, before.

Speaking upon this topic to the Bookmen of Swansea and West Wales, Eliot is as tender-handed as if he had a plover's egg to uncover. He takes up and puts down the faded volumes waiting for the clear-eyed buyer to find. As usual, his procedure is analytic, but by gentle stages. He invites an easy attention by the proposition that minor poetry is poetry we are likely to read only in anthologies. Soon, however, he is closer on the trail as he distinguishes between Herbert and Herrick, Herbert and Campion. He leads his listeners to a major question as he separates the poet who repeats successes of the same kind from one whose work taken as a whole is more than the sum of its parts—the question Yeats had in mind when he spoke of the way poems light one another. Eliot ponders the problem of the long poem as a constituent in the writer's *oeuvre*. Finally, he challenges the bookseller and, potentially, readers, to recognize the genuine qualities in new poetry, without trying to rank it comparatively.

The observation to be made here is that in this friendly and relatively simple discourse Eliot has persevered to the delivery of an important principle that no critic before him had clarified. By asking subsidiary questions he formulates one central one, and at the end the reader can continue the exploration in many different ways. And in this discourse, the critic has been good company. "When we talk about Poetry, with a capital P, we are apt to think only of the more intense emotion or the more magical phrase; nevertheless there are a great many casements in poetry which are not magic, and which do not open on the foam of perilous seas, but are perfectly good windows for all that" (p. 49). Perhaps because for Eliot the poet the sacred and profane may inhabit the same neighbourhood, there is no humbug in him as critic.

By a similar careful procedure Eliot progresses, in "The Social Function of Poetry," to his own characteristic answer. First he indicates answers that have been given, or might be, to this problem. He discards them not as invalid but as probably less universally valid than the one he proposes. It has to do, but on a different level, with the reciprocal exchange of experience between the writer and other people—a phenomenon with which, as I have tried to show, Eliot was rather differently concerned in his essays on dramatists and on the metaphysical poets. He explains here the poet's duty to his language:

We may say that the duty of the poet, as poet, is only indirectly to his people: his direct duty is to his *language*, first to preserve, and second to extend and improve. In expressing what other people feel he is also changing the feeling by making it more conscious; he is making people more aware of what they feel already, and therefore teaching them something about themselves. But he . . . is also individually different from other people, and from other poets too, and can make his readers share consciously in new feelings which they had not experienced before (p. 20).

This is a power which Eliot in various asides on Shakespeare had attributed to him, but which in this essay is considered for its more general bearing. As Eliot develops this point of view, he sees it as a cultural phenomenon of the widest significance. He believes that the language of poetry "makes a difference to the speech, to the sensibility, to the lives of all the members of a society, . . . whether they read and enjoy poetry or not: even, in fact, whether they know the names of their greatest poets or not" (p. 22). It is true likewise that as experience and sensibility change, language changes, and there follows the need of each generation for new poetry—by which (as in "Tradition and the Individual Talent") older poetry retains its life. Further, should a slice of the present, or a particular people, lack living poetry, a deterioration of the whole culture results. There is an obvious relationship between this essay and Eliot's *Notes Towards the Definition of Culture*; in both he is a committed man of letters concerned with the life of a whole society.

In "The Music of Poetry," he is dealing with seemingly more technical issues and this essay should be grouped with the "Reflections on 'Vers Libre'" and "Ezra Pound: His Metric and Poetry," which were rescued from oblivion in *To Criticize the Critic*. But again Eliot directs attention to the relationship between poetry and the ordinary language that we hear. This leads him to the delicate divide, and bridge, between music and meaning. "If, as we are aware, only part of the meaning can be conveyed by paraphrases, that is because the poet is occupied with frontiers of consciousness beyond which words fail, though meanings still exist" (p. 30). He is led more openly than in some of the earlier essays I discussed to the pluralism that I believe was latent there:

> A poem may appear to mean very different things to different readers, and all of these meanings may be different from what the author thought he meant. For instance, the author may have been writing [about] some peculiar personal experience, which he saw quite unrelated to anything outside; yet for the reader the poem may become the expression of a general situation, as well as of some private experience of his own. The reader's interpretation may differ from the author's and be equally valid—it may even be better (pp. 30-31).

The illuminations of "The Music of Poetry" are rich and inexhaustible. Among them is a wise observation on the variations, including dissonance, necessary to the music of the long poem, so that "it may be said that no poet can write a poem of amplitude unless he is a master of the prosaic" (p. 32). And in a decisive footnote Eliot adds that this is a counterpart to Arnold's doctrine of touchstones, testing the greatness of a poet by "the way he writes his less intense, but structurally vital matter." It is a test which readers of the *Four Quartets* must be aware of as they turn from the music of a sestina to passages building poetry out of the rhythms of prose.

"The Music of Poetry," like "Reflections on 'Vers Libre,'" contains observations that nobody else has set down on free verse and on the poet's awareness and choice of metres. There is the vital declaration that "no verse is free for the man who wants to do a good job" (p. 37) together with the recognition that it was a "preparation for new form . . . an insistence upon the inner unity which is unique to every poem, against the outer unity which is typical." While the earlier of these two essays manifests some of the asperity, even irritability, that appears occasionally in Eliot's early prose, "The Music of Poetry" is one of his truest exploratory efforts, with valuable comment on the music of Shakespeare's poetry and priceless indications of new possibilities for verse.

A pair of essays that form a good contrast are "Poetry and Drama" and "The Three Voices of Poetry." D. Nichol Smith said that no critic has been freer than Dryden to admit the reader to his own studio.[37] This freedom is conspicuously present in Eliot's "Poetry and Drama." Without self-consciousness, indeed with evident modesty, he accompanies himself through the decisions, mistakes, successes found in his own writing of plays. This is a dialogue between the accomplished writer and the apprentice writer, although there is plenty to enlighten the ordinary reader as to the ingredients of poetic drama. Anyone who would again experiment in the theatre with a form of verse derived from modern speech has much to learn from it—as from the discussion of verse for drama in the lecture on Yeats. "What is necessary is a beauty which shall not be in the line or the isolable passage, but woven into the dramatic texture itself; so that you can hardly say whether the lines give grandeur to the drama, or whether it is the drama which turns the words into poetry" (p. 260).

"The Three Voices of Poetry," in contrast to "Poetry and Drama," is not so much a dialogue as a meditation. The question posed requires us to think not so much of the writer's relation to his readers or hearers—although Eliot answers it in these terms—as of the way he takes up the material of his art. The first voice, that of the writer speaking to himself or no one, the voice of lyric or, Eliot would prefer to say, meditative poetry, governs *Ash Wednesday* and the *Four Quartets*. The second, that of the poet addressing an audience, whether large or small, enters into *The Waste Land* at times and is present in satiric poems like "The Hippopotamus." The third, that of the creation of a dramatic character speaking in verse, Eliot has of course experimented with widely. But for me what Eliot has to say of the first voice, and, relying on Gottfried Benn for illustration, on the creative germ of lyric poetry, is what matters most. And, in fact, in distinguishing the "voices," and concluding that they are rarely exclusively present, Eliot has done much to advance discussion of a question that has been of increasing interest in modern criticism.[38]

The resort to Gottfried Benn for a helpful analogy in this essay typifies Eliot's awareness of continental thought as of European literature generally, a point that distinguishes his criticism throughout. His preoccupation with this potentially wider area of cultural as well as specifically literary problems marks two of his short books. I have not undertaken to discuss Eliot's *Notes towards a Definition of Culture* or *The Idea of a Christian Society* because I do not think they extend his range as a writer of prose. No doubt both are significant as evidence of his sense of the time he lived in, and the substance of the loyalties he defended. I do want to record my opinion that neither of these books is fascist in tendency, however deplorable may be the ambiguities in the *Criterion* editorials before Eliot had learned the true tenor of fascism and nazism.[39] In any case, he seems to me always ill at ease in speaking of social or political problems, or those of organized religion. "As kingfishers catch fire, dragonflies draw flames," and the life and colour of Eliot's prose lives when he enters the world he intimately knows, the writer's and the reader's experience of literature.

Eliot's persistent sense of a potential underlying unity between European and English literature strengthens his various essays on Dante, his "Virgil and the Christian World," and "What is a Classic?" This is a resource and a concern that Eliot shares with Arnold. The simplicity and order of the essay on Virgil are an accompaniment of the whole theme. It finds an open channel in the major essay, "Goethe as the Sage"; and here, too, there is a major expansion of Eliot's gifts as prose writer and critic.

Eliot's views about Milton seem not to have changed much between the writing of "Milton I" and "Milton II." But his views of Goethe changed radically from the awkward dismissal of him in *The Use of Poetry* to "Goethe as the Sage." And it is striking when a critic can not only overcome an early inadequacy, but overcome it with such magnanimity and thoroughness.

He starts from the principle that in overcoming an initial lack of sympathy with some great writer, it is ourselves that we remake, that an effort of self-criticism is called for. Proceeding from this idea of reconciliation, he goes on to describe the writer who, transcending nationality, deserves to be called European, as possessing abundance in his productivity, an amplitude of interests and sympathies, and a unity derived from the inner cohesion of various works. Dante, Shakespeare, and Goethe are the ones he relies on to exemplify the fulfillment of these tests—I wish he had added Tolstoy.[40] (But he voluntarily confined his discourse to poets.)

Adding to these vital and essential qualities the fact of representativeness (which may sometimes place a man in conflict, as well as in tune with his age), Eliot poses a more difficult, a procreative question. Having restated his position on poetry and belief, and reaffirmed the phenomenon of suspended disbelief, as well as the necessity to reject what is either vile or nonsensical, he builds upon his awareness of what wisdom is. On his first reckoning with this concept, he has told us that "the wisdom of a human being resides as much in silence as in speech" and that "wisdom is a native gift of intuition, ripened and given application by experience, for understanding the nature of things, certainly of living things, most certainly of the human heart" (p. 221). This ineffable understanding is an indispensable quality of great poetry, and in apprehending it we must simultaneously apprehend the poetry as poetry. And it is for the sake of learning wisdom that we must frequent such men as Goethe, overcoming by willing effort any early sense of uncongeniality. By such reconciliation we ourselves may become wiser through the knowledge of literature. "For wisdom is communicated on a deeper level than that of logical propositions; all language is inadequate, but probably the language of poetry is the language most capable of communicating wisdom" (p. 226).

I think it is not too much to say that in this essay (and in many passages of other essays) Eliot has evolved from critical intelligence the free insight of a meditative thinker. It is for this reason that I have chosen him as the final writer to be discussed in this book.

He has respected, at the same time that he has extended, the "Frontiers of Criticism." In that essay, against the claims of geneticists who would account for sources, as well as of those he wittily calls the "lemon squeezer" school, who would write *id est demonstrandum* after every line, phrase, metaphor, Eliot maintains against all comers that the end of literature is understanding and enjoyment, and they are indivisible. He once more defends a priceless freedom. Freedom for the reader to read, freedom from cant or categories for the critic.

Even when one does not agree with Eliot, he rarely advances an opinion that is not worth testing. There is progress in his criticism, there is development, but the start was instinctively in the direction of truth of statement and honesty of apprehension. There were moments of autocracy, there were flashes of irritation along the way, but the movement was toward the wisdom he is entitled to praise. An indispensable and uncommon virtue in Eliot's prose is a clarity which is never obtained at the expense of discretion or sublety of thought. He is capable of—and sometimes later embarrassed by— the formulaic phrase, but increasingly he escapes the need for it. But there are certain constancies, appearing early and late, that identify a sensibility. Throughout, integrity prevails. In his lecture on Yeats he saw the "Character of the Artist" as "a kind of moral, as well as intellectual excellence." Such excellence marks, and is communicated in, Eliot's dialogues with the reader and with the writer.

Thinking of his future readers, it is not hard and it is not easy to place T. S. Eliot among the writers of imaginative prose. The others—from Donne and Browne to Hazlitt, De Quincey, Emerson, and Thoreau—are of the same lineage. Backward and forward, the imagination of each opens light into another's. T. S. Eliot chose the collateral line of Hooker and Andrewes. If he ever read Owen Felltham, we cannot say—but Felltham's desire for a sense of order in life, his neatness and precision, and care for the value of a single word, resemble Eliot's. The praise Eliot gave to Andrewes for "ordonnance, or arrangement and structure, precision in the use of words, and relevant intensity," might without deceit be applied to many of his own collected and uncollected essays. Neither he, nor any modern writer of prose that is not fiction, could re-awaken rhythm and imagery like that of Donne, Browne, De Quincey. Nor could he naturally recapture the conversation in progress of Hazlitt, the free meditative patterns of Emerson, or the singular exploratory narratives of Thoreau. Eliot recognized that this kind of prose, approaching yet respecting the borderline of poetry, perhaps can only have its future in the novel. He learned, by reading great predecessors in the art of prose, that at the heart of both prose and poetry is veracity, to be sought in the best available form.

# Notes

## Introduction

[1] *Biographia Literaria*, ed. J. Shawcross, 2 vols. (Oxford, 1907) II, 12.

[2] See G. P. Krapp, *The Rise of English Literary Prose* (New York, 1915); George Saintsbury, *A History of English Prose Rhythm* (London, 1912); George Williamson, *The Senecan Amble* (London, 1951); F. P. Wilson, *Seventeenth Century Prose* (Berkeley, 1960); James Sutherland, *On English Prose* (Toronto, 1957). Morris Croll's most important articles appeared in *Schelling Anniversary Papers* (New York, 1923) and *Studies in English Philology*, ed. K. Malone and M. B. Ruud (Minneapolis, 1929). They are included in the posthumous collection *Style, Rhetoric, and Rhythm*, ed. J. Max Patrick et al. (Princeton, 1965).

³ W. K. Wimsatt, Jr., and Monroe C. Beardsley, "The Intentional Fallacy," in *The Verbal Icon* (Lexington, Kentucky, 1954).

⁴ Henry James, Preface to *The Awkward Age*, in *The Art of the Novel* (New York and London, 1934), pp. 109-110.

⁵ W. K. Wimsatt, Jr., *The Prose Style of Samuel Johnson* (New Haven, 1941).

⁶ *Selected Essays from the Rambler, Adventurer and Idler*, ed. W. J. Bate (New Haven and London, 1968), p. xxix.

⁷ Emily Dickinson.

⁸ T. S. Eliot, "Bruce Lyttelton Richmond," *TLS* January 13, 1961.

⁹ "The Study of Poetry," in *Essays in Criticism*, Second Series (London, 1889), pp. 2-3.

¹⁰ Henry James, Preface to *The Spoils of Poynton, op. cit.*, p. 120.

## Chapter One

¹ Quotations from Donne's sermons in this chapter are from *The Sermons of John Donne*, ed. George R. Potter and Evelyn M. Simpson, 10 vols. (Berkeley, 1953-1962). References to the volume and page number are given at the end of each passage.

This great edition not only provided for the first time a full collection with accurate text. Its prefaces, especially those of Mrs. Simpson, are notable for interpretation as well as for placing the sermons in the immediate context of seventeenth century events.

In Part II of volume x, Donne's "Sources," Mrs. Simpson considers the degree of Donne's knowledge of Hebrew and Greek, and the various Bibles that he used. See also Don Cameron Allen, "Dean Donne Sets His Text" *ELH* x (1943) 208-227. This at least is clear: Donne knew enough Hebrew to hear the rhythm of parallelism in his favourite books, especially *Psalms*. He knew the Vulgate almost by heart, and the Vulgate gives the Hebrew rhythms a sonority capturable in English. And from the early Fathers to Jerome to Tremellius, Renaissance writers including Milton as well as Donne received the conception of the Bible as containing great literary forms. With the help of polyglot bibles and his own care for meaning, Donne does not hesitate to correct at times a word in A. V. or the Vulgate.

[2] On Donne's attitude toward the literal or allegorical interpretation of the Bible see Dennis B. Quinn, "John Donne's Principles of Biblical Exegesis," *JEGP* LXI (1962), 313-329.

[3] William Fraser Mitchell, *English Pulpit Oratory from Andrewes to Tillotson* ( London, 1932); Evelyn M. Simpson, *A Study of the Prose Works of John Donne* (Oxford, 1948) ch. XI, and introductions to *Sermons (supra)*; William R. Mueller, *John Donne: Preacher* (Princeton, 1962); Joan Webber, *Contrary Music* (Madison, Wisconsin, 1963).

[4] Webber, p. 32.

[5] See also Dennis Quinn, "Donne's Christian Eloquence," *ELH* XXVII (1960), 276-297; Irving Lowe, "John Donne, The Middle Way," *JHI* XXII (1961).

[6] Joan Webber, *The Eloquent "I"* (Madison, Milwaukee, and London, 1968), p. 42.

## Chapter Two

[1] All quotations from Browne in this chapter are from *The Works of Sir Thomas Browne*, ed. by Geoffrey Keynes, 2nd ed., 4 vols. (Chicago, 1964). The references given in my text are to the volume and page numbers of this edition.

[2] T. S. Eliot, *Notes towards the Definition of Culture* (London, 1948), p. 29.

[3] Boris Pasternak, *Safe Conduct* (New York, 1958), p. 15.

[4] Ralph Waldo Emerson, "Thoreau," in *Works*, 14 vols., Standard Library Edition (Boston and New York, 1883-93), X, p. 439.

[5] Frank L. Huntley, "The Relation of *Urn Burial* and *The Garden of Cyrus*," *SP* LIII (1956), 208. See also Mar-

garet A. Heideman, *"Hydriotaphia* and *The Garden of Cyrus*: A Paradox and a Cosmic Vision," *UTQ* xix (1950), 235-246.

[6] Huntley, *Sir Thomas Browne* (Ann Arbor, 1962), pp. 209-210.

[7] *OED.*

[8] Joan Bennett, *Sir Thomas Browne* (Cambridge, 1962), p. 208.

[9] Huntley, *Sir Thomas Browne,* p. 239.

[10] Huntley, *Sir Thomas Browne,* ch. xii.

[11] On these revisions, see the excellent discussion in Bennett, *Sir Thomas Browne,* pp. 230-240. Material casting light on Browne's revision of passages in his notebooks is to be found in Jeremiah S. Finch, "Early Drafts of *The Garden of Cyrus," PMLA* (1940), 742-747.

[12] Professor N. J. Endicott's article, "Sir Thomas Browne, Montpellier, and the Tract of Languages" casts light on Browne's revisions. See *TLS* August 24, 1962.

[13] Huntley, *Sir Thomas Browne,* p. 227.

[14] Peter Green, *Sir Thomas Browne* (London, 1959) (Published for the British Book Council and the National Book League), p. 28.

## Chapter Three

[1] For Felltham's biography see M. D. Cornu, "A Biography of Owen Felltham with Some Notes on His Poems and Letters," University of Washington *Digest of Theses* i (Seattle, 1931), 139-142. This abstract contains information supplementing as well as correcting the article on Felltham in *DNB.* Further details are added in articles by Jean Robertson in *NQ* clxiii (1937), 381-389; *MLN* lviii (1943), 385-388; *MLR* xxxix (1944), 108-115; and by Fred S. Tupper in "New Facts Regarding Owen Felltham," *MLN* liv (1939), 199-201.

[2] The most detailed and accurate account of editions of

*Resolves* is given in a forthcoming book by Ted-Larry Pebworth. (Not yet scheduled for publication.)

See also *DNB* and Cornu, pp. 140-141. In most editions the "century" written first stands, and will here be referred to, as the second century. Finally, in the eighth edition and the ones reprinted from it (9th, 10th, 11th), the original century was revised, and new pieces added. In this study, quotations will be made from the Temple Classics text (ed. Oliphant Smeaton, London, 1904; reprinted from the edition of 1628), except when the later versions of specific "resolves" are cited from my copy of the 10th (1677) edition. The designation of first or second century will be in roman numerals; of individual "resolves" in Arabic, and the page numbers are from Temple Classics edition, unless the tenth edition is specified. The copious use of italics has been removed from citations of passages from this edition.

[3] Quoted in Tupper, p. 300.

[4] There has been relatively little scholarly discussion of Feltham as an essayist or stylist. See Elbert N. S. Thompson, *The Seventeenth-Century English Essay*, University of Iowa Humanistic Studies III (Iowa City, 1928), pp. 74-76, 127-128; Douglas Bush, *English Literature in the Earlier Seventeenth Century* (Oxford, 1945), pp. 190-192; George Williamson, *The Senecan Amble* (London, 1951), pp. 201-203; McCrea Hazlett "New Frame and Various Composition: Development of the Form of Owen Feltham's *Resolves*," *MP* LI (1953), pp. 93-101. Ted-Larry Pebworth's forthcoming study gives a more thorough analysis of the evolution from the genre of "resolve" to something approaching the "personal essay" (his term).

[5] His interest in it was typical of his age. See Philip Allerton Smith, "Neo-Stoicism in English Prose of the Seventeenth Century," *Harvard University Summaries of Theses* (Cambridge, 1942), pp. 363-367.

[6] Hazlett (note 4, *supra*) finds that 28 new resolves were added, 43 discarded; my reckoning is 27 new, 44 discarded.

But as he rightly says, "Felltham's revisions were in some cases so complete as to preserve only a phrase or clause of the original. Such slight connections might escape even the most painstaking comparison" (pp. 93-94).

[7] Jacob Zeitlin, "The Development of Bacon's Essays," *JEGP* (1928), 511, 513.

[8] See Donald M. Frame, *Montaigne's Discovery of Man* (New York, 1955).

[9] Thomas Randolph, "To M$^r$ Feltham on his book of Resolves," in *Poems*, ed. John J. Parry (New Haven, 1917), p. 126.

[10] Williamson (see note 4), p. 202.

[11] From "Elegies on Ben Jonson," in *Ben Jonson*, ed. C. H. Herford and Percy and Evelyn Simpson, XI (Oxford, 1952), 462.

[12] All the italics in quotations from Felltham in this paragraph are mine, in order to single out special words.

[13] See Williamson, ch. 5.

[14] *The Journal of Henry D. Thoreau*, ed. Bradford Torrey and Francis H. Allen (Boston, 1906), VI, 89.

## Chapter Four

[1] A section of Wordsworth's 1807 *Poems* is called "Moods of My Own Mind." I owe this information to Herschel Baker, *William Hazlitt* (Cambridge, Mass., 1962), p. 350, n. Like all students of Hazlitt I am indebted to Mr. Baker's monumental biographical study.

The expression "moods of the mind" is subsequently used by Hazlitt, and by Thoreau (*The Journal of Henry D. Thoreau*, ed. Bradford Terry and Francis H. Allen [Boston, 1906, II, 403]).

[2] *The Round Table*, Vol. 1, No. 1 (Edinburgh, 1817) quoted in Marie H. Law, *The English Familiar Essay in the Early Nineteenth Century* (Philadelphia, 1934), p. 39.

[3] *The Complete Works of William Hazlitt*, ed. P. P. Howe after the edition of A. R. Waller and Arnold Glover,

21 vols. (London and Toronto, 1930), 5.53. References to this edition will hereafter be given in the text, and since the volume numbers are in arabic they will be followed by a period instead of a comma, to avoid confusion. References to other editions will be given in the notes.

[4] *Table Talk*, I, 13 (London, 1824).

[5] *Ibid.*, p. 3.

[6] Cf. Kenneth Muir, "Keats and Hazlitt," in *John Keats, A Reassessment*, ed. Kenneth Muir (Liverpool, 1958).

[7] *Table Talk*, I, 2.

[8] *Ibid.*, II, 4.

[9] *Ibid.*, II, 5.

[10] *Ibid.*, II, 38.

[11] *Ibid.*, I, 182.

[12] *Ibid.*, I, 188.

[13] *Ibid.*, I, 191-192.

[14] *Ibid.*, I, 193.

[15] Baker, *op. cit.*, pp. 51, 52.

[16] *Ibid.*, p. 434.

[17] Earl Leslie Griggs, ed., *The Collected Letters of Samuel Taylor Coleridge* (Oxford, 1956-59), II, 991.

[18] *Lectures Chiefly on the Dramatic Literature of the Age of Elizabeth* (London, 1829), p. 281.

[19] *Ibid.*, p. 293.

[20] *Ibid.*, p. 295.

[21] *Ibid.*, p. 308.

[22] *Ibid.*, p. 307.

## Chapter Five

[1] Horace A. Eaton, *Thomas De Quincey* (New York, 1936) p. 378. For biographical information, I have depended chiefly on Eaton, but I have also made use of Edward Sackville-West's *Thomas De Quincey* (New Haven, 1936) and the earlier life by A. H. Japp, *Thomas De Quincey: his Life and Writings* (London, 1890).

[2] Eaton, 334; Sackville-West, 180.

[3] *Selections Grave and Gay from the Writings Published and Unpublished by Thomas De Quincey*, 14 vols. (Edinburgh, 1853-1860).

[4] Horace A. Eaton, ed., *A Diary of Thomas De Quincey, 1803* (New York, 1927), p. 209.

[5] *Ibid.*, pp. 181-182.

[6] *Ibid.*, p. 156.

[7] *Ibid.*, p. 182.

[8] Eaton, *Thomas De Quincey*, p. 250.

[9] *Ibid.*, p. 251.

[10] The following year (1822) Taylor and Hessey published these articles as a book, for which De Quincey furnished an "Appendix" in lieu of the promised third part, never written. On publishing the book, Taylor and Hessey made De Quincey a "present" of £20; he received nothing for their subsequent reprints. Although he had never formally granted them rights in the "Confessions," they attempted to prevent him from including this work in his collective edition until they were threatened with legal action by James Hogg (Eaton, p. 479).

[11] *The Collected Writings of Thomas De Quincey*, ed. David Masson (Edinburgh, 1890) XI, 294. All quotations in this chapter are from the Masson edition, unless otherwise specified; and future references will give the volume and page number in the text.

[12] On De Quincey's "anti-Hellenism" see René Wellek, "De Quincey's Status in the History of Ideas," *PQ* XXIII (1944), 257-262. Professor Wellek questions the value of an over-systematic analysis of De Quincey's criticism such as the one given by Sigmund K. Proctor in *Thomas De Quincey's Theory of Literature* (Ann Arbor, 1943). I find myself in some disagreement with other points made by Professor Wellek, especially in his use of the term "organic." A thorough study of the criticism is *Thomas De Quincey Literary Critic* by John E. Jordan (Berkeley, 1952).

[13] Quoted in Sackville-West, p. 236.

[14] The original version of the "Confessions" was reprinted

by Ticknor and Fields in the American collected edition, *De Quincey's Writings* (Boston, 1851-1859), and Houghton Mifflin Co. later succeeded Ticknor and Fields as publishers of this edition (with added material). My quotations are from *Confessions of an English Opium Eater and Kindred Papers*, which forms Vol. 1 of the Houghton Mifflin edition. Page numbers only will be given in the text, to avoid confusion with quotations from the Masson edition. Subsequent quotations from "Suspiria" and "The English Mail Coach" are taken, for the same reason, from the same volume of the Houghton Mifflin edition.

[15] Elisabeth Schneider, *Coleridge, Opium, and Kubla Khan* (Chicago, 1953), p. 78. On architectural fantasy see A. H. Mayor, *The Bibiena Family* (New York, 1945) and *Giovanni Battista Piranesi* (New York, 1952).

[16] See n. 14 above. Again, the original text seems to me preferable to the revised one printed in *Selections Grave and Gay* and in Masson's edition.

[17] Eaton, p. 424.

[18] *The Posthumous Works of Thomas De Quincey*, ed. A. H. Japp, 2 vols. (London, 1891) I, 1-24.

[19] See a very interesting description of "impassioned dancing" in the "Autobiographic Sketches" (Masson I, 196-197).

[20] Actually Whitehead gives the name "misplaced concreteness" to the fallacy, but the error is that of "mistaking the abstract for the concrete," in the notion that "simple location is the primary way in which things are involved in space-time" (*Science and the Modern World*, New York, 1947, pp. 74, 133).

[21] *A Writer's Diary* (London, 1953), p. 183.

[22] Oliver Elton, *A Survey of English Literature 1780-1830*, 2 vols. (London, 1912) II, 314. Elton's chapter on De Quincey is probably the best brief analysis of his work, although somewhat uncritical in the discussion of prose rhythm.

[23] De Quincey acknowledged as his chief source the narrative account given by Benjamin Bergmann in *Nomadische*

*Streifereien unter den Kalmücken* (Riga, 1804). He apparently used a French translation of part of this work: *Voyage de Benjamin Bergmann chez les Kalmuks: Traduit de l'Allemand par M. Moris* (Chatillon-sur-Seine, 1825).

The authoritative study of De Quincey's treatment of his sources is Albert Goldman's *The Mine and the Mint* (Carbondale, Illinois, 1965). My own observations about De Quincey's originality in reconstructing the previous accounts of the flight of the Tartars were drafted before the publication of Mr. Goldman's study. Although Mr. Goldman presents De Quincey as "a writer for long periods of time utterly dependent upon the opportunities afforded him by the wind-blown chances of casual reading" (p. 10), he rightly sees him as primarily an imaginative author. His account of De Quincey's handling of the sources for *Revolt of the Tartars* confirms my own independently made comparison.

[24] *A Study of History* (London, 1934) III, 19.

[25] De Quincey's own phrase for Zebek-Dorchi's plot against the Russians is applicable to the whole narrative.

In "Satanic Fall and Hebraic Exodus: An Interpretation of De Quincey's 'Revolt of the Tartars,'" (*Studies in Romanticism* VIII [1968]), Vincent A. de Luca offers a stimulating analysis. Nevertheless, he perhaps overemphasizes parallels with Milton and the Biblical narrative, since echoes of both Milton and the Bible are frequent in De Quincey's prose. This leads to the currently fashionable translation of the narrative into terms of the myth of the Fall and of a "quest for an Edenic homeland" (p. 106).

[26] See n. 14 above.

[27] Robert Hopkins, "De Quincey on War and the Pastoral Design of *The English Mail Coach*," *Studies in Romanticism* VI (1967), is by far the most illuminating study of this work, especially in the demonstration of "the profound significances, historical and cultural, of the Napoleonic Wars for [De Quincey] and for the Victorian era" (pp. 129-130).

[28] See De Quincey's similar image for "the pathetic and

the humourous as but different phases of the same art" that "shine each through each like layers of coloured crystals placed one behind the other" (XI, 63).

[29] *Granite and Rainbow* (London, 1958), p. 40.

[30] *Op. cit.*, p. 263.

[31] Masson points out De Quincey's parody of Gray in his note on this passage (XIII, 57, n. 2).

[32] Quoted in Elton, *op cit.*, II, p. 329.

## Chapter Six

[1] *Journals of Ralph Waldo Emerson,* ed. Edward W. Emerson and Waldo E. Forbes, 10 vols. (Boston, 1909-1914). Citations in the text will be abbreviated as J, followed by the volume in Roman and the page in Arabic numbers. Similarly, references to *The Complete Works of Ralph Waldo Emerson,* ed. by Edward W. Emerson, 12 vols. (Boston, 1903-1904), known as the Centenary Edition, will be identified as W.

*The Journals and Miscellaneous Notebooks of Ralph Waldo Emerson,* eds. William H. Gilman, Alfred R. Ferguson, George P. Clark and Merrell R. Davis (Cambridge, Mass., 1960———) will be an invaluable and indispensable successor to the 1909-1914 edition. Passages in my text are cited from the earlier edition not only because the new edition is still in progress, but because its method of literatim transcription, including cancellations, revisions, and variants make it less readable and impossible to reproduce in the same form. I have of course consulted the volumes so far available.

A new edition of Emerson's *Collected Works* is also in preparation under the auspices of the Center for Editions of American Authors, by Harvard University Press, 1971 ———), eds. Robert E. Spiller, Alfred E. Ferguson, et al.

[2] *The Early Lectures of Ralph Waldo Emerson,* ed. Stephen E. Whicher, Robert E. Spiller, and Wallace E. Williams, 3 vols. (Cambridge, Mass., 1959-1971), I, 1. Cita-

tions in the text will be given as *Early Lectures* followed by the volume and page numbers.

[3] On Emerson's attitude toward evolution see Joseph Warren Beach, *The Concept of Nature in Nineteenth-Century English Poetry* (New York, 1936), pp. 330ff., and Harry Hayden Clark, "Emerson and Science," *PQ* x (1931), 225-260. See also Sherman Paul, *Emerson's Angle of Vision* (Cambridge, Mass., 1952), ch. 2.

[4] *American Renaissance* (London and New York, 1941), p. 3.

[5] In his admirable chapter on Emerson in Robert E. Spiller et al., *Literary History of the United States* rev. ed. (New York, 1953), p. 385.

[6] It interesting that the phrase "a great and beautiful necessity," with much the same import, occurs in Emerson's lecture "English Literature: Introductory" (1835). See *Early Lectures* I, 225.

[7] The best study of the development of Emerson's thought on this subject is Stephen E. Whicher, *Freedom and Fate* (Philadelphia, 1953).

[8] *Ibid.*, p. 164.

[9] We must wait for the publication of Emerson's later lectures, now being prepared by Professors Wallace E. Williams and James H. Justus, for a clearer view of the progress from the London lectures to the related series of 1848-1850, 1858, 1866, upon which Emerson drew for the Harvard lectures of 1870 and 1871. The selection printed by James E. Cabot in 1893 as "Natural History of Intellect" and reprinted by Edward Emerson as "Powers and Laws of Thought" seems to be drawn from the London and Harvard lectures and from other manuscript material relating to the theme. Although the arrangement as it stands is Cabot's, the writing itself is wholly Emerson's.

I am indebted to Professor Williams for this information.

I have kept the title "Natural History of Intellect" because not only in the first three lectures of the London series, but also in the much later Harvard ones, this was Emerson's generic title.

See James E. Cabot, *A Memoir of Ralph Waldo Emerson*, 2 vols. (Boston and New York, 1887) II, 633-634; Edward Waldo Emerson's Notes to "Natural History of Intellect," Centenary Edition XII, 422ff.; Rusk, *Letters* IV, 80 n. 288.

[10] *The Letters of Ralph Waldo Emerson*, ed. Ralph L. Rusk, 6 vols. (New York, 1939), IV, 51.

[11] *The Correspondence of Thomas Carlyle and Ralph Waldo Emerson*, 2 vols. (Boston, 1888) II, 81-82.

[12] *American Prose Masters* (New York, 1909), p. 201. On Emerson's prose style see also O. W. Firkins, *Ralph Waldo Emerson* (Boston, 1915), ch. v. Some pertinent observations may also be found in Jonathan Bishop, *Emerson on the Soul* (Cambridge, Mass., 1964).

[13] *Ibid.*, p. 183.

[14] *The Journals and Miscellaneous Notebooks of Ralph Waldo Emerson*, ed. William E. Gilman, Alfred R. Ferguson, et al. (Cambridge, Mass., 1965), V, 253. See also *Early Lectures* II, 255.

[15] *Partial Portraits* (London, 1919), p. 6.

[16] *Ibid.*, pp. 32-33.

[17] Matthiessen, *op. cit.*, p. 3.

## Chapter Seven

[1] "Natural History of Massachusetts," in *Excursions* (Boston, 1863), p. 54.

[2] *Ibid.*, pp. 64-65.

[3] *The Letters of Ralph Waldo Emerson*, ed. Ralph L. Rusk, 6 vols. (New York, 1939), III, 47.

[4] *Excursions*, p. 71. Thoreau had earlier written this sentence in his Journal.

[5] "A Winter Walk," *Excursions*, p. 122.

[6] "A Walk to Wachusett," *Excursions*, p. 76.

[7] See, for example, Walter Harding, *A Thoreau Hand-*

*book* (New York, 1961). For a different view, see Sherman Paul, who (rightly, I believe) recognizes the organic unity of *A Week* in his *Shores of America* (Urbana, Illinois, 1958), pp. 212-233. This is the best comprehensive book on Thoreau's writing.

[8] *A Week on the Concord and Merrimack Rivers* (2nd, rev. ed. Boston, 1868). Page numbers of passages quoted are given in the text; the title will be cited as *A Week*.

[9] Carl F. Hovde, "Nature into Art: Thoreau's Use of his Journals in *A Week*," American Literature xxx (1958), 165-184.

[10] Hovde, p. 174.

[11] Cf. William Drake, "A Week on the Concord and Merrimack Rivers," in *Thoreau: A Collection of Critical Essays*, ed. Sherman Paul (Englewood Cliffs, N.J., 1962), p. 70.

[12] William Drake, "Walden," *op. cit.*, pp. 71-90.

[13] *Walden; or, Life in the Woods* (Boston, 1854). Page references are given at the end of passages cited.

[14] (Chicago, 1957).

[15] *The Maine Woods* (Boston, 1864) comprises "Ktaadn," published first in *Union Magazine*, 1848; "Chesuncook," published in the *Atlantic Monthly*, 1858; and "The Allegash and East Branch," which appears for the first time in the posthumous volume. A more complete account of the publication of sections in periodicals and of Thoreau's plan for revision and expansion is given in vol. 3 of the new edition of *The Writings of Henry David Thoreau, The Maine Woods*, ed. Joseph H. Moldenhauer (Princeton, 1971), Textual Introduction, pp. 355-404.

[16] *The Shores of America*, pp. 360-362.

[17] *Cape Cod* (Boston, 1865) contains sections which had been published in *Putnam's Magazine* in 1855.

[18] *Cape Cod*, p. 8. Further page references will be given in the text.

[19] This interest is fully documented in John A. Christie, *Thoreau as World Traveler* (New York and London, 1965).

[20] The standard or "Walden" edition of the *Journal*,

edited by Bradford Torrey and Francis H. Allen, comprises vols. VII through XX of *The Writings of Henry David Thoreau* (Boston, 1906). The volumes of the *Journal* are also separately numbered (I-XIV), and I have used these numbers for passages quoted in the text.

A new and more complete edition of the *Journal* and related notebooks is in preparation, to be published by Belknap Press (Cambridge, Mass.).

[21] Paul, *op. cit.*, p. 296.

[22] *H. D. Thoreau: A Writer's Journal* (New York, 1960), pp. XXV-XXVIII.

[23] Albert Schweitzer, *Goethe*, trans. C. R. Joy and C. T. Campion (Boston, 1948), p. 37.

[24] Paul, p. 256.

## Chapter Eight

[1] T. S. Eliot, *The Waste Land, a Facsimile and Transcript of the Original Drafts* . . . ed. by Valerie Eliot (London, 1971).

[2] Quoted in *op. cit.*, Introduction by Valerie Eliot, p. x.

[3] Quoted, *ibid.*, p. xiii.

[4] Quoted, *ibid.*, p. xiv.

[5] *To Criticize the Critic* (New York, 1965), p. 20.

[6] See John D. Margolis, *T. S. Eliot's Intellectual Development 1922-1939* (Chicago and London, 1972), especially ch. 1.

[7] *The Egoist*, V, 1, January 1918, p. 2.

[8] *The Athenaeum*, May 23, 1919, p. 361. Although Eliot declared himself unsympathetic to Emerson, he obviously knew his life and work.

[9] *Ibid.*, p. 362.

[10] *Ibid.*

[11] *The New Statesman*, May 19, 1917, p. 158.

[12] *The Chapbook*, no. 22, April 1921, p. 9. Italics added.

[13] *The Athenaeum*, Nov. 28, 1919, p. 1252.

[14] "Bruce Lyttelton Richmond," *TLS* January 13, 1961.

[15] *The Sacred Wood* (2nd ed., London, 1928), p. 23. Page references to essays from *The Sacred Wood* as they were reprinted in *Selected Essays* (New York, 1950) will be given in the text. Other references to *The Sacred Wood* (2nd ed.) will appear in the notes.

[16] "Lettre d'Angleterre," *Nouvelle Revue Française* XI (Nov. 1, 1923), 619-625.

[17] *The Sacred Wood*, p. 12.

[18] *Ibid.*, p. 11.

[19] *Ibid.*, p. 14.

[20] *Ibid.*, p. 15.

[21] *After Strange Gods* (New York, 1934).

[22] "I Am Christina Rossetti," in *The Second Common Reader* (New York, 1932), p. 264.

[23] *The Listener*, June 26, 1929.

[24] *Ibid.*, p. 907.

[25] *Ibid.*, p. 908.

[26] *Ibid.*

[27] See n. 15, *supra.*

[28] London, 1933. Page references will be given in the text.

[29] *For Lancelot Andrewes* (London, 1929), p. 22.

[30] *Predilections* (New York, 1955), p. 22.

[31] See John Peter, "Eliot and the *Criterion*," in *Eliot in Perspective*, ed. Graham Martin (London, 1970).

[32] London, 1928.

[33] See n. 1, p. 136, in *The Use of Poetry and the Use of Criticism.*

[34] *Selected Essays*, p. 230.

[35] *Ibid.*, p. 343.

[36] London, 1957. Page references to quotations from this book will be given in the text.

[37] D. Nichol Smith, *Dryden* (Cambridge, 1950), p. 25.

[38] Harold Nicolson records the effect of this essay. "I . . . go to hear T. S. Eliot speak on 'The Three Voices of Poetry.' . . . I have never seen such a crowd for any literary lecture. They told me that there were more than 2,500 peo-

ple there, and they remained silent throughout. . . . I had to propose a vote of thanks this evening, but the audience were obviously so moved by Tom's lecture that I did it in ten words." *Diaries and Letters of Harold Nicolson, The Later Years 1945-1962* (New York, 1968), p. 249.

[39] See Roger Kojecky, *T. S. Eliot's Social Criticism* (New York, 1972), especially pp. 87-92.

[40] Turgenev would probably have been Eliot's own choice. It was in reference to the Russian novel that he first formulated the idea of an "objective correlative," expressed in really more understandable terms as "a trick of fastening upon accidental properties of a critical situation, and letting these in turn fasten upon the attention to such an extent as to replace the emotion which gave them their importance" (*The Egoist*, Sept. 1917, p. 118).

# Index

Adams, Henry, 237, 238, 242
Addison, Joseph, 9, 91, 98,
 99, 101, 111, 167, 168
Aiken, Conrad, 234
Alcott, Bronson, 191
Aldington, Richard, 236, 238
Allen, Don Cameron, 270
Andrewes, Lancelot, 7, 8, 11,
 17, 40, 252, 267
Aristotle, 75, 244
Arnold, Matthew, 15, 243,
 245, 253, 261, 264
*Athenaeum*, the, 235, 237,
 247

Auden, W. H., 245
Austen, Jane, 159

Bacon, Sir Francis, 40, 42, 51,
 77, 78, 80, 96, 101, 110,
 168, 181, 186, 189, 193,
 250, 251
Baker, Herschel, 105, 107,
 274
Bate, Walter, 10
Baxter, Richard, 58
BBC, 250
Beach, Joseph Warren, 280
Beardsley, Monroe, 6

Benn, Gottfried, 263
Bennett, Joan, 67, 272
Bentham, Jeremy, 104, 105, 108, 175
Bergmann, Benjamin, 277-278
Bible, 17-20, 27, 28, 37, 225
Blackwood, William, 123
*Blackwood's Magazine* ("Maga"), 122, 123, 140, 142
Bowen, Elizabeth, 240
Bradley, F. H., 234, 236, 239, 242, 251, 252
Bramhall, John, 252
Brougham, Henry, 106
Browne, Sir Thomas, 8, 9, 10, 11, 12, 14, 37, 76, 91, 92, 110, 128, 129, 145, 146, 156, 157, 158, 174, 194, 207, 210, 228, 232, 237, 239, 251, 267; originality, 8; observation, 42, 51, 60-62, 66, 197; point of view, 60, 66; themes, 44-47; scepticism, 48-49; idiom, 49, 52; humour, 51; meditation, 53, 67; note-books, 55; revision, 68; rhythm, 52, 57, 68; structure of prose, 52, 69, 72; design in, 52
*Christian Morals*, 43, 68-72, 186, 219: composition of, 43; *The Garden of Cyrus*, 8, 14, 43, 52, 53, 57, 60-68, 221; *Letter to a Friend*, 68;

*Miscellanies*, 68; *Pseudo-doxia Epidemica*, 8, 42, 48-52, 55; *Religio Medici*, 8, 42-48, 52, 67, 68, 69, 91, 211; *Urn Burial*, 8, 43, 46, 52-60, 63, 67, 68, 70, 71, 186, 221, 239
Brownell, W. C., 185
Burke, Edmund, 10, 105, 109, 111, 112, 130
Burton, Sir Richard Francis, 251
Bush, Douglas, 273

Cabot, James E., 180
Campion, Thomas, 258
Canning, George, 104
Carlyle, Thomas, 76, 174, 184, 190
Cézanne, Paul, 182
Chambers, Robert, 181
Channing, William Ellery, 191
Chapman, George, 242
character, as literary form, 47, 104-105, 108
Charles I, 82
Chaucer, Geoffrey, 97, 257
Christie, John A., 282
Cicero, 75
Clarendon. *See* Hyde, Edward
Clark, George P., 279
Clark, Harry H., 280
Cobbett, William, 104, 106
Coleridge, Samuel Taylor, on imagination, 7; organic

theory, 12, 125; and Hazlitt, 94, 95, 102, 104, 106; on Hazlitt's prose, 109; described by Hazlitt, 107, 115, 117; influence on De Quincey, 125, 139; and Emerson, 170-171, 193; and T. S. Eliot, 233, 245
Cornu, M. D., 271
*Criterion*, the, 242, 245, 264
criticism, literary, 14, 15, 123-124
Croll, M. W., 4

Dante, 57, 244, 256, 264, 265
Davis, Merrell R., 279
Della Porta, J. B., 60
de Luca, Vincent A., 278
De Quincey, Thomas, 7, 9, 10, 11, 12, 42, 45, 92, 99, 182, 185, 223, 239, 241, 267; poetic aims, 121-122; and Coleridge, 121, 125; and Wordsworth, 121, 124, 125, 164; and Milton, 122; literary criticism, 123-131; on seventeenth century, 128-129; on Hazlitt, 130-131; on Johnson, 130; on Burke, 130; on Lamb, 130-131; revisions, 133, 161f; and Browne, 145; sources, 148-151; dreams, 134, 136-142, 144; imagery, 141, 144, 150, 152, 163; narrative, 146, 148, 154; "impassioned prose," 132-

133, 141-146; experiments, 133, 157; style of, 132, 151, 159; on style, 159ff; organic theory of, 127, 129, 159; humour, 161; rhythm of, 145, 161, 163-164; digressions, 163; and unity in prose, 165
"Affliction in Childhood," 132, 142; "Apparition of the Brocken," 142f; "Autobiographic Sketches," 132, 141, 165; *The Confessions of an English Opium Eater*, 14, 123, 131-139, 157, 159ff, 161, 165; revisions, 133; *Dream Fugue*, 131, 155, 157, 158, 239; *The English Mail Coach*, 131, 146, 151-157, 159, 161, 165; *Klosterheim*, 120, 159; "Levanna and our Ladies of Sorrow," 142f; *The Logic of Political Economy*, 120; "Murder Considered as One of the Fine Arts," 161; "Palimpsest, The," 142; *The Revolt of the Tartars*, 147-151, 157, 159, 165; "Savannah-La-Mar," 142f, 155; *Selections Grave and Gray*, 120, 132, 160, 161; *Spanish Military Nun*, 159; *Suspiria de Profundis*, 132, 139-152, 157-158, 165

*Dial, The,* 196-197
Dickens, Charles, 144, 159
Donne, John, 7, 8, 9, 11, 91,
146, 210, 214, 232, 240,
242, 249, 250, 267; poems,
39; on the Bible, 17-19, 20;
on sermons, 17, 19; regard
for words, 21-24; sentences,
24, 36-37; style, 24-26;
imagery, 26, 31, 32;
metaphors, 26-31, 34, 40;
themes, 31-39; use of
experience, 31-33, 40; self-
knowledge, 38; sermons
compared with poetry,
39-40; rhythm, 24, 26, 40
*Elegies,* 33; "Devotions,"
39; *Satires,* 33; *Songs and
Sonnets,* 66
Drake, William, 208
Dryden, John, 10, 91, 124,
127, 262

Eaton, Horace A., 180
*Egoist,* the, 235, 236, 237
Eliot, T. S., 7, 14, 15, 43, 48,
64, 124, 127, 192; lectures,
234, 257; early essays, 235,
236; and Shakespeare, 236;
on prose writing, 237; and
Emerson, 237; on Henry
Adams, 237, 238; on Henry
James, 237; critical prose,
237; humour, 238; on
qualities of prose, 238; on
relation between prose and
poetry, 238; on cadence in
prose, 239; on imagery,
239; on rhythm in prose,
239; on earlier prose
writers, 240, 250, 257;
criteria for prose, 242;
philosophical training of,
233-234, 242; on Aristotle,
244; on dramatists, 247,
248, 259; on Marlowe, 248;
on Spenser, 248; on blank
verse, 249; on the meta-
physical poets, 249, 259;
writing for periodicals,
235, 240-241, 250, 258; and
Bradley, 251; on difference
of prose and poetry, 251;
on prose style, 252; later
lectures, 252, 253, 257-259;
experience and literature,
254-255, 264; on poetry
and belief, 256-257, 265;
later essays and dialogue,
258; as man of letters, 260;
pluralism, 256, 261; on
Arnold, 261; on free verse,
262; and European litera-
ture, 262, 264; and Arnold,
264; on Milton, 264; on
Goethe, 264-265; as medi-
tative thinker, 263, 266;
*After Strange Gods,* 245;
*Ash-Wednesday,* 241, 263;
"Bacon and Hooker," 250;
"The Borderline of Prose,"
238; *The Cocktail Party,*
247, 248; *The Confidential
Clerk,* 248; "Ezra Pound:

His Metric and Poetry," 261; *For Lancelot Andrewes,* 241, 252; *Four Quartets,* 261, 262; "Frontiers of Criticism," 266; "The Function of Criticism," 241-244, 245; *Gerontion,* 248; "Goethe as the Sage," 16, 264; "The Hippopotamus," 263; *The Idea of a Christian Society,* 263; "Marina," 236; "The Music of Poetry," 239, 260, 261, 262; *Notes Towards the Definition of Culture,* 260; *On Poetry and Poets,* 253, 257; "The Perfect Critic," 241-244; "Poetry and Drama," 262, 263; "Prose and Verse," 239; *Prufrock and Other Observations,* 236; "Reflections on Vers Libre," 236, 239, 261, 262; "Religion and Literature," 256-257; *The Sacred Wood,* 241, 242; *Selected Essays,* 244; "The Social Function of Poetry," 259; "The Three Voices of Poetry," 262, 263; *To Criticize the Critic,* 261; *Towards a Definition of Culture,* 263; *Tradition and the Individual Talent,* 241-244, 254, 260; *The Use of Poetry and the Use of Criticism,* 252-257, 264;

"Virgil and the Christian World," 264; *The Waste Land,* 234, 241, 263; "What is a Classic," 264

Eliot, Valerie, 234

Elton, Oliver, 147

Emerson, Ralph Waldo, 8, 9, 11, 12, 13, 14, 37, 41, 42, 44, 62, 83, 92, 158, 195, 196, 197, 209, 226, 232, 237, 241, 267; journals, 13, 71, 167, 168, 173, 176, 189, 191-192, 194; and spirit of the age, 166, 170, 175, 179, 183, 193; and evolution, 168, 183; lectures, 168-170, 179-181, 184, 191; and science, 170-171, 181; and correspondences, 171; and universal mind, 172, 183; and facts, 173-175; self-knowledge, 177, 193; and American mind, 178; and natural history, 180; compared to Impressionists, 182; essays of, and the novel, 181, 183, 189; form of, 182-190, 191-194; on writing, 189; use of myth, 186-188; form, 184-190

*The American Scholar,* 190; "Circles," 173; "Compensation," 173, 183; *The Conduct of Life,* 175, 176, 177, 179; *English Traits,* 174; *Essays,* 40; "Experience," 172, 173; "The

Emerson, Ralph Waldo
(*cont.*)
Fugitive Slave Law,"
177-180; "Illusions," 179;
*Journal*, 13, 71, 167-168,
173, 176, 189, 191-194;
"Napoleon," 187; "Nat-
ural History of the Intellect," 71, 181-182, 186, 188;
*Nature*, 167, 228; "The
Over-Soul," 173; *Repre-
sentative Men*, 174, 187;
"Self-Reliance," 173, 183;
"Society and Solitude,"
187; "Thoreau," 174;
"Works and Days," 180
Endicott, N. J., 272
essay, 4, 6, 9, 10, 11, 12, 13,
16, 42, 64, 67, 93, 95-96,
116, 168; and *passim*
essayist, *see* essay
Evelyn, John, 51
*Examiner*, the, 93, 94, 104,
115

Faraday, Michael, 181
Felltham, Owen, 9, 219;
*Resolves*, and essay, 73, 74,
90, 91; revision of, 8off;
as moralist, 74, 76-77, 88;
on style, 74, 84-85; on the
graces and the muses,
74-75; stoicism, 75; com-
pared with Bacon, 77-78,
82-83; with Montaigne, 83,
88; and Senecan style,
84-85; metaphors, 85-87;

themes, 88-90; and
Browne, 92; and later
essayists, 92
Ferguson, Alfred R., 279
fiction, *see* novel
Finch, Jeremiah, 272
Firkins, O. W., 281
Fletcher, John, 247
Ford, John, 254
Frame, Donald M., 274
Frazer, Sir James George,
242
Fuller, Margaret, 191, 196,
197

Gibbon, Edward, 10
Gilman, William H., 279
Godolphin, Sidney, 109
Godwin, William, 104, 105,
108
Goethe, J. W. von, 193, 210,
231, 265
Goldman, Albert, 278
Goldsmith, Oliver, 91
Gray, Thomas, 161
Green, Peter, 72
Grierson, Sir Herbert J. C.,
238
Grieve, C. M., 245

Hakluyt, Richard, 240
Harding, Walter, 280
Hazlett, McCrea, 81, 273-274
Hazlitt, William, 9, 10, 11,
12, 130, 131, 168, 179, 182,
232, 241, 267; on imagination, 94-95, 100, 104; unity

of feeling, 94-95; and Bacon, 96; on Addison, 98; on Montaigne, 98; on Steele, 98; on conversation and point of view, 101; on style, 101, 106, 113; and conversation, 101, 106; structure, of essays, 96, 102-103, 114-115, 116-117; imagery, 109, 110, 112, 116; rhythm, 109; metaphors, 118; on Burke, 105, 111-112; on Johnson, 111; on Coleridge, 106, 107, 115, 117; on Sir Walter Scott, 107; on Wordsworth, 107, 108, 117-118; on Bacon, 110; on other essayists, 98, 111; on Browne, 110; on Taylor, 110

*Essay on the Principles of Human Action*, 94; "On the Conversation of Authors," 113; "On the Difference between Writing and Speaking," 113-114, 118; "On Envy," 113; "The Fight," 98, 114f; "On Genius and Common Sense," 100; "On Going a Journey," 102, 118; "On the Ignorance of the Learned," 96; "The Indian Jugglers," 102ff; "On a Landscape of Nicolas Poussin," 100; *Lectures of the English Comic Writers,* 98f, 110; *Lectures on the English Poets,* 97f; "The Letter Bell," 114, 116-117, 118; "The Love of Life," 96; "My First Acquaintance With Poets," 115-116; "On Persons One Would Wish to Have Seen," 113; *The Plain Speakers,* 110, 113-114; "On the Pleasures of Hating," 113; "On the Pleasures of Painting," 99; "Reason and Imagination," 113; *The Round Table,* 94ff, 97; *The Spirit of the Age,* 104-109, 118, 183, 187; "On a Sun Dial," 116, 118; *Table Talk,* 99-104, 113

Heidemann, Margaret A., 272

Herbert, George, 27, 52, 249, 258

Herbert, Magdalen, Lady Danvers, 33

Herbert of Cherbury, Edward, Baron, 249

Herrick, Robert, 258

Hoar, Elizabeth, 191

Hobbes, Thomas, 251

Hooker, Richard, 250, 251, 267

Hopkins, Robert, 278

Horace, 78

Hovde, Carl F., 203

Hunt, Leigh, 93
Hunterian Museum, 181
Huntley, Frank L., 60, 63, 64, 67, 68, 71
Hyde, Edward, Earl of Clarendon, 108, 174, 179, 251

James, Henry, 6, 7, 13, 64, 187, 189, 190, 207, 237, 238, 242, 257; on Emerson's lack of form, 188, 189
James I, 28
Japp, A. H., 275
Johnson, Samuel, 10, 42, 67, 68, 92, 111, 124, 130
Jonah, book of, 225
Jonson, Ben, 74, 83, 84, 247
Joyce, James, 236
Jung, Carl, 140

Kant, Immanuel, 170
Keats, John, 97
Kojecky, Roger, 285

Laforgue, Jules, 241
Lamb, Charles, 45, 93, 99, 102, 110, 130, 131, 168
Landor, Walter Savage, 189
Law, Marie H., 274
Lawrence, D. H., 40
Liberal, the, 115
Lipsius, 75
literature, nature of, 246
London Magazine, the, 97, 99

Lucretius, 73

Macaulay, Thomas Babington, 111, 174
MacDiarmid, Hugh, see Grieve, C. M.
Machiavelli, Niccolo, 77, 252
Mackintosh, Sir James, 104, 106
Malthus, Thomas R., 104
Manchester Guardian, the, 234
Margolis, John D., 283
Marlowe, Christopher, 236, 242, 248
Marvell, Andrew, 249
Matthiessen, F. O., 173, 189, 192, 193
Mayor, A. H., 277
Melville, Herman, 42, 152, 154, 222
Middleton, Thomas, 236
Mill, John Stuart, 105
Milton, John, 117, 122, 124, 207, 233, 249, 264
Mitchell, William Fraser, 21
Moldenhauer, Joseph H., 282
Montaigne, Michel Eyquem de, 8, 40, 47, 83, 88, 96, 98, 168, 182, 189, 193
Moore, Marianne, 100, 237, 253
Mueller, William R., 21, 31
Muir, Kenneth, 275
Murry, J. Middleton, 247

narrative, 12, 14, 115, 116, 121, 157; and *see* De Quincey, Thoreau

Nashe, Thomas, 10, 250

*New Monthly Magazine*, the, 99

*New Statesman*, the, 234, 235, 236, 238

Newman, John Henry, 239

Nicolson, Harold, 284-285

novel, 3, 4, 9, 12, 13, 16, 117, 146-147, 156-157, 158-159, 181, 183, 189, 217, 223, 227, 240, 267

Owen, Richard, 181

Pasternak, Boris L., 60, 61

Paul, Sherman, 220, 228, 231, 280, 282

Pebworth, Ted-Larry, 272-273

periodicals, writing for, 11, 13, 15, 93, 96, 99, 120, 122-123, 131, 134, 161, 235, 240-241, 250, 258

Persius, 210

Peter, John, 284

Piranesi, Giovanni Battista, 139

Plato, 57, 66, 171, 182, 193

Plotinus, 171

Plutarch, 168, 189, 193

Poe, Edgar Allan, 239

Pope, Alexander, 119

Potter, George R., 270

Pound, Ezra, 236, 255

prose, imaginative, 4-5, 7, 10, 12, 16, 48, 49, 117, 219; structure, governed by meaning, 5, 49, 52, 96, 164-165, 232; universal themes, and belief, 13, 45, 59, 110, 146, 151, 154, 156, 157; and observation, 14, 42, 51, 60, 61-62, 66, 83, 196; rhythm, different from poetry, 109, 130, 145, 164, 232, 262. *See also* author entries

Quinn, Dennis B., 271

Raleigh, Sir Walter, 240

Randolph, Thomas, 74, 83

Rembrandt van Rijn, 46, 99, 100

Reynolds, Sir Joshua, 103

Richards, I. A., 256

Richmond, Bruce Littleton, 14, 240, 241

Robertson, Jean, 272

Rousseau, Jean Jacques, 102

Rusk, Ralph L., 281

Ruskin, John, 239

Sackville-West, Edward, 159

Saintsbury, George, 4

Schneider, Elisabeth, 139

Schweitzer, Albert, 231

Scott, Sir Walter, 104, 107, 109

Seneca, 75

Shakespeare, William, 29, 97, 100, 117, 119, 124, 125, 126, 236, 242, 244, 260, 262, 265
Shanley, J. Lyndon, 213
Sidney, Sir Philip, 253
Simpson, Evelyn, 21, 24, 39, 270
Smith, D. Nichol, 262
Smith, Logan Pearsall, 240
Smith, Philip Allerton, 273
Socrates, 57
Southey, Robert, 107, 109
*Spectator*, the, 93
Spenser, Edmund, 97, 248
Spiller, Robert, 170, 175, 280
*Stationer's Register*, the, 73
Steele, Richard, 9, 91, 98, 101, 111
Sterne, Laurence, 224
Stevens, Wallace, 100, 252
Sutherland, James, 4
Swift, Jonathan, 9, 10, 224
Swinburne, Algernon Charles, 242, 245
Symons, Arthur, 245

*Tait's*, 123
Taylor, Jeremy, 7, 8, 9, 10, 11, 17, 33, 40, 58, 110, 128, 129, 130, 146, 156, 157, 171, 239, 251
Thackeray, William Makepeace, 159
Thomas, Dylan, 223
Thomond, Earl of, 74, 81
Thompson, Elbert N. S., 273

Thoreau, Henry David, 8, 9, 11, 12, 13, 14, 37, 41, 44, 62, 67, 77, 83, 91, 92, 158, 169, 180, 191, 241, 267; journal, 14, 48, 195, 196, 197, 199, 201, 203, 206, 208, 221, 223, 225, 226; lectures, 169, 195, 196; and periodicals, 195; problem of form, 195, 197, 225; and observation, 196; poems, 196; humour, 217-218, 223-225; themes, 197, 199, 202, 205, 207, 210, 214, 216, 220; narrative, 198, 205, 222, 223, 225, 231; language of, 200; actual and contemplative, 203, 207, 218, 222, 228, 231; contrasted with seventeenth-century writers, 197, 205, 206; and myth, 206, 222; and allegory, 208; and symbol, 208; transcendentalism, 198, 208; compared with Emerson, 209; compared with Browne, 207, 210, 219, 221, 232; compared with Donne, 210, 214, 232; a new kind of prose writer, 217, 219; compared with Sterne, 224; compared with Swift, 224; unity in composition, 223, 225, 226
*Cape Cod*, 185, 219, 222-225, 231; comedy in,

223-224; *Journal*, 14, 48, 195-201, 203, 208, 221, 223, 225, 226-229; and Concord book, 229; *The Maine Woods*, 185; relation to *Walden*, 221; unity of theme, 223; "The Service," 197; "Sir Walter Raleigh," 197; *Walden*, 199, 206, 208, 209, 211-219, 222, 224, 225, 229, 231; satire in, 214; structure of, 211-214, 217; humour, 217-218; and self-knowledge, 218; *A Walk to Wachusett*, 198; *A Week on the Concord and Merrimack Rivers*, 14, 185, 198-211; design of, 199-205; an experiment, 210; contrasted with *Walden*, 211; "A Winter Walk," 197
*Times Literary Supplement*, the, 15, 238, 240, 246, 247
Tocqueville, Alexis de, 174
Tolstoy, Leo, 265
Toynbee, Arnold Joseph, 151
Traherne, Thomas, 186
Tudors, 251
Turgenev, I. S., 285
Tuve, Rosemond, 249

Vaughan, Henry, 84, 87
Virgil, 264

Weaver, Harriet Shaw, 236
Webber, Joan, 21, 24, 39
Webster, Daniel, 177, 178, 242
Wellek, René, 276
Welty, Eudora, 240
Whicher, Stephen, 170, 173, 178, 280
Whitehead, Alfred North, 44, 146, 171, 277
Whitman, Walt, 13
Wilberforce, William, 106
Williams, Wallace E., 279, 280
Williamson, George, 4, 84, 86, 273
Wilson, John, 123
Wimsatt, W. K., Jr., 6, 10
Woolf, Virginia, 124, 146, 158, 207, 227, 232, 240, 247
Wordsworth, William, 94, 95, 100, 104, 107, 108, 109, 115, 117, 124, 125, 164, 193, 253, 254

Yeats, William Butler, 258, 262, 266

Zeitlin, Jacob, 82

Stapleton, Laurence.
    The elected circle.

    Includes bibliographical references.
    1.  English prose literature—History and criticism.
    2.  American prose literature—History and criticism.
I.  Title.
PR751.S8                    828'.08                    73–2460
ISBN  0–691–06261–7